Home Bound

Home Bound

Filipino American Lives across Cultures, Communities, and Countries

Yen Le Espiritu

UNIVERSITY OF CALIFORNIA PRESS
Berkeley · Los Angeles · London

University of California Press
Berkeley and Los Angeles, California

University of California Press, Ltd.
London, England

An earlier version of chapter 7 was published in *Signs* 26 (2): 415–40. © 2001 by the University of Chicago. All rights reserved. I thank the University of Chicago Press for permission to reprint this article.

In chapter 2, the interviews with A. B. Santos and Juanita Santos and Edgar Gamboa previously appeared in *Filipino American Lives* by Yen Le Espiritu. Reprinted by permission of Temple University Press. © 1995 by Temple University. All Rights Reserved.

Table 3 was previously published as table 6.2 in "The Paradox of Assimilation: Children of Filipino Immigrants in San Diego," by Yen Le Espiritu and Diane L. Wolf. In *Ethnicities: Children of Immigrants in America*, edited by Ruben Rumbaut and Alejandro Portes. © 2001 by the Regents of the University of California. Reprinted by permission of the University of California Press.

Library of Congress Cataloging-in-Publication Data

Espiritu, Yen Le, 1963–.
Home bound : Filipino American lives across cultures, communities, and countries / Yen Le Espiritu.
p. cm.
Includes bibliographical references and index.
ISBN 0-520-22755-7 (cloth : alk. paper) —
ISBN 0-520-23527-4 (paper : alk. paper)
1. Filipino Americans—Social conditions. 2. Filipino Americans—Ethnic identity. 3. Family—United States. 4. United States—Relations—Philippines. 5. Philippines—Relations—United States. 6. Transnationalism. 7. Racism—United States. I. Title.
E184.F4 E87 2003 2002007139

Manufactured in the United States of America

12 11 10 09 08 07 06 05 04 03
10 9 8 7 6 5 4 3 2 1

The paper used in this publication is both acid-free and totally chlorine-free (TCF). It meets the minimum requirements of ANSI/NISO Z39.48–1992 (R 1997) (Permanence of Paper).

For Abe, Evyn, Maya, and Gabriel . . . the Filipino parts of me

Contents

Acknowledgments

On August 11, 2001, mourners crowded the Old Mission Church at the Mission San Luis Rey de Francia in Oceanside, California, to pay their final respects to Peachy Rebaya, loving wife and mother, loyal friend and neighbor, devoted parishioner, and active member of the Filipino community in Oceanside. I met Mama Peachy and her husband, Papa Joe, in 1991. Our family was then new to Oceanside and to the Mission San Luis Rey Parish; and I had just begun my preliminary research on the Filipino American community in San Diego. Mama Peachy and Papa Joe warmly welcomed us into the church, into their home, and into their hearts. We treasure the times we shared with the Rebayas at the weekly Filipino mass, where our toddler daughters would sprawl on the floor, next to the Filipino choir, happily coloring and delighting in the always festive music. The Rebayas had since become a part of our family, "regulars" at the children's baptisms, communions, and birthday parties.

The Rebayas also helped me to launch my research project by inviting me to various Filipino community functions and introducing me to their large circle of Filipino friends and acquaintances. Thus it is fitting that I begin these acknowledgments by thanking Mama Peachy and Papa Joe—for their precious support, generosity, and love. But it is also fitting to open this book with them, because their lives exemplify what I wish to document in this book: home making. Born in Nueva Ecija and Baguio City, respectively, Mama Peachy and Papa Joe left for the United States in 1967. With five children in tow, they led transnational lives, immigrating first to Guam, then to Canada, Arizona, Los Angeles, and Sacramento, before eventually settling in Oceanside in 1973. In all these places, they enthusiastically created "home" not only for themselves and their children but also for those around them, especially the Filipino immigrants in their midst. The crowds of people of all different ages, races, ethnicities, and classes that gathered at Mama Peachy's funeral mass were a testament to her and her husband's success at community building. She will be dearly missed.

I also owe a great deal to the Filipino Americans whom I interviewed. I am inspired by their courageous lives and humbled by their trust in me. I am grateful to all those families who welcomed me into their homes and graciously shared with me not only their food but also their wisdom. I hope that I have been able to convey in this book the fullness of their lives—especially the dignity, grace, and resourcefulness with which they transform and remake the social world around them. I want to thank especially Ruth Abad, Fe and Rick Castro, Edgar Gamboa, Anamaria Labao-Cabato, Luz Latus, A. B. and Juanita Santos, Leo and Norma Sicat, and Connie and Angel Tirona.

Over the years many friends and colleagues have enriched my work in different and important ways; their wisdom and generosity have nurtured this book to completion. I owe a special debt to Sucheng Chan for her pioneering research in Asian American studies, for her unflagging support of me, and for her steadfast encouragement of my work on Filipino Americans. For their generative scholarship on Filipino and Filipino American lives, I thank Filomeno Aguilar, Rick Bonus, Cathy Choy, August Espiritu, Dorothy Fujita-Rony, Theo Gonzalves, Emily Ignacio, Martin Manalansan, Jon Okamura, Rhacel Parreñas, Karin Aguilar-San Juan, Charlene Tung, and especially Vince Rafael. To the following friends and colleagues, I express my respect and affection: Jacqui Alexander, Jose Calderon, Mary Yu Danico, Pierette Hondagneu-Sotelo, Nazli Kibria, Elaine Kim, Peggy Levitt, Ketu Katrak, Yvonne Lau, Joane Nagel, Michael Omi, Rubén Rumbaut, Leland Saito, George Sanchez, Nina Glick Schiller, Barrie Thorne, Linda Vo, and Diane Wolf. My deepest gratitude to Antoinette Charfauros McDaniel for challenging me, and all of us, to live, and live up to, the principles of Ethnic Studies. I also want to thank Sonja de Lugo, Leigh Ann Farmer, and Ruby Wirfs for their lifelong and life-sustaining friendships.

I thank Rick Bonus for assisting me with the research while he was still a graduate student at the University of California, San Diego, especially for conducting and transcribing several interviews in Tagalog. I am indebted to Russell Leong, a dear friend and gifted writer, for helping me to coin the title for this book. I am grateful to Pacita Abad for permitting the Press to include her beautiful painting in the cover design, and to Vince Rafael for recommending her work to me. Naomi Schneider has been a supportive and skilled editor during the process of turning my manuscript into a book. I also thank Mimi Kusch for her careful copyediting and Dore Brown for bringing the book through production.

For the past decade, teaching at U.C.S.D. has been a labor of love. I have had the opportunity to teach—and to learn from—extraordinary students who have both inspired and grounded me. My thanks and appreciation to the undergraduate and graduate students in Ethnic Studies who, through their words and deeds, have confirmed for me the inseparability of intellectual and political projects. I also wish to acknowledge my incredible colleagues in Ethnic Studies—Roberto Alvarez, Charles Briggs, Shalanda Dexter, Ross Frank, Ramon Gutierrez, George Lipsitz, Natalia Molina, Lisa Park, David Pellow, Jane Rhodes, Denise Silva, and Ana Celia Zentella—for their unmatched collegiality, exemplary scholarship, and unwavering commitment to social justice. Special thanks to Ross Frank for all our many conversations on I-5 and to Denise Silva for our many e-mail exchanges that included astrology, faith and fate, and a magical chair. I also thank Jody Blanco, Paula Charkravartty, Rosemary George, Nayan Shah, Olga Vásquez, Edwina Welch, and Lisa Yoneyama for making U.C.S.D. such a fertile community in which to work. Finally, I am grateful to Lisa Lowe, my dear friend and colleague, for her faithful friendship and inspiring example.

As always, I am indebted to the loving support of my family. My mother, Hoa Ngoc Ho, continues to amaze me with her ability to anticipate and fulfill my everyday needs. My husband, Abe, is truly my life partner; and my children, Evyn, Maya, and Gabriel, my life. I am deeply thankful for the loving *home* that we have built with and for each other.

CHAPTER I

Home Making

It is one of the unhappiest characteristics of the [contemporary] age to have produced more refugees, migrants, displaced persons, and exiles than ever before in history, most of them as accompaniment to and, ironically enough, as afterthoughts of great post-colonial and imperial conflicts.

Edward Said, *Culture and Imperialism*

We [Filipinos] are now a quasi-wandering people, pilgrims or prospectors staking our lives and futures all over the world—in the Middle East, Africa, Europe, North and South America, Australia and all of Asia; in every nook and cranny of this seemingly godforsaken earth.

E. San Juan, Jr., *Beyond Postcolonial Theory*

The relationship between the Philippines and the United States has its origins in a history of conquest, occupation, and exploitation. A study of Filipino migration to the United States must begin with this history. Without starting here, we risk reducing Filipino migration to just another immigrant stream. Extending Michael Omi and Howard Winant's notion that "racial formation" is the changing product of the negotiations between social movements and the U.S. state, this book contends that Filipino American racial formation is determined not only by the social, economic, and political forces in the United States but also by U.S. (neo)colonialism in the Philippines and capital investment in Asia. The Filipino case thus foregrounds the ways in which immigrants[1] from previously colonized nations are not exclusively formed as racialized minorities within the United States but also as colonized nationals while in their "homeland"—one that is deeply affected by U.S. influences and modes of social organization.[2] Placing the study of immigration within an "agency-oriented theoretical perspective,"[3] I examine in this book how Filipino women and men—as simultaneously colonized national, immigrant, and racialized minority—are transformed through the experience of colonialism and migration and how they in turn transform and remake the social world around them.

Attentive to both the local and global structures of inequality, I argue that Filipino Americans confront U.S. domestic racism and the global racial order by leading lives stretched across borders—shaped as much by memories of and ties to the Philippines as by the social, economic, and political contexts in their new home in the United States.

Focusing on the experiences of Filipinos in San Diego, California, I maintain that the process of migration is not only about arrival and settlement but, crucially, also about home orientation and return. In focusing on the power and appeal of both "here" and "there," I hope to show that immigrants—in this age of transnational flow of labor, capital, and cultural forms—are both spatially mobile and spatially bounded. Immigrants are mobile in that they can physically live across (unequal) borders or return home through the imagination. At the same time, they are bounded by force of law, economic and political power, and regulating and regularizing institutions in the site(s) in which they find themselves. Given that immigrants are multiply located and placed, this book is about how home is both an *imagined* and an *actual* geography; or more specifically, it is about how home is both connected to and disconnected from the physical space in which one lives. Home is defined here both as a private domestic space and as a larger geographic place where one belongs, such as one's community, village, city, and country.[4] I am especially interested in understanding how immigrants use memory of homeland to construct their new lives in the country to which they have migrated.

To explain better the conceptual relations between home as an imagined and home as an actual geography, I will focus on *home making*—the processes by which diverse subjects imagine and make themselves at home in various geographic locations. Because home making is most often a way of establishing difference and a means of jostling for power, homes are as much about inclusions and open doors as they are about exclusions and closed borders.[5] At the interpersonal level, homes are simultaneously places of nurturing and sites of conflict between family members who occupy different positions of power.[6] At the national communal level, homes are places carved out of repressive state, labor, and cultural practices designed to keep outsiders—in this case, Filipinos—from becoming "rooted." Amid this enforced "homelessness," many immigrants articulate their sense of home by overemphasizing ties of biology and geography and/or by building political coalitions across class, regional, national, and racial boundaries. I will pay particular attention to the problematic relationship that women have to home—as immigrant wives, as second-generation daughters, and as women of color in a white patriarchal society. In so doing, I heed Grewal and Kaplan's call to be attentive to "scattered hegemonies"—to the multiple, overlapping, and intersecting sources of power—as opposed to hegemonic power.[7]

TOWARD A CRITICAL TRANSNATIONAL PERSPECTIVE

The globalization of labor, capital, and culture, the restructuring of world politics, and the expansion of new technologies of communication and transportation: all have driven people and products across the globe at a dizzying pace. In the last decade, reflecting the current saliency of transnational processes, scholars have shifted from the dualism inherent in the classic models of migration—the assumption that migrants move through bipolar spaces in a progressive time frame—to nonbinary theoretical perspectives that are not predicated on modernist assumptions about space and time.[8] Recent writings on "transnational sociocultural system," "the transnational community," "transmigrants," the "deterritorialized nation-state," and "transnational grassroots politics" have challenged our notions of *place,* reminding us to think about places not only as specific geographic and physical sites but also as circuits and networks. These writings also have contradicted localized and bounded social science concepts such as community and culture, calling attention instead to the transnational relations and linkages among overseas communities and between them and their homeland.[9]

Transnational migration studies form a highly fragmented field; there continues to be much disagreement about the scope of the field and the outcome of the transnational processes under observation.[10] I engage transnationalism in this book not because I expect that transnational lifestyles—the back-and-forth flow of people, ideas, material resources, and multisited projects—will become the rule in the near future. Indeed, I suspect that the literature on transnationalism has overemphasized transnational circuits and understated the permanency of immigrant settlement. Like Pierette Hondagneu-Sotelo and Ernestine Avila and others, I believe that most immigrants in the United States are here to stay, regardless of their initial intentions and their continuing involvement in the political, social, and economic lives of their countries of origin.[11] At the same time, it is precisely because of the "permanent" status of Filipino immigrants in the United States that I find their ongoing social and emotional connections to the Philippines most surprising and thus in need of study. I am interested in understanding not only how but also why Filipino immigrants who have settled permanently in the United States would continue to maintain transnational families, social networks, and communities.

From an epistemological stance, I find transnationalism to be a valuable *conceptual* tool, one that disrupts the narrow emphasis on "modes of incorporation" characteristic of much of the published work in the field of U.S. immigration studies.[12] While no longer bound by a simplistic assimilationist paradigm, the field has remained "America-centric," with an overwhelming emphasis on the process of "becoming American."[13] The concept of transnationalism, used as a heuristic device, highlights instead the range and depth of migrants' lived experience in multinational social fields.[14] It is important to note that transnational activities are not new. As early as 1916, Randolph Bourne, in his classic essay "Transnational America," argued that the nation might have to accept "dual citizenship" and "free and mobile passage of the immigrant between America and his native land."[15] Given the notoriety of Bourne's essay, we must ask why the concept of transnationalism never really did enter the lexicon of political and scholarly debates on immigration. Instead, *pluralism, melting pot,* and *assimilation*—terms that presumed (and prescribed) unidirectional migration flows—dominated our discussion. Following Barry Goldberg,[16] I contend that scholars and policy experts cast aside the idea of transnationalism because it poses too much of a challenge to the "mythistory" of the United States—one that valorizes the linear narratives of immigration, assimilation, and nationhood. Going against these linear narratives, this book (re)presents Filipino migration as multifaceted movements across borders.

A critical transnational perspective also provokes us to think beyond the limits of the nation-state, that is, to be attentive to the global relations that set the context for immigration and immigrant life. In this age of increasing worldwide interconnection, the boundaries of the nation-state seldom correspond to the transnational social, cultural, economic, and political spaces of daily life.[17] At the same time, today's global world is not just some glorious hybrid, complex, mixity; it is systematically divided.[18] As Doreen Massey reminds us, these deep ruptures and inequalities are not mere "geographical differences" but are produced and maintained within the very process of globalization.[19] A vision of the world as an unstructured and free unbounded space obscures the asymmetrical links between First and Third World nations forged by colonization, decolonization, and the globalization of late capitalism.[20] Calling attention to global structures of inequality, recent social theorists have linked migration processes with the global penetration of Western economic systems, technological infrastructures, and popular cultures into non-Western countries.[21] Although the details vary, these works posit that the internationalization of capitalistic economic system to Third World countries has produced imbalances in their internal social and economic structures and subsequently has spurred emigration.[22] Indeed, all the nation-states from which the largest number of U.S. immigrants originate—Mexico, China (including Taiwan and Hong Kong), the Philippines, El Salvador, Cuba, the Dominican Republic, South Korea, Guatemala, Vietnam, Laos, and Cambodia—have had sustained and sometimes intimate social, political, and economic relations with the United States.

A transnational approach that stresses the global structures of inequality is critical for understanding Asian immigration and Asian American lives in the United States. Linking global economic development with global histories of colonialism, Edna Bonacich and Lucie Cheng argue that the pre–World War II immigration of Asians to the United States has to be understood within the context of the development of capitalism in Europe and the United States and the emergence of imperialism, especially in relation to Asia.[23] From World War II onward, as the world economy has become much more globally integrated, Asia has been a site of U.S. expansion. As a result, contemporary immigrants from the Philippines, South Vietnam, South Korea, Cambodia, and Laos come from countries that have been deeply disrupted by U.S. colonialism, war, and neocolonial capitalism.[24] Since contemporary immigration and modern imperialism are "two sides of a single global phenomenon,"[25] contemporary Asian immigration to the United States can be better understood as "the 'return' of Asian immigrants to the imperial center."[26] In this sense, contemporary Asian immigration erodes the spatial structure of colonialism by interspersing the "colonial self" and the "colonized other" in interpenetrating spaces.[27]

The history of U.S. imperialism in Asia suggests that Asian American "racial formation" has been determined not exclusively by events in the United States but also by U.S. colonialism and neocolonialism in Asia.[28] But the process of Asian American racial formation has been neither singular nor unified. Owing to the multiple contexts of colonialism and its various extensions into the development of global capitalism, Asians in the United States have experienced different processes of racialization specific to each group's historical and material conditions.[29] In the case of Filipinos, who come from a homeland that was a U.S. colony for more than half a century and that continues to persist as "virtually an appendage of the U.S. corporate power elite,"[30] their formation as a racialized minority does not begin in the United States but rather in the homeland already affected by U.S. economic, social, and cultural influences. The prior flow of population, armies, goods, capital, and culture—moving primarily from the United States to the Philippines—profoundly dislocated many Filipinos from their home and subsequently spurred their migration to the United States and elsewhere.

The history of U.S. colonialism in the Philippines reminds us that immigrant lives are shaped not only by the social location of their group within the host country but also by the position of their home country within the global racial order.[31] Writing on the marginal status of immigrants of color in North American society, M. G. Vassanji proposes that "the marginalization of the non-European immigrant is concomitant to the marginalization of the world he or she comes from—a country and culture viewed as alien, backward, poor, and unhappy."[32] With "civilization" constructed as implicitly white, nation-states such as the Philippines continue to be subordinated and defined as racially different and hence inferior and without history or culture. As such, U.S. racism against Filipino immigrants—misrepresented variously as the little brown brothers, the monkeys, the prostitutes, the mail-order brides—is not only a contemporary backlash against the influx of recent Filipino immigrants but is also part of a continuum that goes back to U.S. racism in and colonialization of the Philippines. It is the convergence of these multiple historical trajectories—their location in the United States, in the Philippines, and in the space between—that is the focus of this book.

ABOUT MYTHS: IMMIGRANT SUCCESS AND IMMIGRANT MENACE STORIES

The abundant literature on immigration—both popular and academic—tends to begin with the premise that immigrants are a "problem." It is striking how this literature locates the problem *not* in the political and economic oppression or violence that produces massive displacements and movements of people, but within the bodies and minds of the migrants themselves.[33] Developed during the peak years of mass immigration from Europe, the sociology of immigration, particularly that of the Chicago School, approached the study of immigrants and their absorption into U.S. society as a social problem requiring specialized correctives and interventions.[34] Today, when more than 80 percent of the "newer" immigrants are from Asia and Latin America, immigration is regularly presented in public debates and popular images as a problem to be solved and a flow to be stopped.[35] Contemporary research on immigration has likewise produced numerous cost-benefit analyses of immigrants' impact on the economy, on the labor market, and on local, state, and federal treasuries.[36]

Among all contemporary U.S. immigrants, Mexicans are singled out as especially problematic.[37] According to Leo Chavez, the media have consistently represented Mexican immigration using alarmist imagery. In his provocative study of magazine covers on immigration since 1965, Chavez finds that "Mexicans are imaged as low-income, low-skilled people whose threat of 'invasion' derives from their numbers, reproductive capacities, and competition for jobs with low-educated, low-skilled U.S. citizens."[38] Along the same line, Hondagneu-Sotelo argues that in the early 1990s, with the Proposition 187 campaign in California, the dominant anti-Mexican immigration narrative characterized Mexican immigrants and their children as a growing underclass class who drained the government treasuries fed by U.S. citizen-taxpayers.[39]

In contrast, media images of and stories about Asian immigrants generally celebrate their purported economic assimilation, pronouncing that many Asian immigrants "do not fit the stereotype of the huddled masses" and that "they are educated and middle class, ready and eager to prosper in America."[40] Many scholars have disputed this claim, emphasizing instead the economic diversity among Asian Americans, especially the persistent poverty experienced by Southeast Asian refugees.[41] Even so, the socioeconomic status of certain Asian groups exceeded that of whites, fueling the characterization of Asian Americans as the model minority. Overall, the post-1965 Filipino immigrants constitute a relatively affluent group: in 1990, more than half joined the ranks of managers and professionals; their median household income exceeded that of all Americans and even that of whites; and their percentage of college graduates was twice that of all Americans.[42]

Given the relative occupational, educational, and class advantages of Filipinos in the United States, the story of Filipino migration is often recounted as an immigrant success story—one that validates the myth of the United States as the land of opportunity. Because groups in the

United States are racialized relatively to yet differently from one another,[43] the immigrant success story works as an effective foil to the immigrant menace myth: Filipino and other Asian immigrants succeed because they have the right cultural values, while Mexican and other Latino/a immigrants fail because they do not. Other researchers have called attention to the class diversity within both the Filipino and the Mexican communities.[44] Here I am more interested in the ways in which the "immigrant success" and the "immigrant menace" stories work in tandem to "obscur[e] the operation of racial power, protecting it from challenge, and permitting ongoing racialization via racially coded methods."[45] Embedded in the language of liberal individualism, these "colorblind" myths promote cultural beliefs in innate racial difference, preventing us from seeking structural explanations for social inequality.[46]

From an America-centric perspective, the stories of Filipino and Mexican migration begin when the immigrants arrive on U.S. soil. Thus told, the differences in their socioeconomic profiles become "interiorized"; that is, they become differences in natural abilities, unmediated by global politics and power.[47] But when recounted from a critical transnational perspective, the stories of Filipino and Mexican migration must begin with U.S. military, economic, and market intervention in the Philippines and Mexico, respectively. It is this history of the U.S. exercise of global power in Asia and Latin America—and not of the immigrants' abilities and values—that shapes the terms on which these groups enter and become integrated into the United States. As Hondagneu-Sotelo and others have argued, Mexican migration—and the number, low average education, and working-class status of the migrants—has its historical origins in U.S. geopolitical and economic expansion in Mexico, and in deliberate, active, and continuous recruitment of low-wage workers to fill labor demands in agriculture and other U.S. service industries.[48] In the Filipino case, as I document in this book, the different cohorts of Filipino immigrants—the pre–World War II agricultural laborers, the pre-1970 Filipino sailors in the U.S. Navy, and the post-1965 medical professionals—have their roots in early-twentieth-century U.S. imperialism and colonization of the Philippines and in U.S. changing labor needs. By telling the story this way—that is, by indicating that the socioeconomic profiles of Filipino and Mexican immigrants reflect U.S. global interests and needs for different types and sources of labor—I disrupt the immigrant success/menace binary and call attention instead to shared histories and lives.

A few more words about the fictionality of success. Scholars, the media, and the public often herald the "remarkable success" of Filipino and other Asian immigrants as evidence of the "declining significance of race" in the United States. But economic success—and its converse, economic hardship—provides but one index of racial violations. I am less interested here in debating the economic status of Filipino immigrants, not because I don't consider it important, but because I am haunted more by what Avery Gordon terms "the subtleties of domination."[49] In her highly original and provocative call for scholars to imagine alternative stories about the relationship among power, knowledge, and experience, Gordon urges us not to settle for "narrower and narrower evidence for the harms and indignities" that people experience, but to be as vigilant about the more "subtle violations" that are often unseen and denied:

> [T]he sublimating insecurities and the exorbitant taxes for our unquestioned behavior; the wear and tear of long years of struggling to survive; the exhausting anger and shame at patiently and repetitively explaining or irritably shouting about what can certainly be known but is treated as an unfathomable mystery; the deep pain of always having to compete in a contest you did not have any part in designing for what most matters and merits; the sinking demoralization and forlorn craziness of exchanging everything with the invisible hands of a voracious market; the quiet stranglehold of a full-time alertness to benevolent rule; and the virtually unspeakable loss of control, the abnegation, over what is possible.[50]

It is these subtler violations—the sublimating insecurities, the exhausting anger and shame, the deep pain, the sinking demoralization and forlorn craziness, and the unspeakable loss—that I am most compelled to document in this book about Filipino lives.

HOME AND ABROAD: RETHINKING COMMUNITY, CULTURE, AND PLACE

> I am a turtle, wherever I go I carry "home" on my back.
>
> Gloria Anzaldúa, *Borderlands*

For some time now, scholars have been concerned with how global flows of people, capital, and cultural forms have altered the processes of identity formation. Recent empirical research indicates that amid this transnational flow, many immigrants anchor themselves by carrying "home" on their backs. This practice is most apparent in the case of immigrants, refugees, and exiles who continue to invest in "back-home" lives and ties even as they establish social, economic, and political relations in their new country.[51] Postwar Asian America is populated with transnational migrants—the nonresident Indians, the Chinese "astronauts," the *Viet Kieu* (overseas Vietnamese), the *balikbayans* (Filipino returnees or homecomers)—whose households, activities, networks, ideologies, and identities transcend the boundaries of the nation-states between which the migrants move.[52] The existence of these trans-Pacific lives establishes that the lines separating Asian and Asian American, "so crucial to identity formations in the past, are increasingly blurred."[53] Reflecting the prominence of Asian American transnational lives, many Asian American writers have addressed the theme of exile in their stories and poems, with the strength of the exile's ties to the homeland a constant in much of the literature.[54] In an essay on diasporic politics in South Asian American literature, Ketu Katrak argues that this blurring of the "here" and "there" challenges the linearity of time and the specificity of space "by juxtaposing the immigrants' here and now, with their past histories and geographies."[55]

Cognizant of the lives that are lived in the "space between,"[56] in this book I document the languages and social practices that go into remembering and constructing the homeland—particularly the ways in which Filipino families, identities, and resources cross national boundaries and connect the Philippines with the United States. Living between the old and the new, between homes, and between languages, immigrants do not merely insert or incorporate themselves into existing spaces in the United States; they also transform these spaces and create new ones, such as the "space between." This transnational space, then, is a productive site from which to study immigration because it articulates the tensions, irresolutions, and contradictions characteristic of immigrant lives. Most of the Filipinos whom I interviewed, regardless of their regional and class origins, have kept ties with family, friends, and colleagues in the Philippines through occasional visits, telephone calls, remittances, and medical and other humanitarian missions. In so doing, they have created and maintained fluid and multiple identities that link them simultaneously to both countries. These transnational connections underscore the multiplicity of Filipino lives and work against definitions that would fix them in one identity or one place.

It is important to note, however, that home is not only a physical place that immigrants return to for temporary and intermittent visits but also a concept and a desire—a place that immigrants visit through the imagination.[57] Hamid Naficy defines home in the following way: "*Home* is anyplace; it is temporary and it is moveable; it can be built, rebuilt, and carried in memory and by acts of imagination."[58] While it is true that affluent immigrants have greater access than do the working poor to transnational practices, I would argue that all immigrants—regardless of class—can and do "return home" through the imagination. As Bienvenido Santos poignantly reminds us: "All exiles want to go home. Although many of them never return, in their imagination they make their journey a thousand times."[59] Ketu Katrak has described this return through the imagination—or through memory and written and visual texts—as the "simultaneity of geography, . . . the possibility of living here in body and elsewhere in mind and imagination."[60] People who relocate carry with them not only their physical belongings but also their memories. As Anton Shammas puts it, "We don't ever leave home. We simply drag it behind us wherever we go, walls, roof, and all."[61] In focusing on both actual transnational activities (in the form of home visits, kinship ties, and remittances) and imagined returns to one's native home (through memory and cultural rediscovery), I hope to show that the process of migration encompasses both a *literal* and a *symbolic* transnationalism.

The practice of symbolic transnationalism is most evident—and most poignant—in the lives of U.S.-born Filipinos. How do young Filipinos who have never been "home" imagine the "homeland"? And how do they recall that which is somewhere else, that which was perhaps never known?[62] Largely unacquainted with their home country, U.S.-born children depend on their parents' tutelage to craft and affirm their ethnic self, and thus they are particularly vulnerable to charges of cultural ignorance.[63] In an important article on the "transnational struggles" of second-generation Filipino Americans, Diane Wolf suggests that Filipino youth experience "emotional transnationalism," which situates them between different generational and locational points of reference, their parents', sometimes also their grandparents', and their own.[64] Focusing on these "transnational struggles," I will explore the ways in which immigrant parents, as self-appointed guardians of "authentic" cultural memory and representatives of "home," can opt to regulate their children's, especially their daughters', independent choices by linking them to cultural betrayal.

While it is important to document the transnational aspects of immigrant lives, it is equally important to recognize that immigrants—even as transnationals—remain structured by the national politics and national culture of their host country. Calling attention to the deterritorialization of identity formation in the global age, Arjun Appadurai has advised us to stop thinking solely in terms of physical spaces and to imagine instead a "post-national geography" of "global ethnoscapes."[65] While Appadurai's framework enables us to think about the ways in which ethnic identities extend beyond national borders, it undervalues the enduring importance of local spaces, memories, and practices; underestimates the continuing power of the nation-state; and implies a formation that is not structured by domestic and global power relations or is not shaped by differences in culture, class, gender, race, and national origin.[66] Even as transnational migrants live literally or symbolically across borders, they are not deterritorialized, free-floating people.[67] Instead, they continue to exist, interact, construct their identities, and exercise their rights within nation-states that monopolize power and impose categories of identity on local residents. That is, identities, while constantly in flux, are not free-floating, because the shifting terrain of identities is positioned in histories, cultures, languages, classes, localities, communities, and politics. In a comparative study of rich and poor Asian immigrants to the United States, Aihwa Ong argues that immigrant groups are bound by the "cultural inscription of state power and other forms of regulation that define the different modalities of belonging."[68] As such, the strategies that immigrants use to fashion themselves in the world are not all a matter of choice but are profoundly influenced by who or what the immigrants can be in the *physical spaces*—the local contexts—in which they find themselves. As Guarzino and Smith maintain, "The social construction of 'place' is still a process of local meaning-making, territorial specificity, juridical control, and economic development, however complexly articulated these localities become in transnational economic, political, and cultural flows."[69]

In sum, this book is attentive to the dialectic between the powers of the state to circumscribe life chances and to impose categories of identity on immigrants and on the ability of these immigrants—through their various constructions of home—to contest, resist, or deflect these impositions on their self-constructions. In other words, the process of "subjectification" is a dual process of self-making and being made in relation to nation-states and the wider world.[70]

THE POLITICS OF LOCATION AND HOME(S)

Those with an anthropological concept of culture have often assumed that a natural identity exists between people and places, and that discrete peoples belong to specific, bounded territories, which frame their distinct cultures and local identities. Working against this fixed concept of culture, I explore in this book the politics of location—how immigrants use literal or symbolic ties to the homeland as a form of resistance to places and practices in the host country that are patently "not home."[71] As colonized and racially marked immigrants in the United States, Filipinos have been distanced from the "national" or "America," blocked from full political and economic participation, and alienated from cultural Americaness, which was founded on whiteness. In the context of U.S. (neo)colonial subjugation of the Philippines, globalized capitalism, and racialized and feminized international division of labor, Filipino American lives challenge the myth of a welcoming America—the land of opportunity and fair play—and call attention instead to an exclusionary U.S. national identity that has been built historically by distancing the body politic from the racially different other.[72]

In a stunning indictment of the possessive investment in whiteness, George Lipsitz demonstrates that the construction of the "American people" as white—in the realm of public policy, politics, and culture—has served to maintain white privilege and justify and perpetuate the subordination of people of color.[73] Alexander Saxton points out that U.S. society has been racially exclusive from the very beginning:

> Already in the days of Jefferson and the 'sainted Jackson' . . . the nation had assumed the form of a racially exclusive democracy—democratic in the sense that it sought to provide equal opportunities for the pursuit of whiteness by its white citizens through the enslavement of Afro-Americans, extermination of Indians, and territorial expansion largely at the expense of Mexicans and Indians.[74]

The investment in whiteness has also been made explicit in the imperial ambitions of the United States in Asia. When the Philippines were forcibly turned into a U.S. colony at the turn of the twentieth century, Filipinos joined Africans, Mexicans, and Native Americans in being the "white man's burden," the object of "domestic racial imperialism" carried out through brutal racial violence by the U.S. military and by co-optative patronage.[75] In the United States, the investment in whiteness has been institutionalized in federal, state, and local laws that prevented Asians from immigrating to the United States and forbade those already there to become naturalized citizens, to own land, and to participate in the primary labor force and in the court cases that upheld these laws.[76] Until the passage of the Tydings-McDuffie Act of 1934, Filipinos occupied the ambiguous and stigmatized status of "U.S. nationals"—desired as cheap and unprotected labor but excluded from legal and cultural citizenship.

The assumption of whiteness as a diacritic of citizenship has also been made explicit in the social and cultural construction of Asian Americans, even as citizens, as the inassimilable aliens who "are alleged to be self-disqualified from full American membership by materialistic motives, questionable political allegiance, and, above all, outlandish, overripe, 'Oriental' cultures."[77] This cultural discrimination brands all Asians as perpetual foreigners—a status that marks them simultaneously as marginal and as threatening. Although Filipinos have been in the United States since the middle of the 1700s and Americans have been in the Philippines since at least the late 1900s, U.S. Filipinos—as racialized nationals, immigrants, and citizens—"are still practically an invisible and silent minority."[78] Lamenting the neglect of Filipino Americans in the existing literature on U.S. immigration, ethnicity, and communities, Filipino American critics have declared that Filipinos are the "forgotten Asian Americans"; that "not much is known about them"; and that on this group there is "no history. No published literature. No nothing."[79] Certainly, the institutional invisibility of Filipino Americans is a testament to their ambiguous status as the "foreigner within." However, this invisibility is also connected to the historical amnesia and self-erasure regarding the U.S. colonization of the Philippines in particular and U.S. imperialism in general. Finally, in a country that defines its nationalism in terms of whiteness and patriarchy, Filipino immigrant women in particular are clearly "not home," because they are not white and male.

Responding to this enforced "homelessness," many Filipino immigrants have articulated a sense of home by memorializing the homeland and by building on familial and communal ties. Focusing on the everyday imagining of home and country among Filipino immigrants, I hope to show that homes are not neutral places and that "imagining a home is as political an act as is imagining a nation."[80] Memory of place is significant because it helps to locate the individual in a community, to bind family members together, and to shape personal identity.[81] In immigrant communities, the remembered homeland takes on a special significance: not only does it form a lifeline to the home country and a basis for group identity in a new and often alien and oppressive context, but it is also a base on which immigrants construct community and home life and on which they stake their political and sociocultural claims on their adoptive country.[82] Ethnographies of migrants, exiles, and refugees increasingly find that the "there" of deterritorialized peoples is in part at least an "imagined community," invented "to make present felt absences in their lives."[83]

The idealization of the home country, however, becomes problematic when it elicits a nostalgia for a glorious past that never was, a nostalgia that elides exclusion, power relations, and difference or when it elicits a desire to replicate these inequities as a means to buttress lost status and identities in the adopted country. I am particularly interested in the tensions between the patriarchal control, in the name of culture and nationalism, of immigrant women, especially of second-generation daughters, and the efforts of these women to contest and negotiate these expressions of nationalism through their roles as mothers, daughters, workers, organizers, and lovers. I will pay particular attention to the patriarchal call for cultural "authenticity," rendering immigrant women and second-generation daughters emblematic of the community's cultural survival and obliterating contradictions and intricacies in the process. In so doing, I challenge the depoliticized version of multiculturalism that unproblematically celebrates the survival and reinvention of "ethnic" practices. Instead, I highlight the gendered differentials embedded in these ethnic traditions and show that identities forged from below are often no less essentialized than the hegemonic identities imposed from above.[84]

Dorinne Kondo has argued that for many people on the margins, home, however problematic and provisional, "is that which we cannot not want."[85] On the one hand, in an inhospitable world, home stands for a safe place, for community. On the other, because the construct of home (and culture) is inseparable from power relations, home can simultaneously be an unsafe, violent, and oppressive site for people on the margins such as women and children. As Rosemary George argues, home is both a place of violence and nurturing, a place to escape to as well as escape from, and a place that is established as the exclusive domain of a few.[86] It is this tension—between the necessity and inevitability of a desire for "home" and the accompanying dangers of that desire—that this book explores. In calling attention to the gap between the realities and the idealization of "home," in this book I seek to politicize geography, to argue against the notion of an unproblematic geographic location of home, and to reassess our understanding of belonging and origin—which are not always the same thing.[87] The challenge, then, is to find ways of conceptualizing community and home differently without dismissing its appeal and importance in immigrant lives.

BUILDING ALLIANCES: COMMUNITIES OF RESISTANCE

Migration is significant in the reconstitution of identities because it allows migrants partially to escape from subject identity(ies) constructed and contained by the laws and cultures of any single nation-state.[88] As a multiply constituted people, Filipino American identities and lives are formed and informed by different notions of "home," by the struggles to be "at home" in multiple locations, and by overlapping and competing loyalties to various causes in all these homes. The stresses of migration—the struggles against xenophobia, cultural racism, and economic discrimination—have intensified considerably Filipino immigrants' identification with their place of origin. At the same time, they have also firmly rooted Filipinos in joined struggles with each other and with other kin communities to define and claim *their* place in the United States. In their struggles for a place to be, Filipino immigrants have shifted between multiple and dynamic identities, simultaneously narrowing and enlarging their scope of affiliations. For example, those who do not think of themselves as Filipinos before migration become Filipinos in the United States and/or reinforce narrower regional and linguistic identities. I am particularly interested in documenting the ways in which Filipino American identities are constructed among dialect and regional groups, between immigrant and U.S.-born Filipinos, and among Filipinos of different class background.

To understand the complexities of Filipino American lives, we also need to be attentive to the Filipino community's interaction with other local communities. Throughout the first half or more of the twentieth century, for all immigrant groups coming into California, dominant white American society served as the primary point of reference for their construction of identities as immigrants. However, for most contemporary immigrants in California, the white American receiving culture, while still prominent, is no longer the only or even the primary frame of reference within which immigrant identities are constructed.[89] In Los Angeles, for example, growing numbers of Asian and Latino immigrants have changed the complexion of race relations, producing a multipolar frame of reference within which both accommodation and differentiation occur. As they have become each other's neighbors, African Americans, Asian Americans, and Latinos in Los Angeles (and elsewhere) have often collided as they competed with one another for scarce resources.[90] Yet these communities have also coalesced, united by shared interests and by similar experiences as racialized subjects and oppressed class of "colored" laborers.[91] Filipinos in San Diego have had ongoing relations—both antagonistic and cooperative—with local Asian Americans, Latinos, and African Americans. Mindful that outsiders generally lump all Asians together, Filipino Americans, especially those born in the United States, have at times heralded their common fate to build political unity with other Asian Americans. As the two largest groups of color in San Diego, Filipinos and Latinos (primarily Mexican Americans), despite their disparate socioeconomic profiles, have historically braved many similar injustices brought about by persistent and at times virulent personal and institutional racism against them. Moving beyond an Asian–Euro American dyad, I seek to understand interethnic, and interracial, relations. Coalition work, while essential for the dismantling of white supremacy, is risky. To coalesce, to "open the barred room to persons from different locations with different agendas," is to risk losing one's secure place—one's home.[92] It is these unlikely and risky coalitions across groups—and the historical and social conditions that produce them—that I wish to document in this book.

STUDYING FILIPINOS IN SAN DIEGO

This book is a case study of one community: the Filipino American community in San Diego, California. San Diego has long been a favorite place of settlement for Filipinos and is today the third largest U.S. destination of contemporary Filipino immigrants.[93] As the site of the largest U.S. naval base and the Navy's primary West Coast training facility, San Diego has been a primary area of settlement for Filipino navy personnel and their families since the early 1900s. As in other Filipino communities along the Pacific Coast, the San Diego community grew dramatically in the twenty-five years following passage of the 1965 Immigration Act. New immigration contributed greatly to the tripling of the county's Filipino American population from 1970 to 1980 and its doubling from 1980 to 1990. In 1990, there were close to 96,000 Filipinos in San Diego County; by 2000, the population had risen to 121,147. Although these immigrants comprised only 4 percent of the county's general population, they constituted more than 50 percent of the Asian American population.

I do not claim that San Diego is representative of the United States. As a study of one community, this report has no statistical weight outside itself. Yet I believe that the intimacy and depth of a community study allow us to examine at close range and in rich contextual detail both people's material circumstances and their alternative understandings of and struggles against these local and extralocal circumstances.[94] As Cathy Small suggests, "It is at the mundane levels of daily events and interpersonal relationships that the mechanisms for larger social trajectories exist."[95] Formally, the information in this book came primarily from in-depth tape-recorded interviews that I conducted with Filipinos in San Diego. Such interviews are valuable, because they allow us to listen to individuals' own interpretations, definitions, and perceptions of their experiences, in short, to listen to their life stories—the "truths" of their experiences.[96] As Ninna Nyberg Sorensen proposes, if we are interested in understanding how migration affects people's sense of belonging and identity, then we need to listen to how migrants themselves interpret their situatedness, and how they culturally construct "histories" and "herstories."[97] To protect the privacy of these individuals, I have given them fictitious names in this book. However, I use the person's real name if his or her life story has already been published in my 1995 book, *Filipino American Lives*.

Over the course of eight years (1992–2000), I interviewed just over one hundred Filipinos in San Diego County. My first interview took place in the summer of 1992 with a Filipino priest at our parish church: the Mission San Luis Rey in Oceanside, a suburb in North County, San Diego. This priest promptly introduced me to Joe and Peachy Rebaya—a beloved Filipino couple in their sixties—who had since become known as "Papa Joe" and "Mama Peachy" in our family. Because the Rebayas knew so many Filipinos in San Diego, they were able to introduce me to Filipinos in different parts of the county. From this crucial initial contact, I then used "snowball" referrals to find others to interview. In other words, I chose participants not randomly but rather through a network of Filipino American contacts whom the first group of respondents trusted. To capture as much as possible the diversity within the Filipino American community, I sought and selected respondents of different backgrounds and with diverse viewpoints.

The interviews, tape recorded in English, ranged from three to ten hours each and took place in offices, coffee shops, and homes. My questions were open-ended and covered four general areas: family and immigration history, ethnic identity and practices, family relations, and community development. The interviewing process varied widely: some respondents needed to be prompted with specific questions, while others spoke at great length on their own. Some chose to cover the span of their lives; others focused on specific events that were particularly important to them. I found that the dynamics of gender emerged more clearly in the interviews of women than in those of men. Because gender has been a marked category for women, the mothers and daughters I interviewed rarely told their life stories without reference to the dynamics of gender.[98] Even without prompting, young Filipinas almost always recounted stories of restrictive gender roles and gender expectations, particularly of parental control over their whereabouts and sexuality.

I believe that my personal and social characteristics influenced the process of data collection, the quality of the data I gathered, and my analysis of them. As a Vietnamese-born woman who immigrated to the United States at age twelve, I came to the research project not as an "objective" outsider but as a fellow Asian immigrant who shared some of the experiences of my respondents. During my fieldwork, I did not remain detached but instead actively shared with my informants my own experiences of being an Asian immigrant woman: of being perceived as an outsider in U.S. society, of speaking English as a second language, of being a woman of color in a racialized patriarchal society, and of negotiating intergenerational tensions within my own family. Some respondents drew parallels between their experiences as a Filipino and my experiences as a Vietnamese. For example, a Filipina in her forties instructed me, "We are Filipinos because of our skin color. Just like you. You cannot get away from being an Asian because of how you look like." I do not claim that these shared struggles grant me "insider status" into the Filipino American community; the differences in our histories, cultures, languages, and at times class backgrounds remain important. But I do claim that these shared experiences enable me to bring to the work a *comparative* perspective that is implicit, intuitive, and informed by my own identities and positionalities and with it a commitment to approach these subjects with sensitivity and rigor. In a cogent call for scholars of color to expand on the premise of studying "our own" by studying other "others," Ruby Tapia argues that these implicitly comparative projects are valuable because they permit us to highlight the different and *differentiating* functional forces of racialization.[99] It is with this deep interest in discovering—and forging—commonalities out of our specific and disparate experiences that I began this study on Filipino Americans in San Diego.

The Filipinos I interviewed are about equally divided between first-generation immigrants (those who immigrated to the United States as adults) and Filipinas/os who were born and/or raised in the United States. A 1992 analysis of the socioeconomic characteristics of recent Filipino immigrants in San Diego indicated that they were predominantly middle-class, college-educated, and English-speaking professionals who were much more likely to own rather than rent their homes.[100] Even though these and other statistical data indicate that many post-1965 Filipinos came to San Diego as professionals, I often found it difficult to pinpoint the class status of the people I interviewed. To be sure, there were poor working-class immigrants who barely eked out a living just as there were educated professionals who thrived in middle- and upper-class suburban neighborhoods. However, the class status of many of the immigrants I interviewed was much more ambiguous. I met Filipinos/as who toiled as assembly workers but who—through pooling income and finances and working multiple shifts—owned homes in middle-class communities. I also discovered that class status was transnational, determined as much by one's economic positions in the Philippines as it is in the United States. For example, I encountered people who struggled economically in the United States but who owned sizable properties in the Philippines. And I interviewed immigrants who continued to view themselves as "upper class" even while living in dire conditions in the United States. These examples suggest that the upper/middle/working–class typology, while useful, does not adequately capture the complexity of immigrant lives. Reflecting the prominent presence of the U.S. Navy in San Diego, more than half of my respondents were affiliated with or had relatives affiliated with the Navy. I also found that it was much more difficult to interview the working poor because they had little free time away from work and because they tended to believe that their lives—specifically their lack of material accomplishments—were not "interesting" enough to be recorded.

OVERVIEW

Organized around the concepts of boundary maintenance and boundary transgression, this book integrates the analysis of microstructures of the home, the family, and the domestic realm with macro debates about globalization, the nation, and community.[101] Chapter 2 situates Filipino migration to the United States within the larger history of U.S. colonialism and neocolonialism and capital investment in Asia. While larger political, economic, and cultural forces provide pressures, resources, and opportunities for U.S.-bound migration, they do not shape actual patterns of migration. Instead, this chapter shows that it is often gender, class, and culture—as manifested in family and community relations—that determine who migrates and when. Chapter 3 links the annexation of the Philippines and the subsequent Filipino immigration to the United States to the racialized economic, political, and cultural foundations of the U.S. nation. Drawing on the material and cultural histories of Filipinos both in the Philippines and in the United States, this chapter argues that the racialization of Filipinos is more accurately a case of "differential inclusion" rather than one of "exclusion." Chapter 4 explores how immigrants attempt to "reconnect" with the Philippines through literal and symbolic transnational activities. Chapter 5 describes the evolution of the Filipino American community in San Diego and reconstructs, through the words of local residents, what it is like to be Filipino in San Diego during different historical periods. It situates the growth and dynamics of the Filipino community and polity within the larger sociopolitical contexts by examining intergroup relations within the Filipino American community and between Filipino Americans and other local communities. Focusing on home as a private domestic space, chapter 6 explores the effects of employment patterns on gender relations among Filipino immigrants. To underscore the impact of U.S. imperialist occupation of the Philippines on the emigration of specific types of Filipino labor to the United States, this chapter focuses on the two most "conspicuous" groups of Filipino/a workers: Filipino Navy men and Filipina nurses. Chapter 7 extends the discussion on family relations by examining the relationship between Filipino immigrant parents and their daughters. It explores the ways in which female morality—defined as women's dedication to their families and sexual restraints—becomes a site for racialized immigrants to express cultural resistance against racial oppression. Chapter 8 features the voices of the U.S.-born and/or -raised Filipino Americans, paying particular attention to the strategies that they use to construct multiple and overlapping identities and to rework dominant ideologies about their place in contemporary U.S. society. Chapter 9 summarizes the book's main arguments and calls for home-making projects that transgress borders and work against all pervasive and systemic forms of domination. In all, these chapters tell us how Filipinos in the United States have created "home" for themselves amid constant dislocation, migration, and endless assault.

While the stories told in this book confirm the appeal and importance of home in immigrant lives, they also remind us of the tensions, exclusions, and power relations that exist in any construction of home. My title, *Home Bound*, is meant to convey this doubleness: Filipino immigrants are bound for home, and they are also bound to and by home.

CHAPTER 2

Leaving Home

Filipino Migration/Return to the United States

The United States is the biggest reality in our lives.

Renato Constantino,
"Identity and Consciousness"

Because of the American influence, everything American was considered to be the best. It's like if you made it to America, you were in heaven, and certainly that was prevalent in my family because of my sister sending Sears & Roebuck catalogs, money, packages, and stuff, and just the smell of things makes us want to come to America badly.

Nicholas Azores, Filipino immigrant

Geopolitical upheaval, displacement, dispersal—such has been the way of life for millions of Filipinos scattered around the world. The ferocity of U.S. (neo)colonial exploitation, the mismanagement of the Philippines by the country's comprador elite, and the violence of globalized capitalism have flung Filipinos "to the ends of the earth" as contract workers, sojourners, expatriates, refugees, exiles, and immigrants.[1] Although Filipinos can be found in more than 130 countries, with most earning a living as short-term contract workers, the vast majority of the "permanent" Filipino emigrants have settled in the United States.[2] According to the 2000 U.S. census, Filipinos totaled 1.8 million, comprising the second-largest immigrant group as well as the second-largest Asian American group in the United States.[3]

U.S. colonialism stunted the Philippine national economy, imposed English as the lingua franca, installed a U.S.-style educational system, and Americanized many Filipino values and aspirations. Even long after the Philippines regained its independence in 1946, the United States continued to exert significant influence on the archipelago—through trade, foreign assistance, and military bases. Besides imposing strong and unequal military and economic ties between the two countries, this colonial heritage has produced a pervasive cultural Americanization of the population, exhorting Filipinos to regard the American culture, political system, and way of life as more prestigious than their own. Infected with U.S. colonial culture and images of U.S. abundance peddled by the educational system, the media, and relatives and friends already in the United States—and saddled by the grave economic and political conditions in the Philippines—many Filipinos migrated to the United States to claim for themselves the promises of the "land of opportunity."

Although Filipino migration needs to be situated within the larger history of U.S. (neo)colonialism and capital investment in Asia, these structural forces do not shape actual patterns of migration. Immigrant women and men are neither passive victims nor homogeneous "pools of migrant labor" responding mechanically and uniformly to the same set of structural forces.[4] Instead, they are active participants in the process of migration who vary by gender, generation, class, and culture. I argue that it is these variations—as manifested in community and family relations—that shape how individuals respond to the pressures and opportunities exerted by larger structural transformations. To capture the varied contexts and experiences of migration—to understand who migrates and when and why migrants behave as they do—we need to look more intimately at their lives, examining both the social contexts in which they decide to migrate and the complex social networks and family ties that support the migration process.[5] Attentive to the larger political, economic, and cultural context of migration and to the human agency and subjectivity of the migrants, this chapter shows that it is the intersection of macro and micro forces that shapes the migration—and eventual settlement—of Filipino women and men to San Diego County.

BORDER CROSSERS: FIRST CAME THE AMERICANS

In the United States, public discussion about immigration fundamentally centers on people who cross borders. However, the media, elected officials, and the general public often represent border crossers to be desperate individuals migrating in search of the "land of opportunity." At its worst, this representation is both racist and misogynist, demonizing the immigrants as uninvited and illegitimate partakers of the American dream.[6] From the perspective of immigration restrictionists, immigrants unfairly "invade" the United States, drain its scarce resources, and threaten its cultural unity. Besides fueling nativist hysteria, this anti-immigrant rhetoric makes invisible other important border crossers: U.S. colonizers, the military, and corporations that invade and forcefully deplete the economic and cultural resources of less-powerful countries.[7] Given these multiple forms of border crossings, a critical approach to immigration studies must begin with the unequal links between First and Third World nations forged by colonization, decolonization, and the globalization of late capitalism.

The argument of this chapter is simple: Filipinos went to the United States because Americans went first to the Philippines. In other words, Filipino migration to the United States must be understood within the context of U.S. imperialism in the Philippines and in Asia. In 1898, in the aftermath of the Spanish-American War, the United States brutally took possession of the Philippines over native opposition and uprising, thereby extending its "Manifest Destiny" to Pacific Asia. The often-ignored Philippine-American War (1899–1902) resulted in the death of about a million Filipinos, the violent destruction of the nationalist forces, and the U.S. territorial annexation of the Philippines—ostensibly to prepare the archipelago for eventual independence.

The U.S. occupation infiltrated all segments of Philippine society. Politically, the colonial government structured the Philippine government after that of the United States. It was to win over the existing leadership of the Philippines and to pacify Filipino nationalists that the United States adopted the policy of Filipinization: the gradual substitution of Filipino personnel for American administrators and clerks in the colonial government. As early as 1900, Filipinos began assuming positions in the municipal, provincial, and later, in the national governments. However, Americans still controlled the strategic positions that allowed them to formulate and implement policies. Under U.S. colonial rule, the Philippine national economy changed significantly. Foremost among these changes was the further development of the agricultural export economy (begun under Spanish rule), with sugar in the lead, and the growing dependence on imports for such basic necessities as rice and textiles. By its tariff regulations and the subsequent "free trade" between the two countries, the United States fostered this export-import policy and kept the Philippines an unindustrialized export economy—a condition that depleted the country's economic resources and propelled the eventual migration of many Filipinos.[8]

As a civilian government replaced military rule, the cultural Americanization of the Philippine population became an integral part of the process of colonization. Convinced that education, rather than outright military suppression, was the more effective means to pacify the Filipinos, U.S. colonizers introduced a universal public education and revamped Philippine educational institutions and curricula using the American system as its model and English as the language of instruction. When the Philippine Commission took over civil governance of the Philippines, it kept English as the primary medium of instruction. Filipino historian Renato Constantino contends that through this educational policy, the colonial educational system became an instrument of assimilation or Americanization. With the use of U.S. textbooks, "young Filipinos began learning not a new language but a new culture. Education became miseducation because it began to de-Filipinize the youth, taught them to regard American culture as superior to any other, and American society as the model *par excellence* for Philippine society."[9]

Whereas U.S. invasion, annexation, and subjugation of the Philippines have left indelible moral and physical marks on the country and its people, these violent acts have been largely erased from American public memory or obscured by public myths about U.S. benevolence and the "civilizing mission" in the Philippines.[10] But the facts of imperialism are *not* erasable. The enduring legacies of U.S. empire are *present* in the Philippine economy, its political structure, its educational system, and its cultural institutions—all of which continue to be dominated or influenced by the United States.[11] The impact of the U.S. empire on Filipinos is also very much present in the United States—perhaps most visible in the presence of large Filipino American communities. Linking U.S. (neo)colonial subjugation of Filipinos in the Philippines to the fate of Filipinos in the United States, Oscar Campomanes insists that "the consequences of [the] inaugural moment of U.S. Philippine relations for latter-day U.S. Filipinos are manifold and extend to their politics or forms of recognition and emergence."[12]

COMING TO THE U.S.A.

Filipino migration to the United States—from the *pensionados* to the agricultural laborers to the professional workers—has clearly been the "by-product of U.S. policies towards and in the Philippines."[13] During the first decade of the twentieth century, as part of their effort to acculturate Filipinos and to augment their devotion to the United States, the territorial government sent several hundred individuals to study in U.S.

colleges and universities. Highly selected, these *pensionados* often were the children of prominent Filipino families whose loyalty the colonial regime hoped to win.[14] U.S. policies also accounted for the mass migration of Filipino laborers before World War II. After the passage of successive Asian exclusion laws, labor recruiters from Hawaii and the U.S. West Coast concentrated on the Philippines "as the only available source of permanent labor supply and the only hope of the future under existing laws."[15] As U.S. nationals, Filipinos could bypass exclusion laws and thus became the target of aggressive and well-organized labor-recruitment programs. In the hard-pressed regions of the Philippines, labor recruiters met willing emigrants—individuals who had been displaced and dislocated because of the devastating U.S. economic policies in the Philippines.[16]

The 1920s was a decade of dramatic increase in Filipino migration, with some forty-five thousand Filipinos migrating to the U.S. West Coast. Although Filipinos scattered across the country, the majority concentrated in California. From 1923 to 1929, Filipinos streamed into the state at the rate of more than 4,100 a year. Between 1910 and 1930, the Filipino population in California had increased from only five to 30,470.[17] But Filipino migration proved to be short-lived. By the early 1930s, as the Filipino population grew and as the Great Depression engulfed the nation, white resentment against Filipino laborers intensified. In the midst of the Depression, exclusionists sought unsuccessfully to repatriate the Filipinos.[18] Anti-Filipino forces also brutally drove Filipino men out of various communities, branding them as sexual threats seeking the company of white women at taxi dance halls.[19] Ultimately, Filipino legal status as U.S. nationals had to be changed if they were to be excluded. In 1934, yielding to anti-Filipino forces, the U.S. Congress passed the Tydings-McDuffie Independence Act, granting the Philippines eventual independence, declaring Filipinos to be aliens, and cutting Filipino immigration to a trickle of fifty people a year.[20] This act slowed but did not halt immigration from the Philippines. Filipinos who served in the U.S. armed forces, especially in the U.S. Navy, were among the few who were exempted from this immigration restriction. And they continued to come.

TO SERVE THE (COLONIAL) NATION: FILIPINOS IN THE U.S. NAVY

It was during the Philippine-American War at the turn of the century that the United States established its first military bases in the Philippines.

Since then, the Philippines had hosted—often unwillingly—some of the United States' largest overseas air force and naval bases. In a review of the forms and functions of overseas bases, Robert Harkavy reports that from the nineteenth century until and beyond World War II, most overseas bases throughout the world were "automatically provided by colonial control and were an important aspect and purpose of imperial domination."[21] Even after the Philippines' formal independence in 1946, the Military Bases Agreement, signed one year later, gave the United States exclusive use of twenty-three specific bases, both naval and air, rent free, for ninety-nine years.[22] Although the agreement was signed in 1947, its preliminary terms had been arranged before World War II, in effect making it an agreement between the United States and its colony, not between two sovereign states.[23] In comparing this Military Bases Agreement with similar postwar military arrangements between the United States and other countries, Voltaire Garcia II concluded that "the Philippine treaty is the most onerous" and that its provisions "made the bases virtual territories of the United States."[24] It was not until a 1991 vote for national sovereignty by the Philippine Senate that the last U.S.-controlled base (Subic Bay Naval Station) was turned over to the Philippine government in 1992, some ninety-four years after the first U.S. troops landed in the Philippines.[25]

During the ninety-four years of U.S. military presence in the Philippines, U.S. bases served as recruiting stations for the U.S. Navy. Filipinos were the only foreign nationals who were allowed to enlist in the U.S. armed forces; and the Navy was the only military branch they could join. After the United States acquired the Philippines from Spain in 1898, its Navy began actively recruiting Filipinos primarily as stewards and mess boys. From a total of nine people in 1903, the number of Filipinos in the U.S. Navy grew to six thousand by World War I and hovered around four thousand (or 5 percent of the total Navy manpower) during the 1920s and 1930s.[26] After the Philippines achieved full independence in 1946, the United States no longer could unilaterally authorize recruitment of Filipino nationals, since they had become citizens of their own country. To sidestep this obstacle, U.S. officials inserted a provision in the 1947 Military Bases Agreement (article 27) granting its Navy the right to continue to recruit Filipino citizens. With the onset of the Korean war in the early 1950s, the U.S. Navy allowed for the enrollment of up to two thousand Filipinos per calendar year for terms of four or six years.[27]

Besides serving as recruiting stations, these military bases—centers of wealth amid local poverty—exposed the local populace to U.S. money, culture, and standards of living, generating a strong incentive for enlistment. The economic incentive to join the U.S. Navy was high: the salary of a Filipino enlistee often placed him among the top quarter of his country's wage earners. Filipino recruits also used their service in the Navy to gain U.S. citizenship—the perceived springboard for escaping from poverty.[28] During the 1960s, some one hundred thousand Filipinos applied to the U.S. Navy each year, but few were admitted, owing to a high reenlistment rate of 94 to 99 percent among Filipinos.[29] By comparison, less than 50 percent of the U.S. citizen enlistees reenlist after their first enlistment.[30] By 1970, in large part because of the grave economic, political, and social problems besetting the Philippines, there were more Filipinos in the U.S. Navy (fourteen thousand) than in the entire Philippine Navy.[31] In 1973, when the U.S. Navy reduced the number of Filipino recruits from two thousand to four hundred per year, approximately two hundred thousands applied for the coveted slots. According to the U.S. Navy Chief of Legislative Affairs, in the 1970s about forty thousand potential Filipino enlistees were available at any given time.[32]

Before and during World War I, the U.S. Navy allowed Filipino enlistees to serve in a range of occupational ratings such as petty officers, band masters, musicians, coxswains' mates, seamen, machinists, firemen, water tenders, commissary stewards, officers' stewards, and mess attendants. However, after the war, the Navy issued a new ruling restricting Filipinos, even those with a college education, to the ratings of officers' stewards and mess attendants.[33] During this period, "virtually all stewards were either Black or Filipino."[34] In 1922, when the Navy officially excluded African Americans, the majority of mess attendants were Filipinos. The number of Filipino enlistees first surpassed that of African American enlistees in 1914. By 1922, there were almost four times as many Filipino enlistees as there were African American enlistees. By 1930, the Filipino–African American ratio was ten to one.[35] It was only when the Navy experienced a shortage of Filipino enlistments in 1936 that it reopened its doors (but only partially) to African Americans.[36] Barred from admission to other ratings, Filipino enlistees performed the work of domestics, preparing and serving the officers' meals and caring for the officers' galley, wardroom, and living spaces. When they were ashore, their duties ranged from ordinary housework to food services at the U.S. Naval Academy mess hall. Unofficially, Filipino stewards also have been ordered to perform menial chores such as walking the officers' dogs and acting as personal servants for the officers' wives. Even when they passed the relevant qualifying examinations, few Filipinos were allowed to transfer to other ratings—unless they were the personal favorites of high-ranking officials who agreed to intervene on their behalf. In 1970, of the 16,669 Filipinos in the U.S. Navy, 80 percent were in the steward rating.[37]

In the early 1970s, amid the demands of the civil rights movement and escalating tensions and charges of white racism in the Navy, the U.S. Senate investigated the Navy's record on racial issues. Although most of the senatorial investigation focused on the Navy's discriminatory treatment of black sailors, it also questioned the Navy's practice of recruiting Filipinos as stewards, mess boys, houseboys, and servants for its officers. Admiral James L. Holloway III, Chief of Naval Operations—who himself had four Filipino houseboys assigned to his living quarters—defended the practice as "a continuation of traditional relationship" and a "compassionate" act that provided ambitious Filipinos an opportunity to escape grinding poverty at home.[38] Under the leadership of Navy Admiral Elmo Zumwalt, the U.S. Navy eventually amended its policies to grant Filipino enlistees the right to enter any occupational rating. In 1973, the first year of the new Navy policy, Filipino nationals served in fifty-six of the eighty-seven ratings available for enlistees. But they were not distributed evenly among these ratings. According to Navy statistics for that year, more than 40 percent of Filipinos remained stewards. Of the balance, the majority congregated in clerical positions such as personnel man, disbursing clerk, storekeeper, and commissary man.[39] In 1992, with the ending of the bases agreement, the Navy finally stopped its century-old practice of recruiting Filipino nationals.[40]

These Navy-related immigrants form a distinct segment of the Filipino American community. Because of their shared lives in the U.S. Navy, these Filipino personnel and their families cultivate informal but lasting social networks—often following each other from one post to the next. In fact, many Filipino Navy retirees prefer living near their "old Navy comrades with whom they spent a great deal of time while in the service."[41] In U.S. cities with large naval facilities, Navy families comprise a sizable segment of the Filipino communities—often providing the impetus for and sponsorship of subsequent chain migration. In San Diego, the former site of the largest U.S. naval base and the Navy's primary West Coast training facility, Filipino Navy families are ubiquitous, forming the cornerstone of the Filipino American community there. Aware of the paucity of materials on Filipino

American Navy families, I have explored their lives in more detail in chapter 6.

AND STILL THEY CAME

After an imposed lull brought about by U.S. exclusion laws, Filipino immigration sped up in the 1970s. The 1965 Immigration Act, which abolished the national-origins quotas and permitted entry based primarily on family reunification or occupational characteristics, dramatically increased the number of Asian immigrants. In the twenty years following passage of the 1965 act, about 40 percent of the documented immigration to the United States has come from Asia.[42] The Philippines has been the largest source, with Filipinos comprising nearly one-quarter of the total Asian immigration. In the 1961–1965 period, fewer than sixteen thousand Filipinos immigrated to the United States, compared to more than two hundred and ten thousand in the 1981–1985 period. Since 1979, more than forty thousand Filipinos have been admitted annually, making the Philippines the second largest source of all immigration, surpassed only by Mexico.[43]

The 1965 Immigration Act alone, however, does not explain why so many Filipinos have come to the United States in the last quarter century. The military, business, and cultural ties forged between the Philippines and the United States during the ninety-plus years of (neo)colonial rule have definitely propelled and shaped this movement. Many scholars have attributed the U.S.-bound migration to the grave economic conditions in the Philippines. During the 1960s, the Philippine economy registered high growth when President Ferdinand Marcos implemented an economic plan that depended solely on U.S. war efforts in Vietnam. When U.S. forces withdrew from Vietnam, the Philippines was left with an economic infrastructure ill suited to local needs.[44] By the end of the Marcos era in 1986, the Philippines was bankrupt, and inflation was rampant. Weighed down by a gigantic debt and heavily dependent on agricultural exports, the Philippine economy suffers from massive unemployment and inequality in the distribution of income and wealth. Driven off the land, many peasants migrate to Manila in search of livelihood, but the city does not have enough industries to support its burgeoning population.[45]

In addition, since the 1960s, the Philippines has harbored an oversupply of educated people. With U.S. aid, the Philippines underwent an "educational boom" after World War II. In 1970, one-quarter of the college-age population in the Philippines was enrolled in colleges and universities, a ratio second only to that of the United States. But this growing army of college-educated Filipinos faced extremely limited employment prospects. Heather Low Ruth estimated that in the late 1960s, jobs were available for only half the college graduates in the Philippines.[46] Under such grave economic conditions, many Filipinos sought employment all over the world either as permanent immigrants or as short-term contract workers. For many Filipino migrants to the United States, migration is attractive not so much because of the promise of lucrative jobs or unlimited mobility but because of the differential between their potential earnings in the United States and in the Philippines. As Cathy Small reminds us, this international differential in earnings is not natural, but a "legacy of colonialism."[47]

But the push to leave was also political. Declaring martial law in 1972, President Marcos prorogued the legislature, controlled the media, suspended the writ of habeas corpus, and arrested many of his alleged political opponents. According to a U.S. congressional report, there were between five hundred and one thousand political prisoners in the Philippines at the end of 1978.[48] During the Marcos era (1965–1986), an estimated three hundred thousand Filipinos emigrated to the United States.[49] In 1983, the U.S. Immigration and Naturalization Service (INS) reported that 208 Filipinos had filed for political asylum that year, although only eighteen were granted asylum.[50]

Since the 1960s, the Philippines has sent the largest number of professional immigrants to the United States, the majority of whom are physicians, nurses, and other health practitioners.[51] The overrepresentation of health professionals among contemporary Filipino immigrants is not accidental; rather, it is the result of deliberate recruitment from U.S. hospitals, nursing homes, and health organizations seeking to fill their recurring shortage of medical personnel. The Philippines has become the major source of foreign-trained nurses in the United States, with at least twenty-five thousand Filipino nurses arriving between 1966 and 1985.[52] In fact, many women in the Philippines studied nursing in the hope of securing employment abroad, and many of the nursing programs in the Philippines accordingly oriented themselves toward supplying the U.S. market.[53] Beginning in the early 1960s, as the demand for nursing education exceeded the enrollment slots available in Philippine colleges and schools of nursing, Filipino businessmen and health educators opened new schools of nursing in the provinces as well as in urban areas. Between 1950 and 1970, the number of nursing schools in the Philippines increased from just seventeen to 140.[54]

Like the migration of Filipino Navy men, the migration of Filipino nurses must be understood within the context of U.S. colonialism. Catherine Choy argues that the development of this mobile labor force is inextricably linked to the history of U.S. imperialism and the early-twentieth-century U.S. colonization of the Philippines. The establishment of Americanized professional nursing training in the Philippines during the U.S. colonial period laid the professional, social, and cultural groundwork for a "feminized, highly educated and exportable labor force."[55] In the early twentieth century, Filipino nurse migrants, as U.S.-sponsored scholars, constituted a unique sector of the Philippine intellectual elite. In the mid-twentieth century, as exchange visitors under the auspices of the Exchange Visitor Program, they became Philippine cultural ambassadors in the United States, and U.S. nursing ambassadors upon their return to the Philippines. Like the early-twentieth-century scholarship programs to the United States such as the *pensionado* program, the Exchange Visitor Program reconstructed a global, cultural, and intellectual hierarchy in which U.S. institutions—educational, political, medical—were superior to those of the Philippines. By the 1960s, Filipino nurses entered the United States through two major avenues: the Exchange Visitor Program and the new occupational preference categories of the Immigration Act of 1965. The latter avenue of entry enabled Filipino nurses not only to enter the United States but also to settle as permanent residents. Their personal and professional lives will be examined more closely in chapter 6.

Not all contemporary immigrants from the Philippines are professionals, however. Instead, the dual goals of the 1965 Immigration Act—to facilitate family reunification and to admit workers needed by the U.S. economy—have resulted in two distinct chains of emigration: one of the relatives of Filipinos who had left for the United States before 1965 and another chain of highly trained immigrants who entered during the late 1960s and early 1970s. As indicated in table 1, during the 1966–1975 period, the two groups entered in about the same proportion. However, in the 1976–1988 period, the proportion of occupational-preference immigrants dropped to 19–20 percent of the Filipino total, while the proportion of family-preference immigrants rose to about 80 percent. This shift was the result of tightened entry requirements for professionals in the mid-1970s and their subsequent reliance on family reunification cat-

TABLE 1. PROPORTION OF OCCUPATIONAL-PREFERENCE AND FAMILY-PREFERENCE IMMIGRANTS FROM THE PHILIPPINES FROM 1966 TO 1988

		Occupational-Preference Immigrants	Family-Preference Immigrants
1966–70	Total number	30,350	31,090
	Percentage	49.5	50.4
1971–75	Total number	49,606	46,610
	Percentage	51.5	48.4
1976–80	Total Number	19,035	78,605
	Percentage	19.3	79.8
1981–85	Total Number	18,470	78,431
	Percentage	19.0	80.9
1986–88	Total Number	11,681	45,914
	Percentage	20.3	79.6

SOURCE: Carino, Fawcett, Gardner, and Arnold, 1990: tables 4 and 5.

egories.[56] As a result of these two distinct groups of immigrants, the contemporary Filipino American community exhibits more class diversity than it did in the past, adding to the complexity of the contemporary Filipino experience.

NEEDS, WANTS, AND DESIRES: LEAVING THE PHILIPPINES

Leaving the Philippines was a frightening experience for me. One of the saddest moments in my life was the day we were to leave for the U.S. Even at my young age of seventeen, I understood that I would never return and that even if I did, it would be different, because I would be a different person. I knew that I would never again live in my village, that I was stretching my umbilical cords so far that even if they stay connected, they would never snap back so that I could end up the same place that I started. I remember crying and trying to hide, not wanting to go, while knowing all the time that I must. My emotions were mixed. I was excited by what I knew of America from books, magazines, movies, and former classmates who had lived in America, but at the same time I was feeling insecure.

Dario Villa, Filipino immigrant

In 1976, I left for the United States the week of July 12, Philippine Independence Day. I remember feeling elated as the Pan-Am jet lifted off from Manila International Airport. I was at last free from the tentacles of Marcos's repressive government. But I also felt sad about leaving behind a beloved and wonderful homeland. It was an emotionally wrenching period in my life. I was not just leaving my country and family behind, I was also leaving Lucie, my bride of one month, behind too!

Edgar Gamboa, Filipino immigrant

Leaving one's home country is often a wrenching experience. As vividly illustrated in the quotes above, even after some twenty years in the United States, the pain, sadness, and anguish of leaving are still etched in the minds and hearts of these two Filipino immigrants. If migration entails such agony, then why do so many people head abroad each year? There is a widespread assumption—in the scholarly literature as well as in the popular imagination—that immigrants, especially those from developing countries, come to the United States primarily for economic reasons such as obtaining a higher income and standard of living. These economic explanations are well documented in the "push-pull" and macrostructural approaches to the study of migration. The push-pull approach casts the individual migrant as a calculating economic agent, weighing the benefits and costs of migrating.[57] But individuals do not act in a vacuum devoid of historical and political context. Attentive to history and political economy, the macrostructural approaches detail the broad structural forces—such as colonialism, imperialism, global capitalism—which induce, propel, as well as limit migration.[58]

In my discussion of Filipino migration thus far, I have urged us to pay attention to the "big picture"—that is, to situate the origins of Filipino migration within history and the political economy, especially within the context of U.S. colonialism in the Philippines. While this big picture crucially frames the migration process, it cannot account for the unexpected, the unforeseen, the unintended—the part and parcel of the *hu-*

man experience. In a highly original study of Japanese migration to the East Coast at the turn of the twentieth century, Mitziko Sawada argues that the "imprecise" and "sweeping" process of migration "reflected the specific circumstances of the migrants, who acted according to convention, against convention, or, as the case may be, by trial and error."[59] She urges us to pay particular attention to individual motives—motives that mix economic needs with personal longings, dreams, and fantasies about different worlds and different possibilities. That is, we are to pay attention not only to individual needs but also to their wants and desires.

Migrants from all over the world have many reasons for migrating other than or in addition to economic opportunity and political freedom. They leave to see the world, to "find" themselves, to avoid family demands, to join family members, to escape from an undesired marriage, to marry, and to experience "new sensations."[60] The Filipino migrants whom I interviewed in San Diego are no different. They certainly "vote with their feet," not only against economic and political repression, but also against the suppression of their wants and desires. In the following section, I want to convey, through the life stories of four individuals, the complex and specific circumstances that compel migration. My purpose here is not to be comprehensive or representative; neither is possible. Rather, I hope that these narratives will force us to reach beyond the conventional economic and political explanations for migration and to be attentive to and moved by "the distinctive, interesting, complicated, nonessentialist aspects that more accurately reflect the complexities of human life."[61] These narratives are not complete; I have edited them to highlight migration-related events. To convey as much as possible the person behind the narratives, I have presented them in first-person.

A. B. Santos: "I Wanted to Get Married"

I hate to tell you how old I am. I am a very old man. I was born December 26, 1907, in Saint Nicholas in the province of Ilocos Norte. My mother was a housekeeper. My father was a traveling merchant. He was killed during World War II by the Japanese.

My grandfather was a really devout Catholic. His word was law in our family. When I was about fifteen years old, I overheard that my grandfather wanted to send me to the seminary. When I heard that, I ran away from home to Manila because I didn't want to go to the seminary. My grandfather asked why. I told him that it was because a priest cannot get married and I wanted to get married. Because his word was law, my parents had to obey him. But I outsmarted him by leaving.

So I went to Manila. I met some town mates [there] who were much older than I was; I could have been their son. They were coming to the United States to look for jobs, so I decided to go with them. I did not know much about the United States, but I had heard from the Americans and the other Filipinos that there were many opportunities there. I had an American teacher who used to tell our class that in the United States, as long as you are willing to work and you are not weak, you can survive very well. So I was impressed with this. It was this kind of information that gave me all the courage. My town mates took care of me until we arrived in San Francisco.

We arrived in San Francisco in 1922. At that time, I spoke a little English. People could understand me, but I had to repeat. I was good, especially in writing, because from kindergarten to my first year in high school the instruction was all in English, and the Americans were our teachers. A relative of my town mates was a contractor for a Salinas [California] farm, and he was looking for men to work picking sweet peas. I volunteered to go. About thirty of us young people went with him to Salinas to work. So my first job in the United States was picking sweet peas. I only worked there for two weeks. It was hard work for me. I ached all over, my back, my legs, because I was not used to it.

My grandfather's godson was in San Diego working at the Coronado Hotel. When I wrote to him, he told me to come to San Diego. So I came. I got a job at the Coronado Hotel. It was around wintertime, and my job was to turn on the lights of the executive dining room in the morning, set it up, turn on the heater, and make sure that everything was in order. So that was my job, and I was paid twenty dollars a month with board. I wanted to prove to my parents and my grandfather that I could survive without being a priest. With my very first paycheck, I bought a very expensive hat for my grandfather. And that made him change his attitude toward me. I was no longer the boy who was not going to amount to anything.

When World War II came, I got drafted into the U.S. Army. They drafted me in 1943 even though I was a foreigner, a noncitizen. I reported to Los Angeles. When I got there, they swore me in as a U.S. citizen. I did not even have to file an application. So that was how I became a U.S. citizen. I learned about the First Filipino Infantry Regiment, which was formed in 1942. I requested to be transferred there because I knew they were going to be assigned to the Pacific. In 1944, I began my counterintelligence work in the Philippines. The day that the Japanese surrendered, I ran back to my office and requested a discharge. I wanted to go back to the United States to complete my education. But they told me that they still needed me because I spoke several Filipino dialects, Spanish, and English. They assigned me to work for the U.S. Veterans Administration as a contact representative. That was where I met my wife, Juanita, in 1946.[62]

Maria Rafael: "I Had No Intention of Coming to the United States"

I was born in Manila in 1949. I am the oldest of seven children. My mom was a housewife, and my dad was a security guard. In high school, there is a scholarship to go to the States, and everybody wanted to go. I didn't want to go but they said they had to send the best students to America. I was very active in school so they wanted me to try out. So I interviewed and they told me I was going to America. My goal was really just to compete and win as I was trained to compete, to always be on top. So I came to San Diego in '66 and '67 and I went to Crawford High School. I was an exchange student for a year. I liked it here as an experience but I never really intended to come here and stay here. I felt that the United States was too individualistic. There is not the warmth of being among your friends. In high school, everybody just kind of wants to be by themselves. It was never like that when I was growing up. Here, there was just not the camaraderie that I had and I thought that you were left too much alone to worry about things.

I went back to the Philippines and I married my first and only boyfriend. I met him in college and we were together all through college. But he dropped out in his third year of college; he didn't like school. And I finished. When I came back from the States, one of my friends from the exchange student program was an account executive for a big advertising firm, and she asked me if I would like to work for them. And I said, "I am just out of high school." Over there, working full-time out of high school is something that doesn't happen. It's very rare. People have to finish college before they can even get a job. But this friend said we want you to join our team, and so I was offered a job. I was a market researcher. I worked full-time and went to school at night full-time. I had to maintain my grades because I wanted to keep my scholarship. I was the oldest of a big family, and a lot of pressure was on me to succeed. I was the first college graduate in all of my clan.

I had no intention of coming to the United States. All my children were born in the Philippines. One day, in late 1977, this letter from the

U.S. embassy came to my husband. It said that you are now able to come to the United States. Without even knowing, my husband had been petitioned by his brother. His brother was in the service and he petitioned for everybody else in the family. I told my husband I didn't want to go because I was already working for the Philippines Center for Advanced Studies, which is actually a think tank for President Marcos. I was a research assistant. But my husband wanted to go. He was just an employee. And he was not set in a job. He saw it as an opportunity, and he wanted to take it and see how it goes for him. He's also got brothers here.

I told my husband I am happy here [in the Philippines], and I know how it's there [in the States], it probably will be harder there. I had fun here [in the Philippines]. I said to him, "No, I don't want to go. But if you want to go, go." He said he didn't want to go without me but that he wanted to go. So I said, "Okay, you go first and give it a try." But he said, "No, we have to go together." So I said, "I'll try." I even left my children behind for fifteen months. I didn't want to bring them because I was so adamant about not coming. "Believe me, you are not going to like it there," I told him. I said, "I am not bringing my children. If you like it there and I like it there, then we'll send for the children." So we came to San Diego, where my husband's brother was. He was the one who petitioned us.

I did not look forward to coming to the States like a lot of people did. A lot of people, that's all they want: to go to the States and make a lot of money. That was a goal for them. It was never a goal for me. I resisted coming here. I was transplanted and I could never give up what I had there, and so I am lost. I don't know how to transfer the skills that I had there to here. It was difficult trying to decide whether we should stay here, should we bring the children, should we start out from nothing, which is what we actually had to do. Then I thought of my children. I was not sure if I should deprive them of the opportunity of trying it out here or not and I decided I don't think I should deprive them. I will have them come here and let them see how it is here compared to back there. I didn't feel I should make that decision for them.

My husband is happy here and my children are happy here. But I still have not stopped wanting to go back. And it has been fifteen years. I still don't feel American. My children tell me that you have to stop thinking about the Philippines. I am just biding my time here. I'm here because that's where my family wanted me. I'm here for my family. That's what they want me to do, and I'm just waiting for a time when I can say I'm ready to do things for myself, and what I want to do is to go back and be there and do something else for my country.

So my goal is just to go back. Maybe it's just me. I always feel like I meant more back there. I am used to being in the center of things. Here I only exist.

Cecilia Bonus: "I Just Wanted to Get Away and Be Independent"

I was born in 1957 in Manila. My mother was a housewife mainly; my dad was the main supporter while we were growing up. But when we were all grown up, my mom was a teacher, she was a professor of English. My dad was a businessman. He was in the lumber company, and he also owned a farm. I have five sisters and two brothers. So there's eight of us.

I have a B.S. in nursing. My aunt is a nurse, and I always idolized her when I was a little girl. She was always wearing white and all that. And then right after graduation, I applied for this working visa. This was back in '79. My application to the United States, it just came sporadically; it wasn't really planned. Some of my classmates went and applied, and so I just thought one day, "Oh, maybe I should go apply and go to the United States" because my family was just so protective. I just kind of wanted to get away and be independent. I just tried out but it wasn't really my intention to come over here. So I passed and I said, "Okay, I'll go." We were given the choice of which states we wanted to go to. I don't know why I chose Michigan, but I did. I didn't know anybody there.

I thought I was going to have fun in the States, but then it was so lonely! I went to Sheridan in Michigan. It was a small, a little itty-bitty hospital. A forty-bed hospital, and it was a small town. I never expected it to be that small. I thought of America being big but then [here I was in] this little town. It was a population of two thousand, I think, not a big town . . . Everybody knew each other. It didn't even have a McDonald's, you know; all they had was a low-price store, a little drugstore, a small bank, a small shopping center, and a really small grocery store. And if you wanted to go to McDonald's you had to drive like thirty minutes to get to it. I was so lonely, I was always on the phone, always, always! That was my biggest expense. I probably spent three hundred dollars a month for my phone bill. Talking to my family and my boyfriend in the Philippines. I didn't have a car then, so all my money went to the phone bill. Every time it snowed, every time there was a blizzard, I just got so depressed. I had to call up home.

There was another [Filipino] girl that came with me, but I didn't know her until we were going to fly out over there. We were the only Filipinas in the community. Everybody was white. I didn't even see one black person. Everybody really welcomed us, but I guess it was the first time that they'd seen an Oriental person. They'd never had Filipino nurses come over there. In fact, they were talking to us about typhoons. They thought in the Philippines we were tied in trees when typhoons happened. They had this perception that the Philippines was a jungle. I was laughing because Manila was much more cosmopolitan than that town. These people have never been exposed to different cultures. They have never seen other cultures or people in different countries.

I stayed there for one year. Then I was supposed to go back home. But then on my way back to California, I stopped in Chicago to visit some friends. And these friends were relocating to California and they were going to drive there. So I said, "You guys are driving. That must be fun." I was going to go back to the Philippines and get married because I was engaged to this boyfriend of mine. So I wanted to have some fun, to go interstate so I could see all these states. But unfortunately, we met [with] an accident in Utah before we got to California. And I was stranded in Utah. I had broken bones and I was fractured all over so I had to stay there for a month and a half.

But before I left Chicago, I met the man who became my husband. He was just an acquaintance. I never thought he would ever become my husband. He was working in Chicago. So while I was in Utah in the hospital for about two months, he was the one, he came and visited us with one of my classmates who was in Chicago. Then it all started there—in Utah, because of the accident. When I got better, I flew out to California because I was going to leave for the Philippines. But then he followed me. And then we finally dated, then we came to know each other, and before you know it, I got married to him. So I never got back to the Philippines. I had to refund my ticket. So we got married and he petitioned for me. I still consider the Philippines home but my husband, he likes it here.

Edgar Gamboa: "The Reason I Came to the United States Was Mainly Political"

I was born in Cebu City, Central Visayas, in 1948, the second of nine children. My father's father was a Spanish *haciendero* [landowner] from northern Spain, and his mother was a mestiza, or half-Filipina and half-Spanish. My mother's father was a very successful businessman and the foremost importer of American-made products in the region. My wife Lucie's family is one of the oldest and wealthiest families in Cebu. Her maternal grandfather, who was educated in Spain, was the city's first physician. He also started the island's still-existing electric company, a shipping company, and several other establishments. Lucie's father was a physician who practiced for at least fifty years.

The reason that I came to the United States was mainly political. I had been accepted to medical school, the Cebu Institute of Medicine, in 1970. When the Philippines was placed under martial law in 1972, I joined the Christian Social Democrats, an organization of political moderates, founded by Senator Raul Manglapus. I was president of the Medical Student Government and a member of the National Council of Medical Students, and we used to regularly demonstrate in the streets, protesting extensive government abuses.

Fred Dimaya, one of my best friends in med school, was an active underground student activist for the KM [Kabataang Malcabayan], a student Marxist-Maoist group. In 1972, he actually left for the hills to join the Communist movement. He served as a volunteer medic for the "people's army." He was later captured, imprisoned, and tortured. I had the chance to see Fred again soon after his release from prison. He was a broken man. I heard later that Fred was able to put his life back together. He had met his wife, a student nurse activist, "in the hills," and they had been captured together. I understand that he is now a religious minister.

I graduated from medical school in 1974. At that time, my intention was to stay in the Philippines. But I also fell in love with surgery. I saw how significantly one could help others by being a good surgeon. I wanted to work with the rural and urban poor. I did my postgraduate internship at the Veterans Hospital in Quezon City, where surgical technology and science fascinated me. After that internship, I went back to Cebu to specialize in general surgery.

Many medical graduates and friends were leaving for the United States en masse, but I still felt it was not right to leave behind a country in disarray. Ironically, med graduates from the University of the Philippines, a hotbed of nationalistic fervor, were the first to leave for the United States in droves and contributed more to the "brain-drain" phenomenon than those from any of the other six medical schools in the country.

I vividly remember one incident, when med students were demonstrating against the administration, the dean of the medical school remarked, "All you idealistic students. Your concerns about the poor and about the national state of health, these are all well and good. But soon after you graduate and start your own families, you will quickly grow up and decide to leave the country. I guarantee it." Then he challenged the student body: "Those who are *not* going to leave the country, why don't you stand up so we can see you?" I remember only three of us stood up out of a group of fifty or sixty students. We boldly said, "We can promise you, sir, that we are not going to leave and abandon our homeland. We have a responsibility to care for it." As it turned out, out of the three who stood up, I was the first who left.

I was the first to leave because my dear father, who had more wisdom than I had, on his own asked his staff to send applications to different internship programs here in the United States. One day, he beamed as he handed me a two-page contract from Yonkers General Hospital and said, "Ed, you can start your internship in New York in July."

I was fascinated by the thought of traveling and working in the United States, but it really was not in my plans. However, my papa, who was a very patient man, explained: "Look at it this way, Ed. Why don't you go to New York, do your surgical residency, and then by the time you finish the five-year program, Marcos would have been history. Then you can return to the Philippines as a well-trained surgeon and a more effective physician for your countrymen." My father wanted me to leave because he was concerned that my student activism would eventually get me into trouble. The government kept our names in secret files. Being older and wiser, my father put things in perspective for me: "You have to fight your battles, but more importantly, you have to know which battles to fight. If you stayed here and kept demonstrating against the government, you'll end up in prison, just like your friend Fred, and you won't be able to achieve your goals." So in 1976, I left for the United States . . . the week of June 12, Philippines Independence Day.

In 1985, a decade after I first came to the States, I reminded my wife that it's probably time to pack up and return to the Philippines. We had originally planned on staying only for five years. We actually returned to the Philippines for a visit, soon after our green cards were processed. I looked at the possibility of establishing a surgical practice there, but my wife, Lucie, had reservations. Eventually our discussion centered on what was best for the children. We reviewed the pros and cons of raising them in the Philippines or in the United States. It was a difficult choice to make, but we concluded that educational opportunities, at the university level, were far more superior in the U.S. So we decided to stay, even though we knew that it would be difficult for us to impart [to] the kids the conservative values of the old country. On the other hand, we felt that it would be good for the children to be exposed to a more international culture.[63]

◆ ◆ ◆

The four narratives above reveal that U.S.-bound Filipino migration takes place within the context of the (neo)colonial association between the

Philippines and the United States. The glorification of the United States through the colonial educational system; the historically specific recruitment of Filipino nationals to serve in the U.S. armed forces as health practitioners and as low-wage laborers; and the differentials in wage and job opportunities between the two countries: all provide pressure to migrate to the United States.

The lure of America was particularly compelling. The history of U.S. colonialism and the contemporary saturation of U.S. media in the Philippines made the United States appear to be a source of prestige, power, money—a more exciting and expanded world when compared to the Philippines. The following quote—from a Filipino American man who immigrated at the age of fifteen—captures the lure of America expressed by many of the Filipinos that I interviewed:

> It was my dream to come to the United States. I thought I made it to heaven. We had a lot of American influence in Baguio. There was a U.S. air force recreational base right in the middle of the city. So we used to go there and eat candy bars and dream about America, just what America looks like, like the houses, the smell of hamburgers, the smell of Downey or whatever detergent they had going and stuff, and dreaming that some day that I would make it there, and when I finally did, it was the greatest feeling that I ever had.

This macrostructural context, while important, does not determine or shape specific migration responses. As Hondagneu-Sotelo has shown, social networks are the crucial intermediary dimension of migration.[64] Like a good number of other Filipinos in my study, these four narrators considered migration only after an opportunity became available to them through their families or social networks; that is, only after a town mate, spouse, friend, and/or family member assisted them in some way with the migration process. A. B. Santos's travel to the United States was eased by his older and more experienced town mates; Maria Rafael's migration was sponsored by her husband's brother, who was in the U.S. Navy; Cecilia Bonus's decision to apply for a work visa was prompted by her classmates' desire to work and travel in the United States; and Edgar Gamboa's admission to a U.S. medical internship program was arranged by his father, without his knowledge. Survey data confirm the importance of social networks in the migration process, with the majority of Filipino immigrants reporting that joining family members and friends was their primary reason for migrating to the United States. For example, a survey of a representative sample of just over two thousand adult Filipinos who were issued U.S. immigrant visas in 1986 found that a considerable majority (62 percent) immigrated to the United States primarily for affiliative rather than economic reasons.[65] This finding suggests that the macrostructural approach, while important, does not sufficiently account for the internal structure and social dynamics of the migration process, particularly the relevance of kinship, hometown, and other affiliation ties in inducing and facilitating transnational migration.[66]

I want to call attention to yet another level of analysis, that of the *individual*—not as a calculating economic agent but as a desiring subject with complex needs and wants. As the narratives above indicate, each individual had different motives for leaving and acted within and according to the specific circumstances of their lives. A. B. Santos ran away from home to defy his demanding grandfather and to get married; Maria Rafael migrated against her wishes because she *was* married; Cecilia Bonus left the Philippines because she wanted to unshackle herself from her protective parents and see the world; and Edgar Gamboa came to the United States to escape possible political retaliation *and* to better serve the Philippines. These seemingly different motives all stem from desire: for an expanded horizon, for individual development and fulfillment, for an opportunity to be someone else. But migration is not only about unshackling oneself from a constraining past; it is also about being shackled. Maria Rafael's case is an example of the latter: the desire to migrate was not her own but that of her husband who saw it as an opportunity. Although she desired to return to the Philippines and do something for her country, she continues to live in the United States because her husband and children are happy there. Finally, migration is not only about decisions but also about indecisions and unexpected coincidences. Edgar Gamboa, for example, was torn between his fascination with and desire to practice medicine in the United States and his love for and devotion to the Philippines; ultimately, it was his father who decided that Gamboa should go to the United States to escape possible political persecution. And it was the coincidences in Cecilia Bonus's life—her decision to take a road trip to California from Chicago, her car accident, which left her stranded in Utah—that led to her marriage to a Filipino American and her eventual settlement in the United States. In sum, the four narratives remind us that migration, even when framed by the same set of economic and political transformations, is seldom a coherent, unified, and precise process but reflects instead the specific circumstances of the migrants' everyday lives.

CHAPTER 3

"Positively No Filipinos Allowed"

Differential Inclusion and Homelessness

> What is outside is paradoxically what makes the West what it is, the excluded yet integral part of its identity and power.
>
> Timothy Mitchell, *Colonizing Egypt*

> Sometimes, I am not sure what it means to be an American. I am not equal to anyone. My color is different, and that has mattered all of my life. I feel that not all Americans are equal; they are not . . . . I [feel] that the word *American* really doesn't mean anything if you are a person of color, you know. It really doesn't. I don't know, maybe a lot of people would disagree with me, but that's how I feel. I probably will have people say, "Well, then, why doesn't she go back to where she came from?"
>
> Connie Tirona, U.S.-born Filipina

In 1930, a sign in a West Coast hotel declared "Positively No Filipinos Allowed." This sign exemplifies the ways in which Filipinos in the United States have been excluded economically, politically, and culturally from the "national" or "America." Restrictive naturalization and immigration laws, discriminatory housing policies, unfair labor practices, violent physical encounters, and racist and anti-immigrant discourse have all colluded to keep Filipinos outside the nation, that is, to keep them *homeless.* Given this violent record of enforced homelessness, it would be easy to read the history of Filipinos in the United States as one of exclusion. This reading, though appropriate, is incomplete. While it is true that Filipinos have been kept apart from "America," it is also true that they have been at times forcibly included in it—as the infantilized "little brown brothers," colonized nationals, segregated navy stewards, "cheapened" labor, and subordinate citizens. Since Filipinos have been forced to be not only outside but also inside the nation, I believe that it is more accurate to characterize their encounter with the United States as one of *differential inclusion,* rather than of outright exclusion. In this chapter, I use gender as a primary frame of analysis to link imperialism, racialization, and the differential inclusion of Filipinos as second-class citizens in the United States. I focus here on the repressive labor, legal, and cultural practices that have kept Filipinos from becoming rooted in this country. In subsequent chapters, I will address the self-activity and subjectivity of Filipino Americans as they make themselves "at home" in San Diego as well as in transnational spaces.

In their respective works on Asian and Mexican immigration, Lisa Lowe and David Gutierrez have argued that the economic desire by U.S. elites to incorporate Asia and Mexico into the U.S. sphere of influence conflict with the political desire of these same elites to fashion cultural and political unity through "white manhood."[1] As a result of this conflict, immigrants from these nations are cast "both as persons and populations to be integrated into the national political sphere and . . . to be marginalized and returned to their alien origins."[2] Building on these works, I define *differential inclusion* as the process whereby a group of people is deemed integral to the nation's economy, culture, identity, and power—but integral only or precisely because of their designated subordinate standing. Edward Said has described such outcast populations as people whose existence always counts, though their names and identities do not; they are valuable precisely because they are not fully present.[3] Thus the inclusion of Filipinos has been possible, even desirable, only when it is coupled with the exploitation of their bodies, land, and resources, the denial of equal socioeconomic opportunities, and the categorization of them as subpersons of a different and inferior moral status. Paradoxically then, for Filipinos in the United States, to be included in the U.S. nation is simultaneously to be rendered homeless.

I employ the term *differential inclusion* rather than *exclusion* to counter the myth of "voluntary" immigration and to make visible the deliberate and violent peopling of the United States—through conquest, slavery, annexation, and the importation of foreign labor.[4] That is, I want to challenge the narrative of the teeming masses invading the "land of opportunity" and to draw attention instead to the ways in which groups of color have been coercively and differentially made to be part of the nation. I also want to confront the narratives of inclusiveness—of a welcoming America extending the promise of homes and citizenship to the world's poor and persecuted—and to emphasize instead that the process of inclusion, for racialized groups, simultaneously means legal subordination, economic exploitation, and cultural degradation. Finally, I use the term *inclusion* to underscore that Filipinos, and similarly racialized groups, have always been inside of and played absolutely crucial roles in the building and sustaining of the nation; the term *exclusion*, for me, implies that they could be, and in fact are, outside the nation. In so doing, I wish to show that the process of differential inclusion is intimately connected to the "possessive investment in whiteness."[5]

In this chapter, I situate the differential inclusion of Filipinos in the U.S. nation within the larger context of the American empire. I do so to call attention to the ways in which the history of U.S. imperialism in the Philippines continues to take a toll on the lives of millions of Filipinos scattered around the world—long after U.S. troops and bureaucrats are gone. Although imperialism is most often treated as a matter of economics and diplomacy, it has an embodied presence in the lives of people from colonized nations. The situated knowledges of Filipinos—as colonized nationals, immigrants, and workers—make evident the global dimension of racism: Filipino American lives have been shaped not only by the historical racialization of Filipinos in the United States but also by the status of the Philippines in the global economy. Moreover, by locating Filipino American history within the history of conquest and annexation, rather than within the history of immigration, I intend to highlight the historical and intersectional nature of racial formation. That is, I want to point out the ways in which the lives of Filipino Americans have paralleled and intersected not only the lives of other Asian Americans but also those of Native Americans, African Americans, and Latinos. This chapter is not meant to be comprehensive. My goal is more modest: to illustrate some of the processes by which U.S. colonizers naturalize their power to appropriate and command the Philippines and its people and to link these processes to the second-class citizenship of Filipinos in the United States.

"THE PACIFIC IS OUR OCEAN:" THE AMERICAN EMPIRE

The differential inclusion of Filipinos in the United States began with the U.S. imperialist drive into the Philippines in the late nineteenth century.

Although absent from most of U.S. historical accounts, the colonization of the Philippines was not an aberrant but rather an extension of its "westward expansion" to the "Pacific frontier" and the corresponding transfer of racialized images of Native Americans and African Americans to the Philippines and its people. The U.S. annexation of the Philippines was also part and parcel of a larger global colonizing project: the formal partitioning of most of the world outside Europe and the Americas into colonies and territories ruled by a handful of states. Between 1876 and 1915, a period that historian E. J. Hobsbawm has termed "the age of empire," about a quarter of the globe's land surface was distributed or redistributed as colonies among a half-dozen countries, mainly Great Britain, France, Germany, Italy, Japan, and the United States.[6] The United States acquired during this period some one hundred thousand square miles, primarily from Spain: Cuba and Puerto Rico in the Americas and the Philippines in the Pacific. This partition of the world among a handful of states was the most spectacular manifestation of the growing division of the world into the powerful and the weak, the "advanced" and the "backward"—the legacy of which continues to be evident in today's global inequalities and migration patterns.

Economic interest pushed the United States to cross the Pacific. The particular role that the United States imagined Asia to be playing was as a market for the accumulation of goods and capital.[7] Scholars have long documented the economic and strategic roots of the Philippine-American War. This history tells us that the annexation of the Philippines represented a shift in U.S. economic strategy from a concern for land to a concern for markets. Heinz Ickstadt, for example, argues that the war with Spain, and especially the conquest of the Philippines, opened a new economic frontier, a new westward movement toward the hotly contested and potentially lucrative markets of China and Japan.[8] Similarly, Walter Lafeber contends that it was a thirst for overseas markets and a passion for coaling stations that had led the United States to seize dominion over the Philippines, and also Puerto Rico, Cuba, Guam, and Samoa.[9] The economic motive for the annexation of the Philippines seemed clear: American businesses viewed the Philippines as the "gateway to Asiatic markets"—a "home area" from which to intervene in the Asian-Pacific economic and geopolitical matters.[10] In 1900, Senator Albert Beveridge of Indiana, the most popular advocate of U.S. imperialism during his time, defended the invasion of the Philippines in these terms: "The Philippines are ours forever. . . . And just beyond the Philippines are China's illimitable markets. We will not retreat from either. . . . The Pacific is our ocean."[11] Still others looked to the Philippines for its population's labor potential. For example, the *Nation* reported that the Tagal people were "the most tractable of beings and the most useful, being able to turn [their] hand[s] to anything."[12] Lipsitz contends that these systematic efforts of conquest and colonialism have created economic advantages through a "possessive investment in whiteness" for white Americans.[13]

But as postcolonial theorists have pointed out, neither imperialism nor colonialism is a simple act of economic accumulation and acquisition. They are also subject-constituting projects, supported and impelled by impressive ideological formations that designate certain countries and people as requiring and even beseeching domination from the more "civilized" ones.[14] Below, I explore how the Philippine-American War and the subsequent colonization of the Philippines constituted not only economic or territorial but also subject-making projects—fashioning *both* the American and the Filipino subjects in ways that were, and continue to be, mutually implicated in each other.

Nineteenth-century imperial culture included newly constructed forms of knowledge affiliated with domination. As Said reports, the vocabulary of this "age of empire" was replete with words and concepts like "inferior races," "subordinate peoples," "dependency," "expansion," and "authority."[15] In her cogent discussion of the importance of Asia in the development of the U.S. nation, Lisa Lowe argues that the "project of imagining the nation as homogeneous requires the orientalist construction of cultures and geographies from which Asian immigrants come as fundamentally 'foreign' origins antipathetic to the modern American society that 'discovers,' welcomes, and domesticates them."[16] In the case of the Philippines, the U.S. imperialist drive into the country unleashed a consistent, disruptive, and well-articulated ideology depicting foreign rule over the Philippines as a blessing—a means to a higher form of civilization that would bring progress, well-being, and salvation to a racially, culturally, and even morally inferior country and people incapable of self-rule. These colonial ideologies formally justified and codified the subordinate status of Filipinos as wards of the state, creating a juridical and cultural space for Filipinos as a separate category of beings.[17] They simultaneously helped rationalize and buttress the power of "civilized" white men, who shouldered the "white man's burden" of protecting the weak and dispensing justices.[18]

For Filipinos to be depicted as incapable of self-rule, they had to be infantilized, their intellectual and emotional development impugned. In a study that examines U.S. press representation of the Philippines from 1898 to 1902, Christopher Vaughan reports that Filipinos were most often characterized as "children."[19] This characterization contained the seed of condescension and arrogance from which popular justification for colonization would grow. According to Vaughan, "Since the industrializing United States sought affirmation of its new status as a mature world power, there was a dangerous appeal in the notion that Filipinos were powerless children in need of paternal discipline."[20] Conspicuously absent from these newspapers and magazines were news of actual Filipinos and their opinions about Spain, the United States, and their own leaders, reinforcing the notion that Filipinos were incapable of forming such opinions.[21]

U.S. image makers depicted Filipinos not only as incapable but also as unworthy of self-government. Both official and popular discourse racialized Filipinos as less than human, portraying them as savages, rapists, uncivilized beings, and even as dogs and monkeys. Viewing the annexation of the Philippines as a "divine mission," Theodore Roosevelt in 1901 characterized Filipinos as brute savages, uncivilized barbarians, and the heathen in the hands of satanic forces. President William McKinley suggested as much when he defined his future course of "benevolent assimilation" toward the Filipinos: Americans would have to take them, "educate" them and "uplift and civilize and Christianize them."[22] In 1900, Republican Senator John C. Spooner (R-Wis.) objected to the withdrawal of U.S. troops from Manila because that would "give over Manila to loot, pillage, and rape." Two years later, Representative George N. Southwick (R-N.Y.) painted a similarly dire picture of the havoc that would follow an American departure: the islands would be left to "general slaughter, pillage, rapine, and ruin."[23] U.S. popular discourse likewise depicted the United States and the Philippines as unequally advanced civilizations, with "civilization" standing in for racial difference. As an example, a Christian Socialist columnist contended that U.S. military intervention in the Philippines was positive because it was bringing order out of anarchy among the "savage [. . .] half-civilized [. . .] densely ignorant and superstitious people."[24] In all, the claim of benevolent assimilation "effaces the violence of conquest by construing colonial rule as the most precious gift that 'the most civilized people' can render to those still caught in a state of barbarous disorder."[25]

Filipino bodies were also racialized as medically defective. In a nuanced analysis of the role of colonial medicine in the formation of colonial hegemony, Warwick Anderson delineates the ways in which the language of American medical science in the Philippines fabricated and rationalized images of the bodies of the American colonizers and the Filipinos, biologizing the social and historical context of U.S. imperialism.[26] The scientific papers produced by the colonial laboratory during the early 1900s racialized Filipino bodies as dangerous carriers of foreign antibodies and germs threatening to white bodies and American bodies as vulnerable but resilient, capable of guarding against the invisible foreign parasites lodged in native bodies. In his 1936 extraordinary popular autobiography, Victor Heiser, the commissioner of health in the Philippines, described Filipinos in the following terms: "grown-up children, dirty, unsanitary, diseased, ignorant, unscrupulous, superstitious, born actors, resigned to death, untrustworthy, cowards, a nation of invalids, incubators of leprosy, unhygienic."[27] The fears of these "innately unhygienic" people led to and justified house-to-house sanitary inspections and the quarantining of the "sick" from the communities. As such, American medial discourse, as a privileged site for producing the "truth" about the "tropics," served to consolidate racial hierarchies, naturalizing the power and legitimacy of American foreign bodies to appropriate, command, and contain the Philippines and its people.

These dehumanizing stereotypes call attention to the intimate connection between racialism and colonialism: the discursive construction of Filipinos as unfit for self-government and in need of domination was achieved in part through racial modes of differentiation. In a careful study of nineteenth-century racism and Manifest Destiny, Reginald Horsman explains how racialized hierarchies in the United States served as an impetus for imperial expansion abroad, with the rationalizations originally developed to justify conquest of Native Americans eventually applied to Mexicans and Filipinos.[28] With limited knowledge of the Philippines and its people, U.S. image makers drew on a hodgepodge of racial stereotypes of the "Negro" and the "Indian" to depict the Filipino people. Descriptions of "savage" Filipino men had antecedents in negative depictions of Native American men as barbaric and of African American men as bestial rapists.[29] Along the same lines, the stereotype of the childlike Filipino paralleled long-standing images of African American as children who were deemed too incompetent and immature to participate in government and of Native Americans as "wards" of the state."[30] Theodore Roosevelt, in particular, repeatedly linked Native Americans to Filipinos, employing words like "wild and ignorant," "savages," "Apaches," and "Sioux" to refer to the Filipino people.[31] In the same way, white American soldiers in the Philippines used many of the same epithets to describe Filipinos as they used to describe African Americans, including "niggers," "black devils," and "gugus."[32] Given this racially charged context, when U.S. troops—many of whom were veterans of the "Indian wars"—arrived in the Philippines, "violence quickly ensued, with horrific results for the Filipinos."[33]

By situating Filipino/American history within the larger context of the American empire, we can better see how the lives of African Americans and Native Americans—as subjects of conquest—intersected with native Filipinos at the turn of the twentieth century. If we positioned Filipino/American history within the traditional immigration paradigm, we would miss the ethnic and racial intersections between Filipinos and Native Americans and African Americans as groups similarly affected by the forces of Manifest Destiny.[34] These common contexts of struggle were not lost on African American soldiers in the Philippines. Connecting their fight against domestic racism to the Filipino struggle against U.S. imperialism, some African American soldiers—such as Corporal David Fagen—switched allegiance and joined the native armed struggle for independence. Hundreds of others stayed in the Philippines at the end of the Philippine-American War, married Filipino women, and fashioned new lives for themselves there.[35]

While racial beliefs certainly influenced U.S. actions toward and in the Philippines, they were only part of the cultural structure that undergirded U.S. imperialist policies and practices. Gender beliefs, often working in tandem with and through racial beliefs, also affected the content and scope of the U.S. imperialist project. As feminist theorists have reminded us, the discursive constitution of "otherness" is achieved not only through racial but also through sexual and gendered modes of differentiation.[36] Attentive to the mutually constitutive aspects of race and gender, historian Kristin Hoganson has shown how the racialization of Filipinos as biologically unfit for independence drew on ideas about gender.[37] Through a careful reading of a range of official and cultural discourses of the time, she convincingly demonstrates that the prominent stereotypes of the Filipinos—as uncivilized, savages, rapists, or children—all presented the Filipinos as lacking the *manly* character seen as necessary for self-government. She adds to this list the stereotype of the *feminized* Filipino: the depiction of the Philippines as woman, Filipino men as effeminate, and Filipino women as highly feminine and sexualized.[38] The hyperfeminization of Filipino men and women misrepresented and distorted gender relations in the Philippines, pitting the two sexes against each other. They also bolstered the racialized conviction that Filipino men lacked the manly character for self-government and thus justified the need for U.S. interventions to rectify the Philippine "unnatural" gender order.[39] As will be discussed in subsequent chapters, these racialized and gendered stereotypes continue to haunt Filipino men and women in the United States.[40]

In her compelling reading of Michel Foucault's *History of Sexuality,* Ann Stoler extends Foucault's approach to sexuality and power to imperial settings, urging us to treat bourgeois sexuality and subaltern/racialized sexuality not as distinct kinds, but "as dependent constructs in a unified field."[41] Heeding this insight, I contend that to understand more fully the U.S. desire to colonize the Philippines, we need to shift our attention from American perceptions of the Filipinos to American perceptions of themselves. Adding gender to the historical picture unearths other motives for U.S. imperialist ambitions. Hoganson argues that in addition to being motivated by lucrative markets, U.S. imperialists looked to overseas colonies to address their anxieties about manhood. That is, Americans colonized the Philippines not so much because they doubted the Filipinos' capacity to govern themselves but because they doubted their own. Anxieties about degeneracy in American men can be traced, in part, to the urbanization, industrialization, and corporate consolidation of the late nineteenth century. The upper-class men who could afford the material comforts of modern life and the middle-class men who held supposedly "soft" white collar jobs feared the seeming dangers of "overcivilization," that civilized comforts were undermining their manly fiber and vigor, turning them into soft, self-seeking, and materialistic men. Men who worked in large, bureaucratized corporations also resented not having the kind of autonomy their fathers had enjoyed. Finally, women's increased political activism—especially their perceived encroachment into electoral politics—heightened male unease about the feminization of yet another male space.[42]

U.S. expansionism/imperialism in the late nineteenth and early twentieth centuries played a critical role in the fight for American manhood. In contradistinction to a culturally effeminate and overcivilized East, the West embodied the myth of the frontier, "where the taming of the savage concomitantly implied a regeneration of the civilized."[43] Thus westward expansion (especially the martial spirit and pioneer virtues that were associated with it) was desirable not only for its economic and strategic benefits but also for its potential to revitalize American men and to restore the rightful gender order. The rhetoric of westward expansion—especially its potential to remedy the problem of degeneracy in American men—was continued in connection with U.S. military and economic policies of empire at the turn of the century.[44] Heedful of British imperialists' claims that empires made men, prominent U.S. imperialists—such as Theodore Roosevelt, Albert Beveridge, and Henry Cabot Lodge—looked to the colonization of the Philippines to turn white, middle- and upper-class American men into "ideal" citizens: "physically powerful men who would govern unmanly subordinates with a firm hand, men accustomed to wielding authority, men who had overcome the threat of degeneracy."[45] As "unmanly subordinates," Filipino men were held to starkly different standards of manhood than "civilized men." Although U.S. imperialists applauded the martial spirit in white American men as proof of manly virtue and governing capacity, they considered the warlike Filipinos as savages who harbored an insane desire for combat. In battle, white men were depicted as rational and honorable and Filipino men as frenzied, cruel, revengeful, and merciless. In the eyes of "civilized" observers, combat served a different function for American and Filipino men: it made the former manly and courageous and the latter unmanly and animalistic.[46]

In sum, the colonization of the Philippines cannot be attributed solely to economic and strategic motives. To understand the U.S. desire to colonize the Philippines, we also need to recognize the connections between gender, race, and nation. Because white masculinity was constructed as the bedrock of American democracy, a decline in manly character would impair white men's ability to maintain not only their status relative to women but also their class, racial, and national privileges. To stifle the protests of anti-imperialists, imperialists proclaimed that if white manhood were no longer valued as a prerequisite for full citizenship, the nation would succumb to exterior threats or crumble from within. Fearing for the future of the nation, they argued that war—and the subsequent holding of overseas colonies—would shore up the manly character of American politics, and in so doing prevent national and racial degeneracy. War, they believed, would restore the "proper" gender and racial order in which white men governed and homebound white women participated in the national project, principally by raising heroic sons.[47] In other words, in addition to economic ambitions, American anxieties about male degeneracy—and the concomitant worries about racial and national degeneracy—and convictions about the links between manhood, military service, and political authority all contributed to the allure of the Philippines as an overseas colony. The constructions of the Filipinos as savages, children, and/or feminine figures have to be understood within this historical context: these images had less to do with the Filipinos' incapacity for self-government and more to do with imperialists' desire to cast *themselves* as men who wielded power. In this sense, the Philippines and its people were forcibly and differentially included in the American empire because they were absolutely critical to American economic development, to the reconstruction of white American manhood, and to the larger project of nation building. It was they who (re)defined America and Americanness.[48] As Meyda Yegenoglu argues in her work on colonizing Egypt, the cultural representation of the West to itself is often "by way of a detour through the other."[49]

Against these racializing narratives of the Philippines, Filipinos created alternative visions of their history that called into question U.S. pronouncements of benevolent assimilation. A dramatic example of such an alternative vision was a series of Tagalog nationalist melodramas being performed in and around Manila between 1903 and 1905. In a brilliant analysis of these melodramas, Vicente Rafael demonstrates that the theatrical groups structured their plots to provoke sympathy for the suffering of the motherland, conjure intense longing for freedom, stage debates about the present and future of the nation, and depict U.S. rule as a project of enslaving rather than of uplifting the population.[50] Written and performed largely by urban, working-class artists, these melodramas were extraordinarily popular among working-class audiences and among members of the nationalist elite critical of U.S. rule. They were popular because they provided alternative sources of knowledge and power; their performances evoked a "revolutionary nationalism at odds with the racialized imperial order imposed by the United States."[51] For example, these melodramas challenged the colonial representation of the Filipino population as impeccably bound to gender and racial categories subject to the continuous gaze of the benevolent white. Instead, they cast gender as provisional and conditional—a set of negotiable positions under specific historical circumstances rather than a series of fixed and natural categories. In so doing, they contest the insidious misrepresentations of Filipino women and men as passive simpletons and instead represent them as active interlocutors, speaking and acting ably in the defense of the nation (if not necessarily the state) against the designs of colonizing others.

TRAVELING IMAGES, BODIES, AND BORDERS: NATIONALS BUT NOT CITIZENS

As discussed in chapter 2, the American crossing to the Philippines was immediately met by a Filipino counterflow in the beginning of the 1900s. However, a power differential marked these two crossings: the Americans' voyage to the Philippines was one of conquest to a colonized territory, while the Filipinos' journey to the United States was a "return" of subjugated nationals to the center of the empire.[52] The popular and official discourse on the Philippines from 1898 to 1902 established images—of inferiority, immorality, and incapacity—that traveled with Filipinos to the United States and prescribed their racialization there. Calling attention to the connection between place and (sub)people, Charles Mills argues that the imperial project necessarily involves the racing of space and the spacing of individuals.[53] That is, space is depicted as dominated by individuals of a certain race, and the individual is represented as imprinted with the characteristics of a certain kind of space. Thus whites were deemed "civilized" and nonwhites "uncivilized," and these conditions were said to be manifested in the character of the respective spaces they inhabited. This linking of space with race and race with personhood results in the belief that "those associated with the jungle"—in this case, the Filipino "savages"—"will take the jungle with them even when they are brought to more civilized regions."[54] Commenting on the connection between space and power, David Theo Goldberg writes that racialized power "reflects and refines the spatial relations of its inhabitants."[55] Since "you can't take the wilderness out of the Wild Man," state policies—such as apartheid, Jim Crow laws, and segregation—have to be enacted "to maintain these spaces *in their place,* to have the checkerboard of virtue and vice, light and dark space, *ours* and *theirs* clearly demarcated so that the human geography prescribed by the Racial Contract can be preserved."[56] In this section, I continue my discussion of "differential inclusion" by examining how discriminatory state practices enacted against Filipino immigrants have been part of a coordinated effort to prevent them from *contaminating* the "civilized" space around them.

The first Filipinos to arrive in the United States after the American crossing to the Philippines were literally contained: as living exhibits confined within a forty-seven-acre enclosure at the St. Louis World's Fair of 1904. At the fair's "Philippine Reservation," eleven hundred Filipino natives, along with thousands of other "primitive" men and women from all over the world, were displayed side by side with the artifacts and monuments that showcased Western scientific, cultural, and economic superiority. Thus structured, these exhibits were designed to "educate" the American masses about the innate inferiority of the "little brown brothers" they have been reading about in the papers. This "education" included displays of the "monkeylike" Negritos, the "savage" Igorots and Bagobos, and the relatively "more intelligent" Christianized Visayans; "authentic" simulation of the natives' dwelling and environment; and laboratories for anthropometric and psychometric assessments of the intelligence, physical ability, and personality of the Filipino natives—all designed to demonstrate Filipino racial inferiority and inability of political self-rule.[57] Tellingly, the Scouts and the Philippine Constabulatory forces, as the model subjects of U.S. rule, were depicted as the most civilized. As such, the St. Louis World's Fair helped spread the misrepresentation of Filipinos as "tree-dwellers" and "dog eaters" into homes across the country and drained away whatever sympathy there was for them as a people. The 1904 fair was thus an "elaborate scaffolding" whose aim was to provide "proof" of the Philippines as a primitive space that needed taming.

As inhabitants of that primitive space, Filipinos, whether in the Philippines or in the United States, were presumed to be inherently incapable of assimilation and thus biologically unfit for the privilege of U.S. citizenship. In contradistinction to the liberal claims of universal inclusion, the U.S. nation was founded not by granting citizenship and the attendant rights to all members of society but by establishing citizenship as a legal and political category of white male people that historically excluded nonwhites and white women.[58] The American transformation from republic to empire—as a result of the annexation of the Philippines, and also of Hawaii and Puerto Rico—unleashed a score of tense public debates over immigration policy, citizenship, and human rights. Indeed, many ardent anti-imperialists opposed the annexation of the Philippines not on the noble grounds of self-sovereignty but on the racist grounds that it would open the floodgates to millions of undesirable brown immigrants who would constitute a threat to national unity and a peril to the nation. For example, David Starr Jordan, the founding president of Stanford University, proclaimed that the annexation of the Philippines would expand the "race problem" in the United States, since Filipinos were *naturally* unsuited to democratic institutions and hence to economic and social development.[59] Noting that the formation of America in the twentieth century has had everything to do with "westward expansion" across the "Pacific frontier" and the ensuing movement of Asians onto American soil, Palumbo-Liu argues that one of the fundamental questions for modern America has been how to address and exploit dramatically increased flows of people, moving across borders and inserted into national spaces, and at the same time "neutralize their threat."[60]

The U.S. state resolved the contradictions between its expansionist interests in Asia and its anxiety about the unwanted entry of Asian immigrants through the policy of differential inclusion: a "protective" policy whereby the natives of these annexed territories were designated ineligible for citizenship. Having stripped the people of the Philippines of their right to self-sovereignty, the United States had the sole power through its Congress to determine their colonial status. According to Jose Cabranes, the record of the congressional debates over the status of the Filipinos from 1900 to 1916 reveals a widespread concern regarding the danger of placing the "Orientals" on an equal constitutional footing with the Americans.[61] These debates linked the status of Filipinos to that of other "Asiatics," and not to that of the similarly colonized Puerto Ricans. As an example, in a 1900 floor debate, Representative Newlands of Nevada, noting that the exclusion of Chinese immigrants from the United States had been based on the realization that "American civilization was in danger," argued that the Filipinos posed a similar threat to the nation. Other members of Congress spoke out against the annexation of the Philippines because they did not want admitted into the nation people who were "accustomed to a scale of wages and mode of living appropriate to Asiatics" such as the "cheap half-slave labor, savage labor, of the Philippine Archipelago."[62]

These disparaging statements about the Filipinos were in marked contrast to the more approving descriptions of the Puerto Ricans. Citing race, civilization, and geographic considerations, the majority of members of Congress contended that U.S. citizenship was a possibility for Puerto Ricans, but not for Filipinos. In a typical fashion, Representative Thomas Spight of Mississippi argued in 1900 that Puerto Rico, "only an island away," could be integrated into the United States because "its people are, in the main, of Caucasian blood, knowing and appreciating the benefits of civilization, and are desirous of casting their lot with us."[63] In contrast, he proclaimed that the inhabitants of the Philippine Islands, ten thousand miles away, were unworthy of U.S. citizenship because they "are of wholly different races of people from ours—Asiatics, Malays, negroes, and mixed blood. They have nothing in common with us and centuries cannot assimilate them."[64] Sixteen years later, the congressional debates about the distinction between the Philippines and Puerto Rico remained unchanged. As Representative Huddleston of Alabama noted, "[E]ntirely different conditions obtain in Porto *[sic]* Rico than those which obtain in the Philippines. . . . The people of Porto *[sic]* Rico are of our race, they are people who inherit an old civilization—a civilization which may be fairly compared to our own."[65] These congressional debates culminated in the 1916 Jones Act, which promised eventual independence to the Philippines and the 1917 Jones Act, which extended U.S. citizenship to the people of Puerto Rico. Although differing in their aims, both acts produced the same result: they relegated Filipinos and Puerto Ricans to the status of second-class citizens. By promising *eventual* and not immediate independence to the Philippines, the 1916 Jones Act in effect granted the Filipino natives "ward" status without citizenship rights. In much the same way, the 1917 Jones Act was not intended to confer on the Puerto Ricans "any rights that the American people [did] not want them to have" but rather to reaffirm the indefinite colonial status of the islands.[66] As Cabranes argues, the 1917 Jones Act conferred "a type of citizenship on its inhabitants that strengthened Puerto Rico's ties to the United States but gave its people few of the civil and political rights normally associated with American citizenship."[67] The relegation of Filipinos and Puerto Ricans—as colonized subjects—to the status of second-class citizens underscores the fact that citizenship serves as an index of the historical and persistent racial, class, and gender inequalities of American society. It also calls attention to the ways in which the treatment of Filipinos invoked the national racial thinking on Native Americans and African Americans. Native Americans served as the prototype for American colonial policies and administrative strategy that designated natives of these annexed territories as "wards" of the state; and African Americans represented the justification and model for extending "second-class citizenry" to other subjugated groups.[68]

The differential inclusion of Filipinos as U.S. nationals but not as citizens prevented them from voting, establishing a business, holding private and public office, and owning land and other property in the United States. But it did not prevent them from traveling freely to the United States and from working once there. And work they did. In fact, as discussed in chapter 2, since they could migrate freely to the United States, Filipinos became the favored and at times the only available source of *cheapened* labor to fill the labor shortage in Hawaii and the Pacific Coast created by the successive legal exclusion of the Chinese, Japanese, Koreans, and South Asians. Similarly, owing to their status as U.S. nationals, Filipinos were the only Asians allowed to serve in the U.S. armed forces, especially in its Navy, in sizeable numbers without holding U.S. citizenship.

At the same time, their status as U.S. nationals made them even more vulnerable. Because they had no benefits of citizenship, they had virtually no protection from race-based labor exploitation. Whereas other nationalities theoretically could appeal to their government representatives for assistance, the Filipinos, as colonial subjects, had no representation either in the Philippines or in the United States.[69] Racialized as instruments of production and as physiologically suited for "stoop labor," Filipino agricultural workers were often given the least desirable jobs and housing and earned the lowest wages both in Hawaii and along the Pacific Coast.[70] Similarly, the U.S. Navy relegated Filipino enlistees to the ratings of officers' stewards and mess attendants—the ratings previously assigned to black enlistees. Their colonized status also meant that Filipinos faced, at times, a qualitatively different racism from that faced by other Asian immigrant groups. In an excellent study of race and class relations in Hawaii, Moon-Kie Jung reports that as a colonized people, Filipinos were constructed as a "primitive" race "in an adolescent stage of development."[71] In contrast, as a people who represented an imperialist rival, the Japanese in Hawaii were perceived as an inscrutable race beholden to Japan and carrying out its imperialist design from within. According to Jung, "Whereas the racist discourse concerning Filipinos revolved around the unquestioned assumption of their racial inferiority, underlying the racist discourse concerning the Japanese was the fear that they were not racially inferior."[72] The different racisms faced by Filipinos and the Japanese in Hawaii were evident in the racist slurs to which they were subject. Whereas the racial epithets for the Filipinos—"monkeys," "little brown brothers," and "savages"—evoked their subhuman inferiority, colonized status, and supposed violent nature, the most frequently used racist epithet for the Japanese—"Jap"—seems to indicate that what was most despicable about being "Japanese" was being immutably of Japan.[73] Finally, Filipinos appeared to have encountered more hostility from whites who perceived them as greater threats because of their noninclusion in immigration restrictions against Asians.

In sum, the racist designation of Filipinos as U.S. nationals but not citizens is an example of differential inclusion: the deliberate insertion of Filipinos into the U.S. nation, but in servile positions and under exploitable conditions. Their situated knowledges call attention to the linkage of colonialism, racialization, and second-class citizenship. Coming from a colonized nation, Filipinos could not become U.S. citizens, and yet they were not quite noncitizens, as other Asian immigrants were. Their status as U.S. nationals allowed them to travel freely to and work in the United States but afforded them virtually no protection against race- and class-based exploitation. Because Filipinos—as U.S. colonials—could migrate to the United States when other Asians could not, their mode of entry diverged considerably from that of other Asian groups, and thus their history cannot be folded neatly into the narrative of Asian immigration to and settlement in the United States. Instead, their fate as a colonized people mirrored that of the Puerto Ricans; their status as "wards" of the state paralleled that of Native Americans; and their relegation to servile positions in the U.S. Navy resembled that of African American servicemen.

But in other ways, Filipino lives closely intersected those of other Asian immigrants. Because of their prescribed Asiatic race, Filipinos could not become U.S. citizens in the same way that Puerto Ricans could. Like other Asian immigrants, Filipinos were an indispensable but exploited labor force that helped to build the American West and Hawaii. Yet through law, labor segmentation, and "scientific racism," Filipinos and other Asians in the United States have been placed both " 'within' the U.S nation-state, its workplaces, and its markets, yet linguistically, culturally, and racially marked as 'foreign' and 'outside' the national polity" and therefore "outside the rewards of white identity."[74] In the same way, the 1934 Tydings-McDuffie Act should not be read as a singular policy against Filipinos, but rather as a culmination of anti-Asian legislation that can be traced back to the 1882 Chinese Exclusion Act, the Gentlemen's Agreement Act of 1908, and the 1917 and 1924 Immigration Acts. As Palumbo-Liu argues, "The 1934 act marks a significant attempt to uniformly bar Asian immigration, and redefines America's notion of Asian."[75] The Filipino experience thus underscores the intersectional nature of racial formation and the mutability of racism. Like other people of color, Filipinos suffered from racism, but they did so to different degrees and in different ways.

THREATENING BODIES: "CHEAP, DOCILE, UNMARRIED MEN"

Like other Asian immigrants, Filipino immigrants met with widespread and well-organized hostility upon their arrival in the United States. What seems most conspicuous in these anti-Filipino tirades is a fear of Filipino male sexuality. In the classic *America Is in the Heart,* Carlos Bulosan bitterly recounts the brutalities and indecencies that Filipinos experienced during the 1930s: "I came to know . . . that in many ways it was a crime to be a Filipino in America. I came to know that the public streets were not free to my people: we were stopped each time these vigilant patrolmen saw us driving a car. We were suspect each time we were seen with a white woman."[76] As discussed above, this fear has its origins in the racist discourses of the sexuality of Filipino men as excessive and animalistic in contrast to the supposedly restrained or "civilized" sexuality of white colonial men. This fear also has to be understood in relation to the imposed gender imbalance in the Filipino immigrant community. As I have argued elsewhere, one of the most noticeable characteristics of pre–World War II Asian America was a pronounced shortage of women.[77] Because what U.S. interests desired was muscle power, they gave little attention to the family and community life of Asian immigrants except as it related to the latter's economic productivity. In most instances, families were seen as a threat to the efficiency and exploitability of the workforce and were actively prohibited. In other words, America's capitalist economy wanted Asian male workers but not their families.

To ensure greater profitability from immigrants' labor and to decrease the costs of reproduction—the expenses of housing, feeding, clothing, and educating the workers' dependents—U.S. employers often excluded "nonproductive" family members such as women and children. Detaching the male worker from his household increased profit margins, because it shifted the cost of reproduction from the state and the employer to the kin group left behind in Asia. Asian women were also undesirable because of their reproductive powers: they would bear children who could then claim U.S. citizenship.[78] On the Pacific Coast, where a migratory labor force best suited the growers' needs, the unattached male provided a more flexible source of labor that could readily be moved to meet short-term labor needs and expelled when no longer needed. For example, a Californian grower told an interviewer in 1930 that he preferred to hire Filipinos because they were without families: "These Mexicans and Spaniards bring their families with them and I have to fix up houses; but I can put a hundred Filipinos in that barn [pointing to a large firetrap]."[79] Housed in dilapidated, crowded shacks or in tents, Filipino male laborers endured a harsh climate, unsanitary living conditions, and the lack of privacy. Philip Vera Cruz, a pioneering Filipino laborer, recalled: "The first camp I lived in had a kitchen that was so full of holes, flies were just coming in and out at their leisure, along with mosquitoes, roaches, and everything else. . . . The toilet was an outhouse with the pit so filled-up that it was impossible to use."[80] In Hawaii, where plantation workers remained in one place, plantation managers thought a feminine presence would have a stabilizing effect on the men. But even there, the number of women allowed to immigrate was small. A 1916 labor commissioner report sums up the needs of U.S. businesses this way: "Plantations have to view laborers primarily as instruments of production. Their business interest[s] require cheap, not too intelligent, docile, *unmarried men*."[81] As a result, even fewer Filipinas migrated to the United States than did Japanese and Chinese women. According to Lasker, of the estimated 102,069 Filipinos who arrived in Hawaii from 1907 to 1929, 87 percent were males. On the continental United States, almost all Filipino immigrants were prime-age single male workers. By 1930, men comprised close to 95 percent of the Filipino immigrant population; and 80 percent were between the ages of sixteen and thirty.[82]

In the face of deliberate assaults on their family units, Filipino immigrants struggled to make home; that is, to create and maintain some semblance of family life, often by redefining and extending the concept of "family." With few women, children, and older people around, young male immigrants often stretched the boundaries of "family" to include nonkin. Missing the company of wives and small children, single Filipino men adopted and were adopted by the few families that were around. In the Filipino community in Hawaii, as many as two hundred men would be invited to be godparents at every religious ceremony, from baptisms to weddings. This modified *compadre* system incorporated fictive relatives into the kinship network and enabled many single men to affiliate themselves with a family system.[83] I was fortunate to have interviewed Connie Tirona, one of the few Filipino children in northern California in the 1930s. Born in 1929 in Selma, California, Tirona remembered being the "adopted daughter" of many of the bachelor friends of her parents. These *manongs* bought Tirona her first bicycle and purchased pageant tickets from her "by the fistful."[84] Tirona vividly recalled the joy that her family's visits brought to these lonely *manongs* who labored in the Sacramento-San Joaquin area:

> There were about thirty *manongs* in the labor camps in the Sacramento-Joaquin area that we would visit. . . . It was so beautiful when we visited them. . . . And the *manongs* would fix up their rooms immaculately. They scrubbed their place because "the families were coming!" They picked fresh

> corn and cooked good, wholesome food. . . . After eating they would play guitars and mandolins, and we, as little children of the families, would sing and dance. The *manongs* liked to hear the little kids sing. They had a small makeshift stage for us, and we would go up there with our curly hair and cute little dresses. And they would throw coins at us. It was the biggest thing for them. You could just see the tears of joy on their faces. They would come up and hug us. . . . I especially remember when we sang the Visayan songs. You could see the tears on the faces of those grown men. . . . I remember my younger sister had a beautiful soprano voice, and she would sing this one Visayan song that said something about how hard life was in a strange land. It was a love song. As they listened to her song, tears would form and slowly flow from their eyes. They would drink their wine and cry softly. They would say to my parents, "Thank you for teaching your daughter to sing that song.". . . As I was drifting off to sleep, I could hear them laughing as they started to sing nostalgic songs from the Philippines.

Tirona's fond memories of her visits with the *manongs* testify to the ways in which Filipino immigrant communities, even under harsh conditions, coalesce to sustain each other with conviviality, warmth, and some semblance of home.

This gender imbalance, though the product of discriminatory immigration and labor recruiting policies, became the very basis on which anti-Filipino forces constructed the largely single Filipino men as lascivious and predatory—and especially as sexual threats to white women. Severely restricted by racial segregation and stringent anti-miscegenation laws, Filipino men sought pleasure—and a sense of dignity—in the taxi dance halls where they could dance with white working-class women for "ten cents a dance." As a Filipino old-timer recalled, "the only places that welcomed us with open arms were the gambling houses and dance halls."[85] Racialized as exploitable "stoop labor," Filipino men reclaimed their sensuality and virility on the taxi hall dance floors, touting their young fit bodies in flagrant displays of sexuality.[86] Not surprisingly, white working-class men were the ones most threatened by these "immoral" liaisons between working-class Filipino men and white women. But without access to the state power needed to close taxi dance halls or to prevent Filipino-white marriages, white working-class men often resorted to violence to curb the unbridled "sexual passions" of Filipinos for white women.[87] Between 1928 and 1930, racist concern over "hybridization"—heightened by intense competition for jobs—culminated in a series of race riots in Washington and California meant to drive Filipinos out of various communities. The most explosive and most publicized incident took place in 1930 near Watsonville, California, where four hundred white vigilantes attacked a Filipino dance club, beating dozens of Filipinos and killing one. In the days that followed, hundreds of white men roamed the streets of Watsonville, beating or shooting Filipinos on sight. A Filipino laborer described the violent scene: "The mob came into the pool halls and with clubs bludgeoned all of us and followed us until we were out of the city. Then residences where Filipinos were quartered were ransacked and burned to the ground. Automobiles that contained Filipinos were fired upon, and many of the boys were wounded."[88] As a young child, Connie Tirona was deeply bewildered and angered by these hate attacks on Filipino men:

> If the *manongs* got caught talking to a white woman, gosh, they were beaten up. I can remember one incident in particular. It happened in Watsonville. I remember it so well—when some white men came into the labor camp. I thought they were the Ku Klux Klan. They were on horseback, and they took two Filipinos and tied them with a rope. Then they rode up and down the camp, dragging the two Filipinos after them. They wanted to show the "brown monkeys" that they could not speak to the white women. I was horrified. I could not understand why people do such abominable acts. . . . It hurt me deeply to watch the Filipinos being beaten up . . . I just felt a sense of betrayal.

In a study of anti-Filipino race riots in Watsonville, Emory Bogardus found the threat of intermarriage to be the most immediate concern of proponents of the exclusion of Filipinos.[89] As was the case with black-white marriages, Asian-white marriage and procreation were represented as threats to a white power structure in which race, class, and gender are linked.[90] In an analysis of the circumstances in which anti-miscegenation laws were applied to Asian men in California in the nineteenth and twentieth centuries, Metgumi Dick Osumi reports that in all cases, the passage of these laws was linked to the activities of a coalition of laborers, nativists, press agents, and legislators to restrict Asian immigrants' access to jobs and to settlement in the United States.[91] In the Filipino case, the economic depression of the late 1920s and early 1930s, and the boom in taxi dance halls, resulted in vigorous efforts to prevent Filipino-white marriages and to exclude Filipinos altogether. In 1933, in the wake of the Watsonville riots, the California state legislature, characterizing Filipinos as a threat to the racial order, amended anti-miscegenation laws to include Filipino-white marriages. As discussed above, one year later, the U.S. Congress passed the Tydings-McDuffie Act, effectively halting Filipino migration to the United States.

In sum, Filipinos, constructed as threatening social bodies, were subject to racial segregation that quarantined them, lest they contaminate the social space around them. With few Filipino women around, this spatial segregation was in effect a racialized imposition of asexuality on heterosexual Filipino men. When Filipino men refused to be just working bodies and instead flaunted their sexual bodies, they were racialized as sexually threatening. This perceived threat then provided "justification" for anti-Filipino forces to brutalize their bodies, to enact laws to prevent Filipino-white marriages, and to exclude them from immigrating to the United States. By restricting the migration of Filipinas, and by enacting anti-miscegenation laws that prevented Filipino-white marriages, anti-Filipino forces in effect outlawed home life for most heterosexual Filipino immigrants. In other words, Filipino migrants who left home to help pick crops and provide services essential to the "home" lives of normative domestic subjects were themselves denied a family life. This was not an isolated practice; other Asian men, Mexican men, and African men also experienced stunted family life.[92] This separation of Filipino work life from home and community life must be seen as an example of differential inclusion: Filipino men were included only as working bodies but not as desiring bodies with the right to form families and produce American-born children—which would have allowed Filipinos to be more firmly integrated and rooted in the United States. In this sense, the denial of family life, and the resultant construction of Filipino men as threatening bodies, halted their settlement in the United States and contributed to their perceived and actual state of homelessness.

THE PERPETUAL FOREIGNER: "NOT ALL AMERICANS ARE EQUAL"

I want to end this chapter by reflecting on the life of Connie Tirona. Born in 1929, she lived through many important markers in Filipino American history. When Tirona was born, Filipinos could not become citizens, work in decent-paying jobs, marry whom they desired, live where they wanted, and be protected from physical violence. As a young Filipina growing up in the 1930s and 1940s, Tirona lived in segregated housing, was denied service at restaurants and department stores, was not allowed to attend her high school dances, and worked in jobs where "they put you in the back." During the 1950s, when she and her Filipino immigrant husband tried to buy a house in South San Francisco, they were told by the real estate agent that the house had already been sold. Angered by this persistent racial discrimination, she vowed, "There will come a day when we can buy a house in any neighborhood." By the time that I interviewed her in 1994, much had changed. In 1946, the Luce-Celler bill conferred the right of naturalization and small immigration quotas on Filipino immigrants. Filipino lives were further affected by the racial minority movements of the postwar period, which reshaped the political, cultural, and legal landscape of the nation and brought about significant progress toward racial democracy. As a result of the passage of the hard-fought civil rights statutes and the 1965 Immigration and Naturalization Act, Filipinos today constitute the second-largest immigrant group as well as the second-largest Asian American group; and a sizeable proportion are college-educated, home-owning professionals. Tirona's life reflects these changes. Today, she and her family own a comfortable home in a middle-class neighborhood in San Diego, and most of her children are college-educated professionals. And yet, much has remained the same: she bitterly recalled how her son was harassed by the police in his own neighborhood owing to "racial profiling;" how her pregnant daughter was ill treated by the nursing staff at a local hospital; how she, a U.S.-born citizen, continues to be asked if she speaks English; and how so many Filipinos she knows continue to languish in poverty. Reflecting on all the injustices that have marked her life, her parents' life, and the lives of countless Filipinos, she brooded, "Sometimes, I am not sure what it means to be an American. I am not equal to anyone. My color is different and that has mattered all my life. I feel that not all Americans are equal; they are not."

Post–civil rights United States is often celebrated as a "color-blind" society in which racism is a thing of the past. I end this chapter with Tirona's story because her life experiences challenge the discourse of color blindness and draw attention instead to the ways in which contemporary racism has been "rearticulated" or "recomposed" but not ended.[93] Tirona's assertion that "not all Americans are equal" exemplifies the differential inclusion experienced by Filipinos in the post–civil rights era: even as citizens, Filipinos continue to be racialized as outside the cultural and racial boundaries of the nation. As I have tried to show in this chapter, the racialization of Filipinos begins not at the moment of immigration but rather in the "homeland" already deeply affected by U.S. cultural, political, and economic assaults. This history of conquest—and the concomitant dehumanization of Filipinos—haunts the conception of the Filipino American, persisting *beyond* the repeal of actual laws prohibiting Filipinos from immigration and citizenship. As a result, like other Asians, the Filipino is "always seen as an immigrant, as the 'foreigner-within,' even when born in the United States."[94] In the same way, contemporary Filipino immigration has its origins not in the "liberalization" of U.S. immigration laws but in the history of U.S. imperialism in Asia, which disrupted and distorted the economy, polity, and culture of the Philippines.

◆ ◆ ◆

The brief history outlined in this chapter suggests that the extension of U.S. citizenship to Filipinos must be understood as a product of the unequal relationship between the dominant white American citizens and the subordinated, colonized, and racialized Filipinos—and not as a fulfillment of the liberal promise of equal access and equal representation.[95] By locating Filipino American history within the larger history of the American empire, I have attempted to show how Filipino immigrant lives parallel and intersect not only the lives of other Asian Americans but also those of African Americans, Latinos, and Native Americans. In other words, the conditions of Filipino lives—and indeed of all our lives—are connected to and shaped by the conditions of multiple others' lives. In this chapter, I have listed the impediments to Filipinos making "homes" for themselves in the United States. In the next chapter, I begin my discussion on Filipino home-making projects, paying particular attention to the communities of alliances that Filipino immigrants build and nurture both across and within national borders.

CHAPTER 4

Mobile Homes

Lives across Borders

Part of our existence here in the United States is helping our families, relatives, and compatriots "back home" cope with some very burdensome realities.

Rene Ciria-Cruz, "Why Image Counts"

If people ask me, I always tell them, I am an export of the Philippines. . . . The U.S. is my adopted country. But the Philippines is my home.

Maria Rafael, Filipina immigrant

The majority of U.S. immigration studies focuses on the relationship of immigrants to the United States. They ask the question, How well are immigrants faring within U.S. institutions and with other Americans? To disrupt this unilinear model, I employ a critical transnational perspective to call attention to the border-crossing practices that immigrants engage in as they maintain their relations with the homeland. Drawing on the lives of Filipinos in San Diego, I address in this chapter the question of why immigrants do or do not maintain ties to "home." This question is part of my broader concern with home making—the processes by which immigrants use memory of and ties to the homeland to construct their new lives. Akhil Gupta and James Ferguson contend that the "blurring of 'here' and 'there' disturbs the certitudes of the center as well as in the colonized periphery."[1] In a similar way, I conceptualize transnationalism—the processes by which immigrant groups forge and sustain strong sentimental and material links with their countries of origin—as a disruptive strategy, enacted by immigrants to challenge binary modes of thinking about time and space and to resist their differential inclusion in the United States as subordinate residents and citizens. This section focuses on the border-crossing practices of the immigrant generation; the experiences of the second generation will be developed in chapter 8.

OF *LIFE* MAGAZINE, COCA-COLA, AND ROCK HUDSON: AMERICA(NS) IN THE PHILIPPINES

Most of us are expatriates right here in our own land.
America is our heartland whether we get to go there
or not.

Conrado de Quiros, "Bracing for Balikbayans"

In the epigraph above, the well-known Filipino journalist Conrado de Quiros laments what he perceives as a national tragedy: the fact that U.S. colonial hegemony has deluded Filipinos into thinking of themselves as expatriates "even right *here* in our own land." Other writers have similarly exposed these colonial delusions. Set in the 1950s, Bienvenido Santos's short story "The Day the Dancers Came" focuses on Fil, an elderly *manong,* who eagerly offers his hospitality to a troupe of young dancers from the Philippines only to be rejected by them. Worldly and sophisticated, the young Filipinos derisively regard Fil, and other Filipino *manongs,* as "bums" who cannot fit into their Westernized and hybridized world. As Dolores de Manuel notes, this perception of the Westernized is "ironic," given the fact that "it is Fil who lives in America, while the dancers live in the Philippines"; and yet it is they who regard themselves to be more Westernized than Fil, the migrant.[2] In her critically acclaimed 1990 novel *Dogeaters,* Jessica Hagedorn portrays neocolonial Manila, from about 1956 to 1985, as a world in which American popular culture and local Filipino tradition mix flamboyantly. In entertaining but biting language, Hagedorn satirizes the Filipino's "colonial mentality": the unflinching belief that everything made in the United States—movies, music, fashion, food—is automatically better than anything made in the Philippines.[3]

De Quiros's warning and Santos's and Hagedorn's narratives call attention to the pervasive presence of the United States in the Philippines and thus to the always transnational character of Philippine culture and life. Accordingly, I begin my discussion on Filipino transnational lives not with Filipino immigrants in the United States but with Filipino nonmigrants in the Philippines. In chapter 2, I maintained that a study of

Filipino migration to the United States must begin with the "migration" of Americans to the Philippines—the first border crossers. This argument disrupts the perceived unidirectionality of migration—from impoverished to affluent countries—and calls attention instead to the multiple directions and forms of border crossings forged by colonization, decolonization, and the globalization of late capitalism. Extending this argument, I maintain here that as a result of these violent border crossings, and the ensuing economic, sociocultural, political, and familial ties established between the two countries, the majority of Filipinos live transnational lives before they ever leave the Philippines.[4] This critical approach to transnationalism decouples it from the process of migration and situates it within the larger history of conquest and global capitalism.[5]

Cultural critic E. San Juan Jr. argues that as a result of a century of exposure to U.S. lifestyles, cultural practices, and consumption patterns, Filipinos, even before they set foot in the United States, "[have] been prepared by the thoroughly Americanized culture of the homeland."[6] As discussed in chapter 2, the cultural Americanization of Filipinos was an integral part of the process of colonization. Convinced that education was one of the best ways to pacify the population, U.S. colonizers introduced universal public education and revamped Philippine educational institutions and curricula using the American system as its model and English as the medium of instruction. With English as the imposed language of education, and eventually of government and commerce, Filipinos "fell under the spell of America" and "became almost a part of America."[7] English became "the language of aspiration, prestige, and power," so much so that ongoing efforts since World War II to replace English with Tagalog have been met with indifference in most colleges and universities and ignored by government bureaucracies.[8]

Dolores Realuyo, who immigrated to the United States at the age of fourteen, explained that it was "normal" for her to speak English in the Philippines: "I was schooled in a Jesuit school and most of my teachers were either European, British, or American." As a result, she grew up speaking better English than Tagalog. She spoke Tagalog only to "our maids, my grandparents, and my cousins [who lived in the province]." Dolores's fluency in English underscores Filipino obsession with the language and corresponding neglect of the local dialects: English, the language of prestige, was used among family members, while Tagalog was reserved for communication with maids.

With English came a flood of U.S. printed materials and mass media that reached all Filipinos: textbooks, novels, news services, magazines, music, and especially movies. These cultural products infected Filipinos with American norms, standards, ideals, values, and viewpoints. Filipino historian Renato Constantino, a vocal critic of the cultural Americanization of the Filipino people, charges that U.S. books, newspapers, and magazines fed Filipinos with an avalanche of information gathered, edited, and disseminated by Americans, in effect luring Filipinos into seeing and evaluating the world through American eyes.[9] Many of the Filipino immigrants I interviewed remember growing up reading such American classics as *Nancy Drew* and *Little Women* and such popular American periodicals as *Life* magazine, *Reader's Digest,* and *National Geographic.* One reported that he learned how to perfect his English through listening to "Voice of America." And Hollywood movies reached all corners of the country and mesmerized Filipinos with American ways and attitudes, music and dances, and fashion and style, and fostering among many Filipinos a great reverence for all things American. As Constantino declares: "American movies constitute the greatest single influence on Philippine social life."[10] Deriding what he perceives to be the "aping of American lifestyles," sociologist Antonio Pido laments that "being an educated Pilipino meant preferring apple pie in a country where there are no apples and wearing American suits while the temperatures never went lower than seventy degrees Fahrenheit."[11]

But Filipino ongoing connections to the United States are made and maintained not only through the influence of American media and communications but also through actual transnational social ties forged between Filipino nationals with Americans in the Philippines and with Filipinos in the United States. The century-old (neo)colonial association between the Philippines and the United States activated not only a transnational flow of information, capital, goods, and technology but also of people. Even after the Philippines regained its independence in 1944, American presence in the Philippines continued to be pervasive. As late as 1988, more than a quarter million U.S. nationals were living in the Philippines—the largest concentration in Asia.[12] As a testament to the ubiquitous presence of Americans, Filipinos encountered them in all sectors of their lives: Americans were their teachers, supervisors, commanding officers, employers, and customers, as well as their priests, neighbors, friends, lovers, and family members.

When asked to recall the presence of Americans in the Philippines, my respondents readily listed the U.S. companies and businesses in their hometowns: the Del Monte plant, the Pepsi-Cola factory, the Veteran's Hospital, the Bank of America, U.S. engineering firms, and a host of U.S.-owned hotels and resorts. Indeed, the United States is the Philippines' major trading partner, and more than half of the Philippines' foreign investment belongs to American corporations, financial institutions, or individuals.[13] These U.S. enterprises constitute transnational sites, exposing the local populace to U.S. money, culture, and standards of living—and to Americans. Filipinos who worked for these companies had American bosses, supervisors, co-workers, and friends. Nadia Gomez, whose father worked for an American engineering firm for twenty-five years, related, "When you looked at [my dad's] old pictures, he was always with Americans. They would come over to our house for dinner. . . . My mom would cook for them, and they loved Filipino food." Joe Arroyo, who worked as a mechanical engineer for a U.S. firm in the Philippines, was so close to his American supervisor that the supervisor ended up sponsoring him and his family to the United States. Filipinos also worked for Americans as their maids, nannies, cooks, and drivers. Maria Mateo's father was the driver of an American colonel who retired in the Philippines. As a result, she grew up in the 1940s in a "pseudo-American compound," because her father lived in the servants' quarters on this compound. There she spoke English, watched American television, and interacted with American children—and in the process learned "a lot" about American life "just by the exposure of seeing Americans."

Filipino exposure to Americans was perhaps most extensive in military towns. As discussed in chapter 2, the Philippines housed some of the United States' largest overseas air force and naval bases. For Filipino nationalists, the bases symbolized the colonial legacy and U.S. dominance over the Philippines. For many others, however, they represented economic opportunities. In 1987, U.S. bases were the second largest employer after the Philippine government, providing jobs and an annual salary totaling more than ninety-six million dollars to more than sixty-eight thousand Filipinos. They also fueled local economies, sustaining businesses that catered primarily to base personnel. Many local Filipinos vied to work in these businesses, not only for the needed income but also for a chance to meet Americans. Cora Cruz's family, who lived in the Navy town of Olangapo, provides an example. Cora's parents, who toiled as fish vendors, had a difficult time supporting their eight-member family. To supplement the family income, Cora and her sister were waitresses at a nearby restaurant that catered primarily to U.S. Navy personnel, and her brothers worked "odd jobs" on the base. When asked to assess the importance of these jobs to her family, Cora spoke less about the additional incomes and more about how the jobs prepared them for their eventual move to the United States:

> Because we worked with Americans, it wasn't too difficult for me to adjust when I came here. I was able to pick up a little more English, the American English, which is different from the English that we learned at school. My sister and I . . . had a lot of American friends. And they would come over for dinner . . . and so we were able to practice our English and learned more about America from them.

One of Cora's brothers, who worked on the base as a caddy, befriended the base chaplain, who in turn helped him to enlist in the U.S. Navy. And that was how Cora's family was able to immigrate to the United States—through this brother's petition.

Large numbers of Filipinas also married U.S. servicemen every year. Many women met their husbands while working on a base or at the local restaurants and entertainment establishments. Since the Philippines was the designated "rest and recreation" center of Asia during the Vietnam War, all local Filipinas were racialized as sexual commodities. Cognizant of the pervasive hypersexualization of the Filipinas who lived and worked in military towns, many women I interviewed were quick to claim that they were not "that kind of girl" and that they met their American husbands through other means. This was not an exaggerated claim, given the intrusive presence of Americans in many arenas of Filipino life. As an example, Luz Latus, a nursing student at the time, met her white American husband when her nursing school was asked to host the recently docked sailors "to show them around and tell them about the country." She vividly recalled the details of the night they met:

> All the nursing schools were invited to participate, and the nursing students were asked to be the sailors' hostesses. All of us were very excited, because we seldom were allowed to leave our dormitory. We were picked up by these big buses and driven to Manila Hotel, the biggest hotel in the city. All these well-dressed and clean-shaven Navy sailors were there. There was entertainment—folk dances and all kinds of floor shows put on by the USO. That was where I first met my husband.

Their courtship persisted through transnational correspondence. Several years later, when Luz came to the United States as an exchange student, she became reacquainted with and eventually married her sailor boyfriend.

Since "war brides" were among the first of the post–World War II Asian immigrants, most popular and scholarly accounts of these military marriages have focused on the wives' bittersweet experience as they made their new home in the United States.[14] But as Teresa K. Williams poignantly reminds us, there was also an unknown number of American military husbands, like Williams's father, who chose to stay and raise their family in their wife's country.[15] Ruth Abad's Kentucky-born father was such a man. He came to the Philippines with the Calvary during the Spanish-American War, met and married her mother in 1903, and lived out the rest of his life in the Philippines. Because Ruth's mother was the sole surviving child of the family, her grandmother had extracted a promise from Ruth's father to keep the family intact by remaining in the Philippines. Although her father never returned to the United States, he wanted his children to experience the country that he'd left behind. He registered all of his children as American citizens and sent his oldest son to the United States for most of his primary and secondary years of schooling. But when he readied to send his next two sons, Ruth's grandmother objected to the transnational division of the family, warning her daughter, "Your husband is taking your children away little by little." So it was that the rest of the eight children were raised exclusively in the Philippines. It was not until 1945, at the age of thirty-three, that Ruth left for the United States through the repatriate program—a program designed to return to the United States all the dependents of U.S. citizens who had lived in the Philippines before World War II. Because the United States does not keep emigration records, it is nearly impossible to determine how many Americans had left the United States for other countries. In the case of the Philippines, we know of at least one mass American emigration: at the conclusion of the Philippine-American War, nearly five hundred African American soldiers elected to stay in the Philippines; they married local women and raised their families in their wives' homeland.[16]

In a *Manila Chronicle* editorial, Filipino nationalist Constantino scolds his compatriots for their unquestioning acceptance of anything American: "Instead of holding fast to our national identity, we worked assiduously at the ridiculous job of turning ourselves into little Americans."[17] There is some truth to this charge, as is evident in the following remark made by one of my respondents: "Growing up in the Philippines, I already knew what America was like. I was almost an American because I always tried to imitate that culture. . . . I made an effort to be American. My books were all about 'Dick and Jane,' not about Filipinos. . . . I felt that being white was better." But not all Filipinos were impressed by Americans and their ways of life. Dario Villa, the son of a Filipino Navy man, was angry at what he perceived to be the "blatant racism and sexism" displayed by the Americans that he met in Subic Bay, then home of one of the largest U.S. Naval bases in the Philippines:

> My perception of them was that they were rude and that they had no respect for Filipinos and the Philippines. Their maids were Filipinas; their gardeners were Filipinos; therefore, they treated Filipinos as inferior. I also remember young American sailors in Olongapo City behaving like wild animals, mistreating and abusing Filipinos, especially the women. That experience prejudiced my mind. I carried that baggage of distrust and mistrust with me for a long time. In fact, whenever I would meet someone who said that he or his father was stationed in the Philippines, my immediate thought was, "You were one of those assholes who took advantage of Filipinos," because that was what I saw.

Through their encounter with U.S. institutions, Filipinos also learned about institutional racism. Born in Subic Bay in 1969, Daniel Smith is the son of a Filipina and an African American serviceman. Daniel attributed his parents' chance meeting to "U.S. racial segregation":

> At that time [the early 1960s], there was racial segregation. The military brought it over [to the Philippines] from the United States. When American servicemen go on liberty, they still were segregated. What happened is if you're in the white area and then you're black and happen to be there, the white service men they still beat you up. I don't blame them, cause what you gonna do, mix them up over there [in the Philippines] and back here in the States you have segregation?

In an ingenious business move that could also be read as an antiracist project, Daniel's grandmother started a club for African American servicemen. Because there were few establishments willing to serve African American soldiers, the family business became an instant success. "That's how my mother's family made their money," recalled Daniel. "They played black people music, and the troops heard about that so people started going there. They were successful and ended up owning a resort. They didn't know it was going to be big like that. It grew so big that they started to have live bands." It was at his grandmother's club that his mother, who worked the cash register, met his father, a patron at the club. In contrast to the "captive mentality" derided by Constantino and other Filipino nationalists, Dario's and Daniel's characterization of America(ns) suggests that they, along with many other Filipinos, understood well the costs of colonialism—the fact that U.S. economic, cultural, and military colonization of the Philippines always forms the backdrop to any relations between Filipinos and Americans.

Filipinos encountered the United States not only through Americans who lived in the Philippines but also through Filipinos who visited, resided, or worked in the United States—people ranging from students to teachers, from independent travelers to sponsored workers, and from vacationers to permanent immigrants. Transnational families abound, as family members wait, in some cases for more than a decade, to rejoin their loved ones in the United States. The longest family separation that I documented lasted for sixteen years. Most often, the separation was forced, prolonged by restrictive immigration policies and convoluted petition procedures. In some instances, however, the separation was a deliberate decision, made to accommodate the often-conflicting needs and desires of individual family members. As discussed in chapter 2, when Maria Rafael's husband wanted to move to the United States, she reluctantly agreed but left her three young children behind for fifteen months because she was "just adamant about not staying in the United States." Maria strategized that by leaving the children in the Philippines, her husband would be less likely to decide to stay permanently in the United States. Although her strategy failed in the end, the case reminds us that the household is not a unified social group, but is often marred by gender conflicts and negotiation.

Transnational families, especially in cases where young children or elderly parents were left behind, diligently kept in touch through letters, phone calls, photos, visits, and through resources and money sent home by the migrants. Like their counterparts in the United States, those left behind led transnational lives: they physically lived in one place but built their lives around the material resources, and also the dreams and expectations, of another. These dreams and expectations revolved around the possibility of economic mobility, as promised by the gifts and remittances sent by their relatives abroad. These impressions were often confirmed—or even exaggerated—by the visiting migrants. As Nicholas Sario explained, "It was fashionable for Filipinos who have been in the States for a long time to come back and show off. They were like Santa Claus, and the stories that they told. They told us that there was money everywhere. We just sat down, mesmerized by those stories." But others were offended by the returnees' apparent flaunting of success and material wealth. In the following passage, journalist Quiros likens Filipino visiting migrants to the Thomasites, the first group of American schoolteachers who arrived in the Philippines at the beginning of the twentieth century to "miseducate" the Filipinos:

> [The returnees] bring us stories about how much life in America has proved what the *Reader's Digest* says it is. They also bring us homilies, delivered with the proselytizing zeal of Thomasites, which are forceful for their use of contrasts. It's too hot in the Philippines; it's nice to snuggle by the hearth in America. There's grime and smog in our streets; you can't drive without anti-pollutants in the States. Filipino drivers are maniacs; American drivers follow traffic rules.[18]

Represented as Thomasites, the returning migrants are positioned in this passage as "neocolonizers whose ambitions lie in setting themselves apart from the rest of the 'natives' rather than affiliating with them."[19]

But migrants did not always return with positive stories—or positive feelings—about the United States. The lessons learned there can also be bitter. Dario Villa's father, who was separated from his family for sixteen years, recounted stories of racism in West Virginia, "[where] there were separate trains and [restroom] facilities for whites and blacks" and "[where] he got the same stares from both groups whenever he used either bathroom." Although Dario's father did not disclose how U.S. racism affected him personally, other migrant fathers were more forthcoming. Rose Campos's father, who spent his college years in Ohio, often told his children "about how hard it was living in America and how he couldn't go to restaurants that he wanted to go to or go to the movies." These negative experiences remained with him, shaping his views about inequalities that he actively passed on to his children. "Growing up in the Philippines, we had lots of helpers," Rose said. "But Papa never wanted to hear any harsh words spoken to the helpers. He always reminded us to treat them like equals, because he said you will never know the pain of bondage." For some returning migrants, their experience in the United States filled them with resolve never to go back. Maria Rafael was such a person. Maria went to the United States in 1967 as an exchange student. There she found Americans to be "too unfriendly," "too individualistic," and "too selfish." "There was no warmth, no camaraderie like what we have in the Philippines," she exclaimed. When she left the United States, she vowed that she would never return. This was the reason, as related above, that she was so adamant about keeping her children in the Philippines, in the hopes that her husband would decide against settling in the United States.

In this section, I have sought to provide a glimpse into how transnationalism is lived and imagined by those within the "homeland"—or in Quiros's words, by those who "are expatriates right *here* in our own land." My interest here is more qualitative than quantitative: I want to understand how the transnational terrain of the Philippines—fostered by a history of U.S. (neo)colonialism and by ongoing relationships with Americans in the Philippines and Filipinos in America—shapes the knowledge, consciousness, and identities of the local Filipinos. My findings indicate that these transnational ties—economic, cultural, and social—not only change standard of living of Filipinos but also transform their markers of prestige and status, their dreams, fantasies, and longings, and their sense of future for themselves. Most often, these transnational ties serve as catalysts for eventual emigration to the United States. In a few instances, they shore up resolve to remain in the Philippines. Ideologically, these transnational encounters construct and project onto the popular consciousness a mixed portrait of the United States as the land of unrivaled economic opportunity but one that is marred by corrupt and even "immoral" people and policies. As will be discussed below, the representation of the material West as desirable but problematic is a recurring theme in the migrants' conceptualization of the United States.

"OPERATION HOMECOMING": *BALIKBAYANS* AND TRANSNATIONAL POLITICS

In July 2000, my husband returned to the Philippines for the first time since he left his hometown in Pangasanan at the age of seven, almost thirty-one years ago. At the Ninoy Aquino International Airport in Manila, he was pleasantly surprised to discover that the immigration checkpoint had a separate priority line marked *balikbayan* (returnee or homecomer),[20] reserved for returning overseas Filipinos like himself. But he hesitated, unsure if he qualified as a *balikbayan,* since he no longer spoke a Filipino language and his memory of the Philippines had dimmed considerably in the intervening years. But when he inquired about his status, the immigration official assured him that his Philippine birth made him a *balikbayan* and warmly welcomed him "home."

In 1973, the Marcos government turned *home*—the term most used by Filipino migrants to refer to the Philippines—into state policy when it initiated "Operation Homecoming," a program designed to encourage Filipinos living abroad, especially in the United States, to come "home" for a maximum of four months around the Christmas holidays. Officially named *balikbayan,* the returnees were offered a combination of reduced airfares, extended visas, tax breaks, and priority immigration and customs service upon arrival at the international airport in Manila. Begun as a limited one-year initiative, the program has been expanded and extended long after the demise of the Marcos regime in 1986.[21] The routinization of the *balikbayan* procedures testifies to the state's continuing effort to court overseas Filipinos and to the high volume of these return trips. In 1996, according to the Philippine Department of Tourism, nearly one hundred and forty-three thousand Filipinos returned to the Philippines to visit.[22] However, it would be overreaching to attribute these return trips to the effectiveness of the *balikbayan* program; none of my respondents mentioned the program in discussing their trips "home." On the other hand, the program is important for what it signifies: the Philippines's failure to contain its excess population, its increasing dependence on overseas remittances, and its active attempts to reincorporate its "nationals" abroad into its market and polity.[23]

In the past decade, scholars have documented the sending states' growing dependence on migrants' financial resources and their ensuing efforts to claim the dispersed populations as "citizens."[24] "Operation Homecoming" was one such effort. The Marcos regime's interest in overseas Filipinos was part of its plan to spur the tourist industry, to generate foreign exchange, and to lure remittance dollars to the Philippines. But the initiative must also be understood as an example of transnational politics, designed to secure the endorsement of the overseas population for the regime. Indeed, Marcos had launched the initiative to invite Filipino migrants to return and judge for themselves the results of his martial law regime, in the hope that it would improve public opinion in the United States about the perceived loss of democracy in the Philippines.[25]

Marcos had reasons to fear the wrath of those overseas—many of whom had emigrated precisely to escape his rule. As soon as martial law was declared in the Philippines in 1972, the Filipino American community galvanized to depose Marcos.[26] Critical of Marcos's corruption and alarmed by his political repression and violation of human rights, these opposition groups—through countless forums, marches, rallies, and press conferences—alerted the Filipino American community and the larger American public to the plight of political prisoners in the Philippines and to the regime's use of torture and execution of alleged opponents. Convinced that U.S. economic assistance legitimized Marcos's dictatorial rule, the groups vigorously lobbied the U.S. Congress to stop such aid. Throughout the Marcos years, "Stop U.S. aid to the Marcos regime" was a familiar chant heard at virtually every picket line in front of Philippine consulates across the United States. After the brutal assassination of Marcos's chief political rival, former senator Benigno Aquino, on August 21, 1983, the U.S.-based anti-Marcos organizations stepped up their campaign to oust Marcos. They jointly sponsored speaking engagements by prominent Filipinos; featured underground videos, photographs, and skits that exposed the regime's violation of human rights; and urged the U.S. Congress to shift its support from the discredited Marcos to the candidacy of Cory Aquino. It is important to note that they maintained the transnational flow of information, thereby providing crucial information to anti-Marcos groups in the Philippines about the international and U.S. public opinion on the crisis as well as updating Filipino Americans on the political situation at "home." When Marcos was finally overthrown on February 26, 1986, the "people's victory" was claimed not only by Filipinos in the Philippines but also by U.S.-based anti-Marcos forces, which had doggedly organized for some fourteen years.[27]

Edgar Gamboa participated in both the Philippine- and U.S.-based anti-Marcos movement.[28] Like thousands other Filipinos, Edgar left for the United States to escape "the tentacles of Marcos's repressive government." An ardent anti-Marcos activist, Edgar, then a medical student at the University of the Philippines, joined street demonstrations, adding his voice to the growing protest against what he perceived as extensive government abuses. As an aspiring physician, Edgar had hoped to stay and practice medicine in the Philippines. Although many of his medical school friends were leaving for the United States, Edgar believed "it was not right to leave behind a country in disarray." But, for his own protection, he reluctantly agreed and left for New York City in 1976. Soon after his arrival, Edgar joined the Movement for a Free Philippines (MFP) and resumed his protest against the Marcos dictatorship. According to Edgar, "[MFP] mostly did propaganda, lobbying Washington against sustaining the Marcos regime with foreign aid. We in the MFP also financially supported the grassroots antigovernment movement in the Philippines." The day after the assassination of Senator Benigno Aquino, Edgar was among the first who marched in protest in front of the Philippine consulate in Manhattan. "Nothing had been formally organized," he remembered. "A few of us just showed up at the embassy carrying placards denouncing the assassination. . . . I carried [my two-year-old son] on my shoulders as we walked up and down Fifth Avenue." Edgar beamed with pride when he recalled that "the network crews came and taped the impromptu demonstration. It was shown in the evening news."

After he moved to San Diego in 1985, Edgar continued his anti-Marcos activism, especially in the months leading up to the demise of the Marcos regime and the election of Cory Aquino in 1986. Edgar's life story typifies that of a transmigrant: his resolve to "restore democracy" to the Philippines heightened, rather than lessened, as he became incorporated into the United States.

Cory Aquino herself was a transmigrant. Because Aquino had been so closely associated with the Philippine quest for democracy, it is easy to forget that she was a long-time U.S. resident before going "home" to run for election. Aquino and her husband represented a sector of the displaced dominant class that emigrated to the United States and built a political base there among the politicized constituency of Filipino émigrés but that continued to own and oversee considerable land and business holdings in the Philippines.[29] Once elected, Aquino invited many Filipino émigrés to return to the Philippines to join her administration at various levels of government—in recognition of the crucial role they played in ousting Marcos and in placing her in power. A good number of Filipino migrants accepted Aquino's invitation to return and help the fledgling government. Paz Jensen was one. Born in Manila, Paz came to San Diego in 1967 when she married her American husband, who was of "Norwegian/Danish/German" heritage. Reflecting her family's prominent class background, Paz had "strong connections" to the Aquino family and administration: her sister was an assistant to Vice President Laurel, her father was related to Aquino's husband, one of her former students was married to Aquino's son, and one of her former classmates was Aquino's physician. When the phone calls came soliciting her advice and help, Paz took a year's leave of absence from her teaching job at a community college and returned to the Philippines. Paz had high hopes of bringing more foreign investors to the Philippines and establishing new overseas markets for Philippine products. But like many other returnees, she soon became disappointed and disillusioned by what she perceived as the lack of progress and foresight exhibited by the new government. "Everything I tried to do failed," she said. "It was very difficult because [the Aquino administration] did not have policies. . . . [It] did not have a long-range plan." When her leave of absence ended, Paz returned to her career and family in the United States. But soon after her return, her marriage ended in divorce. Paz suspected that her year away from home had taken a toll on the relationship:

> My husband said, "You can't be there and be a wife." Which meant I had to choose between him and my country. And at that time, I was so idealistic

> about helping my country that I chose the Philippines. So we had a friendly divorce. It's sad that it happened, especially because my efforts in the Philippines failed.

When I asked Paz why she invested so much of herself and her time to helping the Philippines, she replied simply, "Because I still consider it my home."

The U.S.-based "people's power" movement reveals a seeming paradox: that the migrants' involvement in homeland politics strengthens or even requires their incorporation into the United States.[30] As such, it challenges the essentialist position that immigrant incorporation into the United States is bipolar, that is, that one either gravitates toward the pole of nativism or the pole of assimilation. In order to discredit the legitimacy of the Marcos government, the Filipino migrant community had to learn how to access U.S. media, lobby the U.S. Congress, mount mass campaigns to sway public opinion, and familiarize itself with U.S. foreign policies. It also had to build coalitions with sympathetic U.S.-based groups such as the labor movement and race-based organizations. In particular, the migrants allied with U.S.-born Filipino American activists who had been drawn into the "people's power" movement through their involvement in the civil rights and anti-Vietnam war struggles.[31] Characteristic of its transnational nature, the U.S.-based movement targeted the infractions committed by both the Philippine and the U.S. governments. As Filipino activists in the United States exposed the wrongdoings of the Marcos government, they simultaneously called attention to U.S. dominance in the global economy, criticized U.S. tacit support of the Marcos regime, and pressed for more assistance and support for the candidacy of Aquino.[32]

The well-publicized anti-Marcos movement is but one instance of Filipino engagement in transnational politics. Even among the first-wave immigrants who came in the 1920s, the issue of Philippine independence of U.S. colonial rule was just as pronounced a political concern as the racially oppressive conditions facing them as immigrant workers.[33] On a day-to-day basis, Filipino migrants have tended to "back-home" needs through voluntary organizations such as hometown associations, cultural clubs, professional and advocacy groups, and alumni school networks. Most of the more than 150 Filipino American organizations in San Diego, especially the hometown associations, regularly provide funds for small development projects in their respective hometowns, for disaster relief, for education of the youth, and/or for local fiestas. The

Philippine Medical Association in San Diego, like its counterparts elsewhere, sends physicians to the Philippines on yearly medical missions. Working together on homeland projects can alter the dynamics of local community politics. For example, the disastrous 1990 Luzon earthquake and 1991 Mt. Pinatubo volcano eruption temporarily united the often-fractious San Diego community around the shared goal of aiding the victims "back home." According to the coordinator of these relief efforts, "That was the first time that Filipinos in San Diego really came together. . . . I think all of the local hometown associations were represented in some kind of donations." In the aftermath of the natural disasters, the umbrella group Council of Pilipino American Organizations of San Diego County (COPAO) effectively coordinated local relief efforts and delivered money, food, medicine, and temporary shelter to the victims in the Philippines. San Diego Filipino leaders continue to point to these relief efforts as examples of how united the community could and should be.

Cognizant of the importance of overseas contributions, many local officials in the Philippines sponsor lavish welcoming receptions for *balikbayans* that feature "immense banquets for several hundred guests, musical entertainment, and laudatory speeches by town officials in which *balikbayans* are individually recognized."[34] A former COPAO chairman related that his community work—especially in relation to the 1990 and 1991 disaster relief efforts—had enabled him to meet high-ranking Philippine officials such as then-Secretary of Defense Fidel Ramos, who became Philippine president. He also befriended Ramos's sister, who was then a consulate in San Diego: "I got to know her because of my participation in the community. As a community leader, *they have to know me* because we work together." The assertion that "they have to know" him is telling: it underscores the migrants' awareness of their role as important brokers of social and political capital and as benefactors of their home country.[35] Because the overseas community can influence and even shape the political destiny of the homeland, as evident in the movement to oust Marcos, home governments have been ambivalent about the degree to which the transmigrants are in fact welcome in the country. In the case of the Philippines, even as the government aggressively courts Filipino *balikbayans,* it does not allow them to participate in the electoral process or to obtain dual citizenship. As such, the Philippine state's reincorporation of the Filipino migrants is ambiguous at best. As Vicente Rafael cogently notes, overseas Filipinos are "neither inside nor wholly outside the nation-state." Indeed, being a *balikbayan*—a returnee or homecomer—is contingent on one's permanent residence abroad; that is, the term "means that one lives somewhere else and that one's appearance in the Philippines is temporary and intermittent, as if one were a tourist."[36]

GOING HOME: OF STATUS, REVENGE, AND RESISTANCE

In an essay on the notion of "home" in Asian Pacific American literature, Luis Francia asserts that Asian Pacific American writers' preoccupation with "home"—that actual and mythified land across the Pacific—arises partly out of America's rejection of Asian Pacific Americans as "full-fledged participants in a pluralistic American enterprise."[37] Asian Americans' longing for home is thus in part a response to their enforced homelessness, an articulation of their deep and abiding dissatisfaction with and anger at the processes of racialized exclusion in the United States. In this context, "homeland" becomes a site for migrants from the "margins" to reestablish a sense of parity—to reinforce or raise their social standing. The place of origin offers a space for claiming and valorizing status, because status claims can be most appropriately interpreted in a historical and community context, "where certain practices, goods, and artifacts have mutually intelligible meanings to community members."[38] For many migrants then, the trip home is in effect a chance for public validation and recognition in their country of origin. Such validation is especially meaningful to the many migrants whose status has been lowered through migration to the United States.

Filipino enlistees in the U.S. Navy constitute one group that has experienced downward social mobility. Although they make much higher wages than at home, many are relegated to servile positions, passed over for promotions, and racially harassed as brown men in a country that favors whites (see chapter 5). But in the Philippine context, to be a U.S. Navy enlistee is a marker of high and enviable status—one that connotes U.S. citizenship and residence, a higher income, and access to desirable consumer goods. Vicente Rodriquez, an enlisted Navy man, described the advantages bestowed on families with sons in the U.S. Navy: "When the Filipino leave the Philippines to join the Navy, he has nothing. Then all of a sudden, the house that he left behind started to improve. And then all of a sudden the family started to acquire properties, buying land, buying business, jeepney, tricycles, sari-sari stores." Thus for Navy enlistees, it is in returning "home" that the real promise of the migration process—of success, prestige, and a better life—can best be fulfilled.[39] Reynaldo Cablay's account of his migration and its meaning exemplifies the importance of status claims and valorization in a transnational context. A native of Manila, Reynaldo explained why he joined the U.S. Navy in 1966: "It was my only chance to get out of the Philippines and get ahead." When he discovered that Filipino enlistees were restricted to the ratings of officers' stewards and mess hall attendants, he felt "bitter and miserable" because "they brought us in the Navy to be butlers." Although Reynaldo "hated every bit" of his life as a steward, whenever he visited the Philippines, he felt only pride about his job—or more accurately, for what the job signified in that context. He described his first visit to the Philippines after a six-year absence: "When I went back, it was great. People really looked up to you because I was an American citizen. It was a good feeling." He characterized his return as "kind of a revenge," an occasion to "go back and show everybody how far I had gotten," especially those who used to mock his humble upbringing:

> It was something that I really wanted to do. I just kind of had to rub it in. Out of revenge to all those people that made fun of me when I was a kid taking care of my pigs and not having a father. I wanted to show them that I could do better than them. To show them that I could take care of my family by myself. I also showed off to my friends who graduated from college and everything but they still didn't have a job. I was making twenty times more money than they were even with all that schooling.

In the same way, for Ricardo Ruiz, who joined the U.S. Navy in 1964, "going home" afforded him an opportunity to claim a higher social status: "Whenever I take a vacation in the Philippines in my own town, they treat me like I am a celebrity because I broke from the shackle of hardship in our town." For Reynaldo Cablay and Ricardo Ruiz, it is partly this status validation that shores up their resolve to stay and do their best in the U.S. Navy—regardless of the indignities afforded by the job.

For the migrants, then, status assertion in a transnational context represents one form of resistance: a refusal to be incorporated into subordinate positions within the United States. Yet the migrants' status claim is in effect a claim about the superiority of the United States and the desirability of international migration. By depicting the United States as the land of opportunity and prestige, and emigration as the optimal means to achieve "a better life," the migrants may unwittingly buttress the national interests of the United States and the economic interests of transnational capital, respectively. In so doing, they may inadvertently justify both at home and abroad the exploitation of racialized labor. But not all returnees chose status valorization—and the concomitant endorsement of the United States—as their form of resistance. In an example of "transnationalism from below,"[40] some returnees challenged their subordinate positions by exposing the "truths" about the promise of America, even when it meant devaluing their own status in the process. For example, Pablo Gutierrez did not hesitate to tell his former town mates how, despite his college degree in business management, the only job he could get in the United States was as a custodian. Like many other immigrants in the United States, Pablo could not find employment that matched his education:

> I applied to different jobs, but I was so disappointed. Most were looking for local background, local experience, even if you're a college graduate. From where we came from, you can take pride with your college diploma. But here, it's just a piece of paper. I looked at jobs that would make me apply what I studied in college. But nothing happened. Don't tell me I didn't try! If you're picky, then you won't get a job. So I gathered my strength to get a part-time job, my first janitorial job.

Whenever he visited the Philippines, he would tell his friends, "You know what my job is? I'm just a janitor over there." But they were still impressed: "They say, 'Well, yes, you're a janitor but you still earn more than I do.' " To counter his friends' tendency to "pine for the United States," Pablo instructed them about anti-Filipino racism in the United States: "I tell them I'm Oriental, so I don't stand much of a chance, this homeboy! Homeboys can only work in the lower fields. I tell them it's different because you're brown skin. Skin color is always primary. That's the game here in the States." He also discouraged his town mates from emigrating by depicting the United States as a "lonely" place for immigrants: "I say don't be envious. . . . I tell them the reason why I visit home is because I get lonely in America. People don't have time for each other there." Pablo attributed this condition of estrangement to the ever-present pressure to work and make money: "The lifestyle in the United States is like this: You sleep at night, you wake up in the morning, go to work, then go home. Life is oriented toward the weekend. Thank God it's Friday! In [the Philippines], . . . any time is Friday there, when friends pull you out for a good time." Andy Panado, in a recent trip to the Philippines, likewise warned his friends about the "uncaring" and "cutthroat" nature of the United States:

> Many of my town mates still see the U.S. as being the most wonderful place in the universe, basically. And I don't. It's still a place where you really work hard. You have bills to pay. In the Philippines, you still have bills to pay but for some reason people can still go through the day. Over here, if you don't pay your bill, you have the collector at your door.

Implicit in these critiques of the United States is a denunciation of the harsh demands and practices of a capitalist society—one that devalues leisure time, interferes with personal relationships, and mistreats its less-fortunate members. From this vantage point, Pablo Gutierrez and Andy Panado inverted the often-heard representation of the Philippines as "undeveloped/unproductive" and the United States as "developed/productive" by characterizing the former as a country whose personal relationships and quality of life are superior to those of the latter. This inversion is evident in the following statement made by Pablo Gutierrez: "Yes, the Philippines can be messy there, but you know your neighbors. And Filipinos have control of our life. Americans, they are controlled by money." By calling attention to the "costs" of migration and capitalism, these migrants in effect are exposing and challenging the unequal power between nations within a global system of racialized capitalist relations.

FOR THE LOVE OF FAMILY: REMITTANCES, OBLIGATIONS, AND DISAPPOINTMENTS

In her work on Tongan migration, Small argues that Tongan migrants did not leave Tonga expressly to become Americans. Instead, they left Tonga to be better Tongans; that is, to better fulfill their obligations of helping their family "back home."[41] Small's argument decenters the United States, redefines the immigrants' dream, and calls attention to the family as a foundational base for transnational social relations. The rise of global capitalism, and especially the continuing global marginalization of "postcolonial" states such as the Philippines, has moved the family into a new transnational arena; the survival of the family and its members increasingly depends on family labor that straddles national borders. When my respondents speak about their connections to the Philippines, it is their ties and obligations to their family "back home" that weigh most heavily on their minds and in their hearts. In this sense, migration is not necessarily—or at least not always—an act of leaving. For the majority of the people I interviewed, their departure was a move designed to improve the lot and status of their families back home, and not only or primarily about the pursuit of personal success. It is in the shouldering of the various obligations of their extended, transnational family that they attempt the near-impossible task of "leaving [home] but staying there."[42]

A significant economic manifestation of these transnational familial relations is the remittance flows to relatives and friends in the Philippines. According to the Philippine Overseas Employment Administration, between 1989 and 1993, Filipino Americans remitted approximately five billion dollars, averaging well over one billion dollars each year.[43] By 1989, consumer goods sent via *balikbayan* boxes contributed 4.2 billion pesos (or one hundred and ninety million dollars) annually to the Philippine economy; of that, 3.3 billion pesos (or 80 percent) went directly to Filipino families in the form of basic commodities.[44] These numbers are rising. In the first half of 1994, overseas Filipinos remitted almost eight hundred million dollars through official bank transfers—a likely underestimate, since this amount does not include cash carried back by returning relatives and friends.[45] The Philippine government covets these remittance dollars because they provide the critically needed foreign exchange to alleviate the nation's mounting external debt and balance of payments trade deficit. As such, the Philippine economy is built in part upon the exchanges among family members who live in different countries. As Small suggests, it is "family relationships [that] support the weight of the remittance economy."[46]

Close to 90 percent of the Filipino migrants I interviewed indicated that they or their family had sent remittances to the Philippines: to help an ailing parent, to finance a sibling's college education, to alleviate an emergency situation, to purchase property, or to provide extra spending money for family members during the holidays. Whatever the reason, remittance sending is widely perceived as a migrant's obligation: to secure a better life for one's family back home. Leo Sicat, who "send[s] money home regularly," viewed remittance sending as a nonnegotiable responsibility: "We cannot get away from that. The people back home always need that support." But this sense of duty stems not only from traditional demands but also from a deep awareness of the income and resource differentials between the Philippines and the United States. When asked why her family continues to send money to the Philippines, Maricela Rebaya, who came to the United States in 1985 at the age of fourteen, declared, "No matter how difficult life is here, it's still better off than anyone over there." Her extended family in the Philippines is large: there are twelve brothers and sisters on her mother's side and eight on her father's side. Of this clan, only three had migrated to the United States. The family's economic situation back home has worsened, ever since the death of her grandfather in 1988 and the subsequent collapse of the family business. As a result, the extended family increasingly looked to the three who lived in the United States for assistance. For Maricela's parents, who worked multiple jobs to make ends meet, this additional obligation stretched the family's meager budget at times to its barest. "We live at a very minimal level," confided Maricela. Still, they considered themselves "fortunate" and pledged to remit "as much as [they] can." As Maricela saw it, their lives were intimately connected to the lives of those back home: "For us staying here doesn't mean that's just for us. When we earn extra money, we send it home. It's a big help for them. So when we're here, we try to make better of ourselves so we can help them. Basically that's the main idea of why we're here." In another example, Julia de Lugo, an assembly worker with meager means, recounted how her remittances were put to use in the Philippines:

> My husband's people in the Philippines, they were very poor. I had to help them. My husband's brothers wanted to go to school. So we sent them money. One was a doctor. One is a lawyer. And then my sister-in-law had kids. We also sent them to school. My husband and I had a house built there just because maybe we would go home [to retire]. One of the nieces stays in the house now.

Julia de Lugo's account highlights the transnational equation understood by many migrants: even if one has a low-paying, low-status job in the United States, one can still funnel hard-earned money into a relative's education, building a house, or retiring back in the Philippines—all of which work to increase one's status back home and thus help to blunt the sharpness of life in the United States.

The frequency of sending and the amount of remittances vary over time, as family members pass away or move to the United States and as the migrants' own economic needs increase. Not surprisingly, immediate family members receive the major share of the remittances, with the bulk going to elderly parents, then siblings, and then other relatives. Vicente Rodriquez, who joined the U.S. Navy expressly "for the money," sent half of his monthly paycheck to his mother. He also wrote her "once a week, even in my busiest time." But when his mother passed away five years later, he wrote home "less and less" and cut down on the monthly remittances, now sent to support his older sister and her family. Nemesia Cortez, a widow with two daughters to support, was clear about the limit of her obligations: "Before, when my mother was alive, I sent her money. But once my mother was gone, we had to be on our own. My relatives have to know that I am a single parent, supporting my own kids. They think that we pick money up under the tree." Continued migration has also altered remittance-sending patterns. As more family members migrated to the United States, the locus of migrants' economic and social support network shifted gradually away from the Philippines to the United States. As Reynaldo Cablay explained, "I used to send money home to take care of my mother and my sister. But now all of my family is here. I'm not directly responsible for anyone else back home." He then paused and added, "But if they asked, I would send money if they needed it."

Although most migrants worked hard to bring their aging parents to the United States, the experience could prove disappointing and frustrating for all concerned. For the elderly migrants, especially those who did not drive or speak English well, life in the United States can be especially unkind. Rose Salunga, a sixty-year-old Filipina, referred to the United States as "a country for the young. If you are old, there is nothing for you here." That was why Pablo Gutierrez's father visited the Philippines every year: "My father lives here with us, but every year, he'd go home, because he'd get lonely." Abraham Ocampo, who came to the United States at the age of sixty and now operates a Filipino senior center in San Diego, explained why so many elderly Filipinos became disillusioned with their experience in the United States:

> They go home because they are disillusioned about coming here. They are accustomed in the Philippines to be taken care of by their children, and yet their children could not take care of them because they are busy. So they were angry with their children. They were hurt. I try to tell them, don't expect very much from your children because they are busy. They are busy with raising money. They are paying high mortgages for their own homes. They are sending their children to school. They have to work double time. They have to work double jobs in order to be able to finance their livelihoods.

Alejandra San Juan, a fifty-five-year-old migrant, explained why she planned to return to the Philippines to retire: "We don't want to be thrown in the nursing home. We cannot expect our children to take care of us, because they have their own lives too. And we understand that, but we're scared to be living in the nursing home." These statements hint at yet another paradox of transnational families: for many migrants and their families, family obligations are at times better fulfilled in a transnational rather than in a national context. That is, when family members are apart, regular remittances and periodic visits are sufficient to fulfill one's obligations; but when family members are united, additional day-to-day duties are expected, many of which the migrants cannot meet because of their already overstretched lives.

Yet remittances cannot compensate for the daily pain and strain of transnational separation. As Basch et al. write, "Family members, separated from the majority of their kin, endure vast stretches of loneliness and isolation socially, culturally, and emotionally."[47] Rose Alvarez described how she longed for her family in the Philippines: "My mind always goes back to the Philippines. I miss the life there. I miss my brothers and sisters there. We had a very happy family. Every Saturday and Sunday, we would sit and sing. But it will never come back." Remittance-based relationships also entail other personal and emotional costs, one of which is a perceived shift in the quality of these very relationships. Decisions over who should receive remittances and how much to send are difficult negotiations, fraught with disappointments and suspicions. Julia Cortez recounted that her mother had a "nervous breakdown" over sending money to the Philippines. Julia explained: "My dad's mom was jealous of my mom sending money to her mom in the Philippines. She didn't think that it was right. She thought that my dad was forgetting about her. She made both of my parents feel really guilty." Remittance sending can also lead to marital conflicts. Ruby Cruz related that her parents fought bitterly over money sent to the Philippines:

> My dad's always proving himself to his relatives back home. So whenever they ask him for money, he just gives it to them. My mom told me that we had given our relatives over ten thousand dollars so far. That makes my mom really, really mad because she worked two jobs so that my brother and me wouldn't have to work when we are in college. But now that money is gone.

Ruby herself resented her father's generosity toward his relatives in the Philippines: "It's not really very fair. I mean, because my dad has sent money to my cousin who went to nursing school. You know, why should she have money to do whatever she wanted, but my brother and me have to struggle and be limited and we're here and we are his kids." As the following quotes suggest, migrants also felt taken advantage of by relatives who bombarded them with requests for money and goods:

> The only time you receive a letter is when they need money. They are not going to write you a letter just to say, "Hey, how are you guys doing?"

> When we go home, people expect us to bring presents. Even those relatives who are very distant already, they come to you. The people there seemed to

be fake; they tended to be close to you only because they expected some money from you.

> One of the reasons I don't want to go back is that when people first see you, their first reaction is that you owe them money. That you have responsibility to take care of them since you are making more money and you should share your wealth with them. I don't have any responsibility to them. I already took care of my own family. I understand they are poor, but they shouldn't impose on you. My brother-in-law says he wants to fix up my house in the Philippines so it can be a memorial house for our family. But they write and ask me for the money to fix it. They ask many thousands dollars from us. I told them, "No more!"

Implicit in these charges is the migrants' frustration over the perceived shift in the quality of their relationship to relatives back home from one based on love and affection to one based on the amount of money and goods remitted. What these charges do not make explicit is that transnational exchanges are not one way. Those who stayed in the Philippines are obligated to oversee the assets of those who left, to look after abandoned land and houses, and to care for relatives left behind. By shouldering these responsibilities, they offer their overseas relatives a place of importance and comfort when they return to visit.[48] In other words, to maintain transnational connections, there are responsibilities at both ends. When these obligations are met, transnational families can represent a creative strategy for coping with the violence of global capitalism. But when they are unmet for whatever reason, they can tear the family apart, leaving the migrants without access to the longed-for "home" that could buffer them from the assaults of migrant life.

TRANSNATIONALISM AND COMPROMISES

A sample survey of Filipinos who were issued visas to the United States in 1986 found that a substantial percentage (36.2 percent) expected that they eventually would return permanently to the Philippines, even though almost three-fourths (74.3 percent) stated that they also planned to become U.S. citizens.[49] When I asked my respondents if they wanted to return to the Philippines to live, most answered affirmatively.[50] Some had never stopped longing for "home." Maria Rafael, even after two decades in the United States, still considered her stay here as "temporary":

> I am just biding my time. I am here because that's what my family wanted me to do. . . . I'm just waiting for a time when I can say I'm ready to do

things for myself and what I want to do is go back and be there and do something for my country. I still can't call America my country after all these years. So my goal is to go back. I haven't been able to consider myself an American. I am just here. I could not sing the American national anthem. I still cry whenever I sing the Philippine national anthem. It probably will always be that way.

Many missed what they perceived to be "the unhurried, gentle way" of Philippine life and resented the "work, work, work" frenzy of U.S. life. Paul Nemenzo, an energetic man who devoted most of his free time to community work, indicated that even after thirty years in the United States, he continues to maintain the dream of retiring in the Philippines: "I really miss life back home. In my hometown, people are so friendly. I knew everybody. And here, sometimes your neighbors, you don't even talk to them, because all they want to do is work, work, work. You can be neighbors for fifteen years and never talk to each other." Luz Lozada, a beautician who had lived in the United States for a decade, also disliked the intense work environment: "We have been here for almost ten years now and I still want to go home. I don't like living here that much. Just work, work, work, pay your bills, and work again. There's no time for anything else." Pablo Gutierrez, a college-educated migrant who had toiled as a custodian for fifteen years, likewise preferred life in the Philippines: "Living there is different. You enjoy life there. You feel different, like you're very free. That's what I like most. Close family relations. Close friends. We all help each other."

However, even as they longed for the Philippines, most of my respondents have resigned themselves to the fact that they will have to remain in the United States at least until retirement age. Work opportunities keep them there. As Jose Faeldo, a cook who is in his mid-thirties, exclaimed, "Sure, I'd like to go back. But unless I win the lottery or find a pot of gold, I'll have to stay here. There is no work there. Maybe I can go home later when I retire, when I am old." Brian Verano, an accountant who had lived in the United States for eighteen years, made a similar prediction: "I probably won't go back to the Philippines [to live] until I am really, really old. I don't want to go back now because there is no work there for me." Their children's well-being also keeps them tied to the United States. Vicente Rodriquez, a retired U.S. Navy man, reluctantly agreed to remain in the United States for his children's education:

I retired in the Philippines with the intention to stay there forever, coming back here no more. But my sons, my children, were determined to go back

> here, so was my wife, for some reason, I can't understand why. So I've been forced to go with them here. I don't want them to sacrifice for me. I'd rather sacrifice for them. And also, I've been persuaded by a lot of my friends who say that the education in the U.S. is better than the education here in the Philippines. That's a good point. So . . . that's the reason I'm here. But I'm going back after their education.

Vincente Rodriquez's preference to return and his wife's wish to remain in the United States corroborates a number of case studies documenting how male and female migrants differ with regard to their desires to return "home" permanently.[51] As Hondagneu-Sotelo reports, Mexican migrant women were more likely than men to wish to stay because they believed their children enjoyed better education and nutrition in the United States than would be possible in Mexico. On the other hand, Vicente Rodriquez's decision to abide by his family's wishes suggests that men, and not only women, understood well that staying promised the best opportunities for their children. Others give up their plans to "go home" because the United States is "the country of [their] children" and the children want to stay here. As Leo Sicat contemplated, "I thought I wanted to go back there and retire but now probably not, because the kids don't want to go home. And they've been telling us that we'll be the babysitters of their children. So I guess that's another family tie that we have here in the U.S." Felicia Gonzaga, a mother of three and grandmother of five, agreed: "Our children are here; our grandchildren are here. So it's hard to leave them. It's not easy for them to go to the Philippines, it's easier for us but not for them."

How do they reconcile these conflicting wishes? For the majority of my respondents, the answer was to divide their lives between the two countries; that is, to have a transnational life. Jose Menor, a successful physician who makes annual trips to the Philippines, outlined his preference: "My desire is this. When I retire I probably would go home to the Philippines to stay and spend my time there and enjoy. But only stay for a couple of months, three months, six months, and back to this country. I would like to have two homes." This arrangement is necessary for the following reasons: "I don't think I could bring my children back home to stay for good. And I don't think we could stay for good for so many reasons. One is the health reason, and the accommodation. If you get there and you have a medical problem, what could you do? So I would like to have a home back there which I could do easily, and a small home here in this country." He paused and added wistfully, "My heart is still Filipino. If there is a possibility of dual citizenship, I'd do that."

Juanita Lopez described how she and her husband have decided to reconcile their differing attitudes toward returning "home":

> I miss the Philippines so much. The environment. It's so different from here. It's so relaxing. I love the food. And my brothers and sisters are there in Manila. . . . [But] my husband thinks the Philippines is too crowded for him, overpopulated, smog all over the place, too noisy for him. But he is willing to stay there for a few months and then come back here. I compromise with him, you know, because my children are here and I don't think they even consider leaving for the Philippines. That's a good compromise; we stay with our children for several months a year and go home for several months.

Juanita Lopez's words alert us to the fact that in an age of growing global inequalities, migrants around the world have had to learn to live with compromises: of being neither inside nor wholly outside both their home and host countries; of living apart from loved ones in order to better provide for them; of working in higher-paid but lower-prestige occupations; and of living in one place while longing for another. In this context, returning "home"—in transnational visits, retirement, remittances, as well as in memory—represents not only an opportunity to regain lost status and to rekindle old relationships, but also a personal resolve to remain stubbornly *home bound* even as the violence of globalized capitalism flings them "to the ends of the earth."[52]

◆ ◆ ◆

In this chapter, I have shown that Filipino immigrants have no wish to exile their country from their minds and hearts. On the contrary, they keep alive their ties to the Philippines by engaging in activities such as sending remittances, visiting their hometowns, and communicating with family members back home. In so doing, they confirm that "identity is less about *rootedness,* but more about *routedness.*"[53] At the same time, I do not want to overstate the frequency of these transnational activities. In the next chapter, I will argue that most Filipino migrants do not live in transnational "circuits" but instead are quite rooted in San Diego, where they have built homes and communities. Although they may keep attempting to re-create the Ilocos region, or Bicol, or Manila in their lives in San Diego, they do so with Filipino Americans—and other local residents—who have become most essential in their daily lives, with whom they interact, and on whom they and their children depend.

CHAPTER 5

Making Home

Building Communities in a Navy Town

Community is simply the way people live a life together.
Cherríe Moraga, *This Bridge Called My Back*

It has been said that whenever two Pinoys had gotten together, they formed a club.
Fred Cordova, *Filipinos*

Filipino American lives in San Diego have been marked both by enforced homelessness and by active home making. Like other U.S. cities, San Diego has been carved out of repressive state, labor, and cultural practices designed to maintain white privilege and to keep "outsiders" from becoming rooted. As racialized immigrants and citizens, Filipinos in San Diego have endured housing, job, social, and interpersonal discrimination—all designed to reinforce their marginal status. But they have also created community to challenge these discriminatory practices and to provide crucial social sustenance and financial support to each other. I focus on San Diego to draw attention to the local as an important terrain. Amid the proliferation of scholarly discussions on the "global" and the "transnational," I want to understand how issues such as territory, identity, and home making are made relevant by individuals through ongoing struggles with others within *particular* sociospatial contexts.

At the same time, I believe that we need to situate the study of community formation within an international and historical perspective. Couching the study of Filipino American home making within the wider context of U.S.-Philippine relations, I argue in this chapter that U.S. colonial rule, recruitment practices, and labor conditions have preselected the regional and class composition of different Filipino immigrant cohorts and thus have profoundly affected their process of group formation and differentiation in San Diego and elsewhere. Specifically, I trace the negotiations, collisions, and (dis)solutions that the San Diego Filipino community has had to enact as it transformed from a predominantly Navy community to a more occupationally diverse community after 1965. By situating the process of community formation within its historical, global, and local contexts, I show how the processes that form community are never complete but instead are always (re)constituted in relation to historical and material differences. I find particularly useful Doreen Massey's conceptualization of communities as "constellations of social relations" that are "open, porous, invented and particularized as a product of interaction."[1] Like Massey, I contend that the shapes and characteristics of communities will change over time. Sometimes, they cohere; at other times, they may splinter or even dissolve.

SAN DIEGO: THE MAKING OF A "NAVY TOWN"

Until 1998, San Diego was the site of the largest U.S. naval base and the Navy's primary West Coast training facility, the Naval Training Center (NTC).[2] Established in 1921 along the north shore of the bay, the training center housed seven camps, each a specialty branch for a particular phase of training. By the end of World War II, more than two hundred and sixty thousand recruits had completed training at NTC.[3] The opening of the training center accelerated San Diego's development into a "Navy town." By 1930, the Navy had already become the "*sine qua non* of San Diego's very existence."[4] Since World War I, the growth of the city and the growth of the Navy had become inextricably intertwined. San Diego leaders had determined that close ties to the military were essential for desirable urban development, and the city's Chamber of Commerce did all it could to lure the Navy to town. Indeed, the Naval Training Center had its inception when William Kettner, congressman from the Eleventh Congressional District of California *and* spokesman for the San Diego Chamber of Commerce, persuaded Franklin D. Roosevelt, then assistant secretary of the Navy, to establish a naval training facility on the shores of San Diego Bay. As a result, it was the Navy that put San Diego on the national map, that stimulated retail and residential development, and that established San Diego as the "aviation capital of the West." In 1930, more than one-third of the city's population was already employed by the Navy. To attract tourists and settlers alike, the city proudly advertised itself to the world as a Navy town. As an example, in a full-page advertisement in *National Geographic* magazine in January 1942, the Chamber offered the Navy's ships, airplanes, and men in uniform as the city's primary tourist attraction.[5]

The making of San Diego into a Navy town must be situated within the larger context of the "possessive investment in whiteness."[6] As the Chamber of Commerce courted the Navy, its real estate operators worked to block the migration of African Americans, Mexicans, and Asians into town. Since the early 1900s, widespread use of racially restrictive zoning covenants kept poor and nonwhite residents out of the most desirable areas of San Diego and confined them in what came to be called Southeast San Diego.[7] The Chamber, in collusion with the municipal government, actively maintained segregated housing projects, schools, and recreation facilities. The Navy—with its "near lily-white" force—did not threaten the goal of whiteness. As late as the 1930s, the Navy was 94 percent white, with fewer than five hundred African American and about four thousand Filipino sailors out of a total of eighty five thousand.[8] Economic segregation also abounded: before World War II, the rate of unemployment was three times higher among women and nonwhites than among white males.[9] After World War II, racial segregation, de facto and de jure, remained a fact of life in San Diego. As late as the 1970s, the only concentrations of African Americans and Mexicans outside Southeast San Diego were on the sites of former defense housing projects at Linda Vista and Midway.[10]

"STRAIGHT TO STEWARD SCHOOL:" LIFE AT THE NAVAL TRAINING CENTER

In 1930, at the age of nineteen, Ricardo Reyes, facing bleak future prospects in his hometown in Bulacan, reluctantly followed a town mate's urging and enlisted in the U.S. Navy. He became one of the approximately four thousand Filipinos who served in the U.S. Navy that year. Like most new recruits from the Philippines, he was sent directly to the Naval Training Center (NTC) in San Diego, where he attended "steward school" to learn how to do "housekeeping type of jobs." In the following decades, countless other Filipino Navy men traveled this same path: moving from their hometown in the Philippines straight to steward school at the NTC in San Diego and then to a naval career as the Navy's "brown skinned servant force."[11]

TABLE 2. FILIPINO POPULATION IN THE UNITED STATES, CALIFORNIA, AND SAN DIEGO, 1910–2000

Year	United States	California	San Diego
1910	2,767	5	—
1920	26,634	2,674	48
1930	108,260	30,470	394
1940	98,535	31,408	799
1950	122,707	40,424	NA
1960	181,614	67,134	5,123
1970	336,731	135,248	15,069
1980	774,652	358,378	48,658
1990	1,406,770	733,941	95,945
2000	1,800,000	918,678	121,147

SOURCES: Up to 1950, the data are from H. Brett Melendy (1977), whose sources include the annual reports of the U.S. Immigration and the U.S. Census of Population and Housing for each area. Melendy's records for San Diego through 1950 were for the city itself; the numbers from 1960 to 1900 are those for San Diego County. The figures for 1960 to 2000 were collated from the U.S. Census of Population and Housing for each area.

When Ricardo Reyes arrived in San Diego in 1930, there were reportedly close to four hundred Filipinos living in San Diego (see table 2). Like Filipinos elsewhere, these old-timers were primarily laborers, some of whom were nonsponsored students who scrambled to maintain themselves by combining work and study.[12] While the farmworkers concentrated in the agricultural communities of El Centro and Escondido, the urban laborers lived and worked in downtown hotels and restaurants.[13] By the 1950s, this community had transformed into a predominantly Navy community as Filipino Navy men and their families flocked to San Diego. For the majority of Filipino Navy men, San Diego was their first U.S. destination—the home of the NTC where they received their basic training. Although thousands of the recruits who had completed training at NTC were from the Philippines, their lives and deeds went unrecorded—even as San Diego transformed itself into one of the largest military complexes in the world.

In 1996, a Filipino American student at the University of California, San Diego, upon learning of my research on Filipino Navy men, gave me three editions of *The Anchor* (1964, 1975, 1979), a yearbooklike publication that records the daily life of a recruit at the NTC. The books belong to three different men in his family: his father, his uncle on his mother's side, and his cousin. They mark his family's entry into the United States and attest to the importance of the U.S. Navy in his—and other Filipinos'—family history. As I scanned the photos of these three books, I saw staring out at me from the pages the faces of young Filipino men. Some appeared eager; others shy; and still others uncertain. But all were made silent, their destiny seemingly determined, their deeds all but forgotten, their lives written out of history. I have listed all their names in the notes—a small attempt to inscribe them back onto the pages of history, to record for posterity that they were there.[14] And indeed they were. As the only non-American recruits, Filipinos comprised approximately 20 percent of each recruit company, far outnumbering African American and Mexican American enlistees. A 1977 Navy-sponsored study indicates that Filipino naval personnel, then numbering around twenty thousand, represented the second-largest minority group in the Navy.[15]

As I turned the pages of these now-yellowed memory books, I tried to piece together the experiences of these young Filipino men during their recruit training—to imagine what their lives must have been like during their first nine to twelve weeks in the United States. In all three editions of *The Anchor,* I saw pictures of young men getting their first hair cut, donning their new Navy uniforms, attending worship services, eating in mess halls, exerting themselves in physical training, visiting the San Diego Zoo and Sea World, and executing military drills. The sequencing of the photos suggests a uniform experience—of men arriving at the NTC, going through recruit training, and finally graduating. But the recruit training experience only appears uniform because the experiences of Filipino men have been written out of these pages. As an example, all three books include a section entitled "In Processing" with the following pronouncement: "In his new company the recruit will meet young men from all walks of life and *sections of the country.*"[16] But the Filipino recruits came from the Philippines rather than from other "sections of the country," their presence thus ignored and their (former) status as colonized nationals unacknowledged, forgotten. In another section entitled "Indoctrination," the text once again privileges U.S. citizens and renders Filipinos—as foreign recruits—invisible and irrelevant:

> [In the classrooms], he gains a better understanding of the government of *his* nation and the role he plays in it. Through lecture and discussion he becomes aware of his responsibilities as a *citizen* and the responsibilities that *his* country has assumed in the world today. [emphasis mine]

Although many of the Filipino Navy recruits eventually obtained U.S. citizenship, they were not yet citizens at the time of the recruit training. Moreover, as Lisa Lowe and others have argued, even as citizens, Filipino

Americans—and other Asian Americans—continue to be marked as "foreign" and "outside" the national polity.[17] Thus when the text refers to "his nation," and "his country," it does not have in mind the Filipino recruits—whose faces appear alongside other men in the company photos but whose nation exists in an unequal relationship to the United States.

The Anchor also promotes other fictions. In the following paragraph, which appears in the 1964 edition of *The Anchor*, the text perpetuates the myth of the U.S. Navy—and by extension, the United States—as "the land of equal opportunity":

> One of the most important steps in the "in processing" stage is the administration of the Navy's General Classification Test. The results of these tests together with a later meeting with a trained classification interviewer will lead to the selection of a career pattern in the Navy, and to special schooling after his graduation from recruit training.

This paragraph is "fictional" because it represents the career placement of the recruits as a color-blind process—one based solely on test scores and individual desires. But as discussed in chapter 2, Filipinos, until 1973, were confined to the ratings of officers' stewards and mess attendants, regardless of their educational level and personal ambitions.[18] This text, then, does more than erase the experiences of Filipino enlistees; it also deliberately conceals the practices of institutional racism rooted in the legacy of U.S. colonialism. But the words and deeds of Filipino Navy recruits—their lives—expose these lies and draw attention back to the possessive investment in whiteness practiced by the Navy and its leaders. J. J. Cruz, who joined the U.S. Navy in 1958, stated that he had no choice in "the selection of a career pattern in the Navy": "My ambition then was to become a radio operator, which I was in the Philippines at that time, but when I got here in San Diego and after the boot training, I was sent to the steward school. I knew then that there was no way out." Having a college education did not change matters. In the mid-1960s, Leo Sicat was studying chemical engineering at the University of Santo Tomas when he read in the *Manila Times* that the U.S. Navy was recruiting Filipinos. Leo still recalled with pride how he was among the seven—out of 350—who survived the stiff competition of the examination day.[19] Although Leo was "not very fond of the military," he was lured by the promise of the "good life in the United States" and joined the Navy in 1966, just as he was about to graduate from college with a chemical engineering degree. Leo learned almost immediately that, regardless of his advanced training, he still had no say in the selection of his career in the Navy:

> When we were recruited, we were promised to be only a steward. We told the recruiting officers about our experiences and that we wanted to become a personnel manager, a hospital corpsman, a yeoman, or an ocean mate. But they told us that we were not going anywhere but straight to steward school.

We cannot dismiss these texts in *The Anchor* as mere words in seldom-read memory books. Instead, we need to see them as part of a larger meaning-making system—designed to forge images, histories, and narratives that (re)present the U.S. nation as racially homogeneous, democratic, and just. As such, these texts both echo and extend the ideologies and practices of the "racial contract" of the time.[20] As I examined these yearbooks, I searched for clues of the racist ideologies and practices experienced by Filipino recruits at the NTC. If all recruits were represented and viewed themselves as having come from "here," then how must they have treated the Filipino men who came from somewhere else—an "inferior" nation? And if all recruits were told that they could select their own career path, then how must they have viewed the Filipino enlistees, who were all sent to steward school? Their initial contact with and impression of Filipinos—as men relegated to servile positions—would only be reinforced once they left the NTC and encountered Filipino Navy men as stewards, mess attendants, and cooks. For Ricardo Reyes and his generation, who retired from the Navy before the 1970s, their whole Navy career was confined to the steward rating. Ricardo, who retired in 1958, stated, "For our generation, we did not make it out of the steward rating. But during those Depression years, the main concern of anyone was to survive the hard times."

From my interviews with other Filipino enlistees, I learned that the training period at the NTC was difficult for many men. Homesickness was acute. Ricardo Reyes characterized his own boot camp experience at NTC as "very difficult." He explained: "I became very lonely. I was trained to be close to my parents, and when you become alone, that was the most difficult transition . . . because we are human beings, we can only take so much of the loneliness." Certainly, homesickness was a condition shared by all young recruits—regardless of race. *The Anchor* (1964) describes the (dis)orientation of young recruits this way: "Having left civilian life behind him, the recruit at once finds himself in unfamiliar surroundings where he is governed by a new code of regulations, where words and phrases have acquired new meanings, and where new obligations and responsibilities have been placed upon him." But unlike his American counterpart, the Filipino recruit lost more than his civilian life; he lost a whole world—the life he once had. Vicente Rodriquez, who joined the U.S. Navy in 1967, described the dislocations that he experienced during recruit training at the NTC: "It wasn't easy for me. . . . I came here in November. It was cold. And the food is different. And the people around you, the language is different. So everything is different, including lifestyle." To combat the homesickness, Vicente wrote home "almost every day" during his stay at the NTC. Moreover, when the Filipino recruit exchanged his civilian clothes for his Navy uniforms, he in effect pledged to switch his national allegiance—to give his loyalty to the U.S. Navy, to salute the U.S. flag, and to defend the United States in battle.[21] One could just imagine the psychic cost to these men of making that switch. In the next section, I discuss how Filipinos in the Navy have managed to build community and home within the often-hostile institution of the U.S. Navy.

MAKING COMMUNITY: "WHEN YOU SEE FILIPINO, HE HELP YOU"

Since their arrival in the United States in the early 1900s, regional loyalties and provincial ties have shaped Filipinos' choice of residence, their network of friends, and their patterns of organization. The proliferation of hometown and regional associations—commonly perceived by Filipinos as evidence of divisiveness and disunity within their community—has been widely reported not only by the Filipino American press but also by returning Filipinos and the Philippine press.[22] In one of the core literary works of Filipino American literature, *America Is in the Heart,* author Carlos Bulosan notes disapprovingly that a "tribal" orientation had "obstructed all efforts toward Filipino unity in America."[23] The Filipinos who served in the U.S. Navy were no exceptions. Jon Sario, who joined the U.S. Navy in 1966, recalled that the Filipino enlistees often "go by groups": "[Filipinos] worked together, but when they go on liberty, when they go out there on their own free time, they have their separate ways: the Caviteños have their own group, and the Ilocanos have their own group." Interregional tensions—even brawls—were not uncommon. J. J. Cruz recounted one such incident: "One time, in our barrack, there were about seventy-five of us there. This was the stewards group, and the Caviteños were fighting the Ilocanos and I happened to belong to neither group, so I just sat there and watched them fight."

Since U.S. bases in the Philippines doubled as recruiting stations for the

U.S. Navy, for many years they preselected the regional composition of the Filipino Navy population, drawing the majority of the enlistees from the areas adjacent to the bases. Though Filipino enlistees in the U.S. Navy hailed from all regions of the Philippines, most came from Cavite and Zambales, two Tagalog provinces.[24] This is because these two provinces housed two major U.S. naval recruiting stations: Sangley Point Naval Base (Cavite) and Subic Naval Station (Zambales). While Filipinos from any region could and did apply to the U.S. Navy, those from these two provinces had a distinct advantage. Living near the recruiting stations, these Filipinos benefited from their firsthand contacts with U.S. naval personnel. Vicente Rodriquez, who lived close to Subic Naval Station, attributed his passing the Navy entrance exam in 1967 to his frequent contacts with American GIs there:

> It helped because I was driving jeepney. I was with the Americans already. I was driving them wherever they want to go, showing them around. . . . Most of the [Filipino] guys, they're not used with the American language: English. When they see an American, they're nervous. But not me. Because I'm already around with the Americans.

Those who lived near the recruiting stations also benefited from "coachings" by Filipinos already in the U.S. Navy. In Cavite, for example, Filipino enlistees or retirees regularly conducted seminars on how to join the U.S. Navy to paid audiences. Informal advice was plentiful. Young Filipino men who contemplated joining the U.S. Navy regularly sought guidance from other men in their hometown. Vicente Rodriquez's town mate helped him to fill out his application and provided him with a smuggled copy of the Navy entrance exam. By the 1970s, when approximately two hundred thousand Filipinos applied to the U.S. Navy each year, Filipino enlistees became correspondingly more diverse along regional lines. Young men who lived in faraway provinces mailed in their applications by the thousands; many more trekked to the surrounding areas of the recruiting stations, awaiting a chance at a career in the U.S. Navy. A 1977 study of Filipino Navy men at three major U.S. Naval bases found that the single most frequently used dialect was Tagalog. Other common dialects included Ilocano and Pangasinan; a few respondents also mentioned Zambal, Cebuano, Visayan, Waray, and Kinaray.[25] Reflecting the dominance of the Cavite-derived Navy population, the first hometown association in San Diego was the Cavite Association of Southern California founded in 1965 by fourteen families.[26]

Filipino enlistees also became more differentiated along class line. As the pool of potential enlistees swelled, naval entrance requirements became correspondingly more stringent: eligible enlistees had to be high school graduates, fluent in English, and have an IQ of at least ninety.[27] Many Filipino enlistees in fact exceeded these requirements, especially during the economic and political crises of the Marcos era, thus widening the class divide among Filipino Navy personnel. As one of the "early Navy people," Ricardo Reyes referred to the post-1960s Filipino recruits as "a different breed": "During my time [the 1930s], the schooling is very low, like I know one of my shipmates could not write his name. He just put an 'X' on his paycheck. . . . After about 1960, there are a lot of highly educated Filipinos that join." Vicente Rodriquez who joined the U.S. Navy in the late 1960s concurred: "When I was taking the [Navy entrance] test [in 1967], I asked what kind of background of the other people taking the test. Most of them are high school graduates. But there's also plenty who are college graduates, and some of them were taking college. I said, . . . damn, I don't have no chance with these guys, you know."

However, regardless of their regional and class backgrounds, the overwhelming majority of Filipino enlistees began and remained as stewards in the U.S. Navy. Even as late as 1970, 80 percent of the Filipinos in the U.S. Navy were in the steward rating.[28] It was this shared "location" within the U.S. Navy—that of a "brown skinned servant force"[29]—that compelled Filipino Navy personnel to expand their social frame of reference and adopt an all-Filipino identity. In other words, it was through their racialized class experiences, especially the realization of a racial caste system in the Navy, that an all-Filipino identity was made. The Filipino Navy men I interviewed were bitter about being confined to the steward rating. Reynaldo Cablay "hated every bit" of his steward duties and "deplored" the fact that "they brought us here in the Navy to be butlers." J. J. Cruz agreed: "We were ashamed of what we were doing. We didn't like it. We felt that the Navy was treating us wrongly in the way that we could not be what we wanted to be." J. J. also "detested the officers" who were "crybabies" and who "thought that they were so intelligent and that the people working for them were dumb." Like other Filipino Navy men I interviewed, J. J. learned quickly that "only the minorities were stewards." He understood that Filipinos were recruited to replace African Americans in that rating: "At that time the black people in the Navy were moving out of the kitchen. And they had to have another group of people to replace them. So we Filipinos were replacing them." In an astute observation, Ricardo Reyes linked the casting of Filipinos as stewards to the maintenance of "white privilege": "At that time, the American people are used to having one or two maids, things like that, that's the reason why it was carried to the Navy that the higher upper class of whites should be served."

Filipinos were also routinely harassed and passed over for promotions. Anita Sotelo discussed the racism her father faced as a Navy sailor: "My father wrote in his diary that once . . . [in the 1930s] . . . when he was taking a train from San Diego to back East, he would not sleep at night because he was so afraid that he was gonna be beaten up by the white Navy people." Raul Calderon's father, who spent twenty years as a steward, was often humiliated by the officers: "When [my father] was stationed on the USS Enterprise and he was the cook for all the white officers . . . they would tell him to redo the coffee, the coffee was not good and they would make fun of him and then they would ask him questions like, 'Why are Filipinos so stupid?' " Having little recourse, Filipino servicemen like Raul's father "would spit in the food" to relieve their anger. Vicente Rodriquez faced so much racism in the Navy that he wished many times that he was white: "Because they look at you different. Sometimes they insult you, some kind of racial insult." Vicente angrily recounted how he was repeatedly passed over for promotions because of his race: "The white guy always gets the job. I should have been more aggressive," he said. "I should stand up and say godammit, wait a minute. I am more qualified at this goddamn job. Here's my qualifications." Survey data corroborate these men's sentiments. A 1977 comparative study of Filipino and American servicemen at three Navy bases found that "a substantially larger percentage of Filipino respondents felt that they do not have the same opportunities for receiving the desired training and advancement enjoyed by their American shipmates."[30] In sum, it is the coincidence of their race and class location—especially the recognition of their shared "location" within the U.S. naval hierarchy—that made it possible for the Filipino Navy community to imagine and build an all-Filipino identity and group consciousness.

But a community is not automatically borne out of a shared structural location, but out of shared lives. Their common experiences in the U.S. Navy—their training, their job duties, their living arrangements, their leisure activities—bonded Filipinos from different ethnoregional and class backgrounds. For some, the bonding began almost immediately: at the naval entrance exam. J. J. Cruz described this bonding: "You didn't know anyone, but while you're taking the test, all of a sudden, all of you guys, and there's two thousand of you guys, are all friends. And then you all become close, and then closer and closer until forty of you guys that's remaining become even closer." Filipino enlistees also sought out each other in recruit training centers and in stewards' schools, where they comprised the majority of the students.[31] On graduating, they entered the fleet, often clustering in kitchen-help services. Because the stewards' division lived and ate together and because there was usually little social mixing with their American shipmates, Filipinos in the U.S. Navy developed a camaraderie that at times transcended regional and class boundaries. J. J. Cruz recounted how Filipino stewards managed to build community aboard ship: "The ships that I was on, we didn't have any dining tables. There was only one stool for the head steward, so we were eating standing up. . . . We didn't have any seats. We had to make our own [seats], like coffee cans. But somehow we overcame this by cooking Filipino food and eating together." Ricardo Reyes, who was born and raised in the town of Bulacan, treasured the friendships that he made with Filipinos from other regions of the Philippines:

> I have lots of Filipino friends in the Navy. Ya know, after years, we became friends with people from Bicol, from Zambales, from Cavite, from the Visayan Islands. When you put in so many years, onboard ship especially, you become shipmates. . . . It's just a matter of learning how to have a good relation, even though it is not your province, that you can work out the internal differences and things like that. We become very close.

Filipinos did not only work together, they also played together. In Navy towns across the United States and in other parts of the world, Filipino navy men mingled with Filipinos from the local community and especially sought the company of young Filipinas. The local community, in turn, welcomed the young sailors into their homes and helped to ease the men's loneliness with home-cooked meals and reminiscences of the homeland. Maria Sotelo, a native San Diegan, remembered that during the 1950s, her Navy father would "bring all these Filipinos from the ship home for dinner" because he wanted his daughters to marry Filipino men. Reynaldo Cablay met his wife in 1968 at the Philippine Hut, a Filipino restaurant in Charleston, South Carolina, catering primarily to the local Filipino Navy community. According to Reynaldo, "There was a lot of Filipinos in Charleston because it was a Navy town. . . . It was a good feeling to be in a different country and see your own countrymen." In 1970, when Vicente Rodriquez was transferred to Whidbey Island in Washington, he did not know anyone. But that was soon to change. While out jogging one morning, he was "picked up" by a car "full of Filipinos" who were en route to a party in Vancouver, Canada. Vicente recalled with fondness the instant camaraderie shared by the group:

> So I jumped in the car. I was in a sweat suit, right? I said, "When are we gonna get back?" "Monday morning."... Once we get to Canada, they already have set up for the party because there are plenty of Filipinas there. In Whidbey Island, there's no Filipinas. But in Vancouver, there are plenty.... So I was there and enjoyed that party. See, I didn't know these people, these Filipinos. But all of a sudden, we were close.

Vicente concluded the story by remarking, "When you see Filipino, he help you." Although Vicente admitted that he "would be more excited to meet someone from [his] hometown," he also said, "Just meeting Filipinos cheer me up, any Filipino." For Filipinos new in town, the Navy commissary provided yet another place to meet up with other Filipinos. "You just go to the commissary and you can say hi and exchange addresses and things like that with the Filipinos there," said J. J. Cruz.

The families of the Filipino servicemen also formed close bonds. Maria Sotelo, a Filipino Navy wife, described the closeness shared by the Filipino Navy community in Hawaii in the 1950s: "There was a big Filipino Navy community in Hawaii. Most of the locals were Ilocano, but the ones in the Navy were from all over. I belonged to a Filipino Navy Wives' Club, and we did many things together. We still keep in touch. Now, once a year, we have a reunion." Corazon Espiritu felt the same way about the Filipino Navy community in South Carolina of the early 1970s: "There were about a hundred families. We all lived near the base. It's really nice because you know you can communicate with other Filipinos. We had birthday parties and weddings and everything. We were so close." Some Filipino families developed such close relationships that they tried to relocate together—often by requesting the same reassignments. Eloisa Brucelas, a twenty-year-old self-identified "Navy brat," recounted that her family was part of a three-family entourage that moved together from San Diego to the Philippines, then to Japan, then back to San Diego. "These were our uncles and aunties," said Eloisa. "All the children grew up together. They are family to us." Eloisa also appreciated the thriving community life that Filipino Navy families created at these overseas bases. For example, when her father was stationed in the Philippines and then in Japan, the children, under the tutelage of their mothers, would stage elaborate Filipino cultural nights for the community, especially for the single Filipino men stationed there—in much the same way that Connie Tirona and her family did for the lonely *manongs* in the 1930s.

"MAN, THIS MUST BE HEAVEN": SETTLING IN SAN DIEGO

As a Navy town, San Diego has been a prominent area of settlement for many Filipino Navy men and their families. In 1969, when Joselito Paralejas came to San Diego for his basic training at the NTC, he was awed by the city's beauty and climate: "When I first saw San Diego and all the palm trees, I said, 'Man, this must be heaven.' And the weather also reminded me of home." Joselito vowed that, as soon as he could, he would return to the city and raise his family there. He did just that in 1975. Others, like Raul Cantada, selected San Diego because of its perceived proximity to "home": "I picked San Diego because in my mind, it is closer to the Philippines than if I would go to the East Coast."[32] Still others, like Ricardo Reyes, who, after twenty years in the U.S. Navy, opted to return to San Diego to settle permanently because "it is a Navy town . . . and it makes you feel good when you talk Navy." The prominence of the Filipino Navy families in San Diego is evident in the following statistic: From 1978 to 1985, more than 51 percent of the 12,500 Filipino babies born in the San Diego metropolitan area were delivered at the U.S. Naval Hospital.[33]

The U.S. Navy also brought civilian Filipinos to San Diego, mainly to join relatives who were Navy personnel. Immigration scholars have long documented the prevalence of chain migration; that is, the presence of relatives and co-ethnics often determines where newly arrived immigrants will initially settle in the United States.[34] In a survey of Filipino immigrants conducted in the late 1980s, more than 90 percent of the respondents gave the presence of relatives as the primary reason for selecting their intended destination in the United States. Only 6 percent indicated that economic factors, such as the availability of work, influenced their choice of where to settle.[35] Of the one hundred Filipinos whom I interviewed, close to 50 percent settled in San Diego because their father or another close relative worked for the U.S. Navy. Raul Calderon's family experience illustrates that most chain migration occurs through direct sponsorship. Raul's father, a U.S. Navy steward, first sponsored his father, who in turn sponsored six more family members. "Almost all of them came to San Diego, because that's where we lived," said Raul. Other Filipinos came to San Diego simply because they knew someone who lived there. As Jacinta Juarez, a twenty-year-old Filipina who migrated to the United States in 1987, recollected: "We came to San Diego because my uncle was stationed here. We've always heard of America, and the only thing we know in America is San Diego because that's where my uncle was."

Between the 1940s and 1960s, the majority of the Filipino families in San Diego was affiliated with the U.S. Navy. Reflecting this Navy dominance, a pioneer Filipino organization in San Diego was the Fleet Reserve Association, and the first community center was the Filipino American Veterans Hall on Market Street. Barred from renting or purchasing homes outside the business district, the downtown section of the city, especially around Market Street, was the vibrant center of the pre-1960 San Diego Filipino community. There Filipinos ran small restaurants and pool and gambling tables and sponsored dances and other cultural events. Growing up in the 1940s in a Navy family, Maria Sotelo remembered that "Market Street and the whole Gaslamp Quarters used to be real Filipino. That's where they used to hang out and a lot of Filipinos were gambling there." Maria's father and his Filipino Navy friends—much to their wives' consternation—used to spend their paydays at the gambling halls on Market Street. Even into the 1960s, the area around Market Street retained its prominence for San Diego Filipinos. Roberto Cenidoza, who came of age during the 1960s, conjured up fond memories of his visits there: "Another part of my memory is going to the Filipino American Association up on Market Street, in downtown San Diego. Still there. I used to take dance classes there and we would have pageants there. And get-togethers. And that was the center for Filipino activities back in the sixties and seventies. That was really living."

In 1949, Ruth Abad, along with thirteen other Filipinas, formed the Filipino American Women's Club, the first Filipino civilian club in San Diego, because "there was no organization for the women."[36] The majority of the pioneer women were wives of Navy men; the rest were married to farmworkers or urban laborers. Ruth Abad's husband, a Filipino immigrant whom she met and married in San Diego, was a "dining room man" at a local private girls' school. Coming from different regions of the Philippines, the women did not share a common dialect; English became their language of choice. They did not want male members: "We didn't want any challenges from them," recalled Ruth. "We felt that we were more outspoken when we were among ourselves."

At the beginning, the men doubted their efforts. "It was discouraging at first because the men did not trust that we could start the Women's

Club," Ruth remembered. "They said, 'Oh, it will not last. These women will pull each other's hair out.' " But the women were determined, their resolve fortified by the virulent racism directed at Filipinos at the time. Ruth, who immigrated to San Diego in 1945, recalled that Filipinos lived segregated lives in downtown San Diego:

> After we got married in 1946, my husband and I lived in downtown San Diego. A lot of Filipinos used to live there, on Forty-fifth and Forty-sixth Streets. Almost all of our neighbors were Filipinos. That was where the cheapest houses were. But then, in 1950 or 1951, they built Highway 5 right through our neighborhood. That sent the people away.

She also remembered that hotels such as the U.S. Grant, the Coronado, and the El Cortez "did not allow Filipinos to hold their dances in their ballrooms"—even as Filipinos toiled in their kitchens and restaurants as dishwashers and busboys. Filipinos also could not eat, live, and work where they wanted. "We started this club so they, the Americans, would acknowledge Filipinos. They look down on us. They don't give us jobs," said Julia Elizado, one of the original thirteen founding members. The women firmly believed that anti-Filipino racism stemmed from cultural ignorance and campaigned to "show the public the culture of the Philippines." This strategy propelled the women into the mainstream political arena. "We got in touch with all the leaders in town, with the human relations people," declared Ruth. "We invited them to our programs, and we asked them to include us in their programs. We wanted to show off our culture, our costumes, and our folk dances." The women also pushed open the doors of exclusive hotels and staged their cultural performances there. And they claimed public spaces, such as Balboa Park, where they sang, served Filipino delicacies and performed Filipino folk dances. The Filipino Women's Club also took seriously its charge to build community. It sponsored many activities for the local Filipinos: Mother's Day and Father's Day celebrations, dinners and dances, Tagalog and folk dance classes for the young generation, and a Miss Sampaguita beauty contest for the teenagers.[37] And they took care of the "transient" members of their community, the numerous young Navy recruits "who had nowhere to go." "We used to feed the Filipino sailors who just came from the Philippines," explained Carmen Reynila, a former club president. "We would talk to the commanding officer that . . . we would be inviting the Filipino recruits for Thanksgiving and Christmas. It really felt good for them. First of all, they'd have the rice. The food is so different here."

But deciding who should or could be members of the *Filipino* Women's Club was not a simple matter. White and Mexican women who were married to Filipino men wanted to join the organization. When a vote was taken, ten out of the thirteen founding members favored restricting membership to "anyone with Filipino blood." Ruth Abad, whose father was a white American, was among the minority who voted to accept the non-Filipino women. "Because I am half-American, I voted for it," she explained. "But the majority of the Filipino women wanted to show that they can build this organization without the American women's help." This dispute reminds us that the "Filipino" community was never all Filipino. Intermarriages were not uncommon, especially given the shortage of Filipinas at the time.[38] Moreover, Filipino Navy men, who traveled the world, sometimes married women from other countries. An example of such international unions was the marriages that took place between Filipino Navy men and Panamanian women during the 1920s and 1930s. Given the importance of Panama to U.S. interests, the U.S. Navy maintained a prominent presence in that country during those decades. Maria Sotelo's father, who joined the U.S. Navy in the 1920s, was assigned to Panama, where he met and married Maria's mother. Two children were born in Panama, the next six in San Diego. Theirs was not the only interracial family. According to Maria, many of the wives of Filipino Navy men were "Spanish, from Panama, Colombia, and Mexico. A lot of us were half. So we were the majority." But this did not mean that the communities were quick to embrace each other. Maria remembered well the tension between the Panamanian and Mexican communities: "In those days, there was a lot of bigotry toward Mexicans. My mother hated the fact that people looked at her and thought she was Mexican . . . so she never spoke Spanish to us. . . . She raised her children to make sure that you tell people you are not Mexican." Her mother's insistence that they disidentified with "anything Spanish"—lest they be mistaken for Mexicans—was so strong that even to this day, Maria has a difficult time acknowledging her Spanish heritage.

Maria Sotelo's family story also gives us a glimpse into another slice of the Filipino Navy experience. Maria's father joined the U.S. Navy during the early 1920s, when Filipinos were still allowed to serve in a range of occupational ratings. He was an accomplished musician and thus began his Navy career as a bandmaster. This rating separated him from the Filipino Navy stewards who came to San Diego during the 1930s and 1940s. During World War II, the family lived in Navy housing in Point Loma. Because of her father's rating, the Navy could not segregate him as it did the Filipino stewards. "At that time, no one other than whites could live north of Broadway," remembered Maria. "So instead of coming out and saying only whites could live in this housing area, they would say that only certain *ratings* could live in this area. At that time, most Filipinos were stewards, so they had to live across from the naval station. But because a few of them were musicians, they did not fit that category." As a result, Maria's family and two other Filipino families, whose fathers were also musicians, lived among white families. This posed a dilemma for the family, especially the children: "We had two lives at that time. We had our school and our neighborhood life, which was all white. In those days, I think all of us were embarrassed that we ate rice. In our neighborhood, they ate potatoes." But their social life was "basically Filipino." After school hours and on the weekends, the Sotelo children would trek to the Filipino side of town to visit friends, attend dances, participate in the Filipino girls' clubs, and enter and win beauty contests. It was at one of these community dances that Maria met and eventually married her husband, a young Navy recruit from the Philippines. These dances were well supervised: "My mother was very strict, but she let me go because I could stay at the door and take tickets. And she was there too. My mother believed in the duenna thing. She had to go when we went out to watch over us."

Even though the pre-1965 Filipino community was predominantly Navy connected, there were already signs of class cleavages when a small group of professionals migrated to San Diego during the 1950s. Some, like Juanita Santos, who held a B.S. in pharmacy, migrated as a "GI bride" to San Diego in 1952. Others, like Carmen Reynila, came to the United States to further their college training. Carmen came to San Diego to study Medical Technology at Mercy Hospital. While there, she met her husband, married, and settled in San Diego. With their college education, these women stood out and apart from the local community. As Juanita Santos recollected, "I was a minority. I was the first one to work at a pharmacy. And you know what, they [the other Filipinos] used to look down on me because I was one of the *educated* ones." But Juanita also distanced herself from the "wives of Navy men":

> The first time that I attended a Rizal Day celebration sponsored by the Filipino community, I wanted to crawl under a chair. I was not looking down on them, but the people who were on the program did not speak very well and the program was not the way it should have been. The following year, I waded in, and I helped them, because they had to be taught.

These class gaps would widen after 1965 as Filipinos became the largest group of white-collar professionals to have immigrated to the United States.

"NOW WE DON'T KNOW EVERYBODY LIKE WE USED TO": THE POST-1965 COMMUNITY

In 1960, the San Diego community was still small: 5,123 people according to census data (see table 2). By most accounts, its size and its Navy connection made for a cohesive community. Anamaria Labao Cabato, who grew up in the 1960s in Southeast San Diego, recalled, "We could fit the Filipino community into one small building, the Filipino American Veterans Association Hall. . . . That was the place to hang out in the sixties." Roberto Cenidoza also remembered the sixties with fondness: "The Filipino community back then was smaller but very cohesive. . . . My parents took us to all their cultural events at Balboa park, their involvement in the Filipino Women's Club, Cavite Association. . . . And all the neat dances they would take us. I was at El Cortez Hotel at twelve years old dancing with the older folks." Dario Sario, then a college student at San Diego State University, stated that all his Filipino college friends "were sons and daughters of Navy people." Reminiscing about the pre-1965 community, Juanita Santos exclaimed, "We used to be very, very close. We were one big family. When we had a picnic, oh, my Lord, everybody would come. Now we don't know everybody like we used to."

As I suggested above, the reality was probably more complex than what these narrators recollected: regional, racial, gender, and class differences were always simmering beneath the appearance and expectation of homogeneity and solidarity. By the 1970s, in the wake of the passage of the 1965 Immigration Act and increasing global inequalities, these differences grew, as the Filipino community in San Diego tripled in size (to 15,069) and split more decisively along class lines. Largely owing to incoming migration, the community would triple once again between 1970 and 1980 and double that between 1980 and 1990; in 2000, more than 121,000 Filipinos resided in San Diego County (see table 2). Class differences became more pronounced as college-educated professionals—who immigrated as occupational preference immigrants—moved to San Diego and planted themselves in middle-class suburban communities.[39] A 1992 survey of approximately eight hundred Filipino students in the San Diego Unified School District—the Children of Immigrants Longi-

TABLE 3. SOCIOECONOMIC STATUS OF THE FAMILIES OF SECOND-GENERATION FILIPINO IMMIGRANTS IN SAN DIEGO, CALIFORNIA

	Father (%)	Mother (%)
College graduate	29.9	47.4
High school graduate	26.0	17.9
In labor force	74.3	77.4
White collar	40.0	57.9
Blue collar and low-wage service	42.5	28.1
Family Economy		
Class position in 1992		
Wealthy	3.4	
Middle Class	85.0	
Working Class	11.0	
Poor	0.3	
Family owns home in 1995	73.0	
Family's economic situation (1992–1995)		
Better	43.0	
Worse	18.4	
Same	38.1	

SOURCE: Espiritu and Wolf 2001: Table 6.2. Reprinted with the permission of the University of California Press.

tudinal Study (CILS)[40]—found that 30 percent of the respondents' fathers and almost 50 percent of their mothers had at least a college degree or more; indeed, very few parents had less than a high school degree (see table 3).

Alex Camino is one such professional immigrant. Born in 1933 in the province of Antique in southern Philippines, he graduated valedictorian from high school and aspired to be a physician. After finishing medical school in 1961, Alex, like many Filipino medical graduates at that time, left for the United States on the Exchange Visitor Program for postgraduate training. As discussed in chapter 2, because of a shortage of medical personnel, U.S. hospitals actively recruited Filipino medical graduates: "The training hospitals in the U.S. would write medical schools in the Philippines and say, 'Give us your medical graduates and we will provide you with a plane ticket.' " Alex calculated that 80 percent of his graduating class took advantage of the Exchange Visitor Program and traded their labor for postgraduate training in hospitals across the United States, especially in the Midwest and Northeast. Alex opted for a small teaching hospital in Ohio, where he was given a monthly stipend of one hundred and thirty dollars. By the time that he finished his residency in pathology in 1967, Alex, like many of his Filipino counterparts, no longer wished to return to the Philippines. He was married by then and the father of a young son. He also feared that he would not be able to practice as a pathologist in the Philippines: "There is no way you can apply your knowledge in the Philippines because of the limitation of the highly technical equipment." After deciding to stay in the United States, he applied for an internship at Mercy Hospital in San Diego, where a friend of his was interning. That was how Alex and his family moved to San Diego—not through the Navy or family sponsorship but through his own career trajectory.

But not all post-1965 immigrants were middle-class professionals. As discussed in chapter 2, most immigrants who came through family sponsorship represented a continuation of the unskilled and semiskilled Filipino laborers who had emigrated before 1965. The CILS survey mentioned above found that 43 percent of the fathers and 28 percent of the mothers were either in blue-collar or low-wage service jobs. Pablo Gutierrez is one such working-class immigrant. Born in 1956 in Cavite City, Pablo, who dreamed of becoming a radio announcer, had a difficult time finding steady employment after graduating from high school. His brother, who was in the U.S. Navy, sent money home regularly to support the family. In 1980, this brother "petitioned everyone" to come to the United States. When the family first arrived in San Diego, all five squeezed into a barely furnished studio apartment. All family members had to work to make ends meet. Pablo's father and two of his brothers worked for a microelectronics company, assembling circuit boards. The only job that Pablo could find was as a janitor. He first cleaned business offices "where all the janitors were Filipino" for three dollars and twenty-five cents an hour. After one and a half years, Pablo shifted to cleaning the food court at a local mall. There, the employees were also primarily Filipino, along with some Mexicans. Finally, after several part-time jobs, Pablo landed a full-time job as a custodian at the U.C.S.D. Medical Center, "picking up the syringes and isolation bags." When asked how he feels about his work, he replied, "I didn't come here for status. I came here for survival. This is just work for eight hours. After eight hours, I'm a normal person like you."

Alex Camino's and Pablo Gutierrez's experiences give us a glimpse into the divergent lives led by professional and working-class Filipino immigrants in San Diego. Their work, residential, and leisure lives seldom intersected. Alex worked as a well-paid pathologist, Pablo as a low-waged custodian. Alex resided in a custom home in an affluent neighborhood that is "almost all white." About fifteen miles south, Pablo lived in a crowded studio apartment in a working-class community consisting mostly of recently arrived Vietnamese and Latino immigrants. "I was so lonely when I first came," remembered Pablo. "I saw some Vietnamese people and I thought at first they were Filipinos. I ran to greet them, 'How are you?' But they answered me in another language!"

Their different lines of work also involved them in different after-work activities. As one of the pioneer physicians in San Diego, Alex Camino worked hard to shore up health-care services for local Filipinos. When Alex came to San Diego in 1969, he counted only three Filipino physicians. Three years later, at the urging of local Filipino leaders, the group, now five strong, opened a free clinic at a Filipino-owned barbershop in downtown San Diego to serve the Filipino senior citizens living in nearby hotels. "These were the old-timers who came as farmers and busboys and things like that. There were so many of them. They are single. They still have families in the Philippines but they never communicate," explained Alex. "They haven't seen doctors for years. And it dawned on us that we got to do something, and the reason apparently that these Filipino old-timers haven't visited a physician is the difficulty in trying to express themselves in English. . . . They were so enthusiastic to see Filipino doctors, you know, that speak their dialect." This fledgling voluntary effort eventually became institutionalized as the Operation Samahan Health Clinic, which offers primary health-care services, as well as a wide range of social services, to low- and moderate-income groups in San Diego County.[41] In 1980, when Alex counted about thirty Filipino physicians in San Diego, he and a friend founded the Philippine Medical Association (PMA) "to protect the welfare and to enhance the image of Filipino doctors in San Diego." His active involvement in the Filipino community, and his frequent fund-raising efforts for local and state political candidates, eventually landed him an appointment as a California medical commissioner and as a board member of the San Diego Stadium Authority—accomplishments that he acknowledged with a great deal of pride.

Pablo Gutierrez was likewise an activist—but in the local union. He joined the union because he has long been involved in union work in the Philippines and because he understood well the plight of workers. He explained the interests of management in the following way: "They make everyone work hard just to save up on budget and pocket the rest of the money. That's how management thinks." Pablo also knew that racism exacerbates the already difficult conditions of service workers of color like himself: "When you're minority, of course, they think you always bow and bow and conform. But not my kind, because I came from the Philippines, I fight." He related an incident when he fought against what he perceived as harassment from the director of the housekeeping department:

> The director wanted me to stay overtime. I said, "I don't want to, and you can't force me." I talked to him, holding a newspaper. He thought I was reading the newspaper, so he grabbed it away from my hand and slapped it on his desk. And he started talking like this to me, pointing his finger at my face. So, I took the matter to the union labor relations. That's harassment. First of all, I am Filipino, and he's white. He looked like a redneck.

Dealing Pablo a victory, the labor-relations committee ordered the supervisor to apologize for his behavior. But the matter did not end there. The harassment continued covertly: "But my friends helped me out. A friend of mine, he was Mexican, he told me, 'Be careful, they're watching you.' I said, 'I appreciate your advice.' That's why a union was established there, because of incidences of harassment like these." When asked why he had not looked for "white-collar" work, Pablo again called attention to race: "I'm Oriental, so I don't stand much of a chance. . . . I mean, it's different when you're local born. And it's different because you're brown skin. Skin color is always primary. That's the game here in the States. So, if that's the game everywhere, I'd rather stay where I am now." At the time of the interview, Pablo had moved to a rented duplex in a community populated with "Navy people, mostly retirees." Although all his close friends were Filipino, Pablo cherished his friendship with his Mexican co-workers: "Our traditions are like one. I feel warmth when it comes to Mexicans. We inherited similar cultural things, the Mexicans and Filipinos."

Although Alex Camino's and Pablo Gutierrez's lives do not and cannot represent the range of experiences of Filipino professional and working-class immigrants, they do tell us several important things. Foremost, they make evident the increasing geographical dispersion of the post-1965 Filipino community, with many professional immigrants settling in suburban neighborhoods beyond the reach of their compatriots who lack comparable economic means. This is strikingly different from the pre-1965 situation, when social exclusion, housing segregation, and Navy housing localized the community in the South Bay communities of National City, Chula Vista, Paradise Hills, and Imperial Beach. Today, San Diego Filipinos also reside in the relatively newer and more affluent North County suburban communities of Mira Mesa, Rancho

Penasquitos, Scripps Ranch, and Poway. Given this geographical distance, most Filipinos who live at opposite ends of the county may know very little about each other. More important, this north-south separation also reflects differences in class and immigration history, with most newly arrived professionals residing in North County and most Navy retirees and working-class immigrants living in the South Bay. Consider the two boards of directors of a local dance troupe. According to its executive director:

> In the North county . . . we've got a financial adviser on the board, a senior financial analyst, an accountant who has his own business, a mechanical engineer, [and] an auditor working for the Department of Defense. . . . Here in the South Bay, the board members are Navy retirees, civil servants, a couple of nurses, maybe one or two teachers. They do not have the business skills that the North County people have.

This perceived class difference often translated into stereotypes about the "dangers" of the South Bay communities. As Luella Rodriquez, a young Filipina who lived in North County, stated, "People from the North are scared of going down south because of all the stories that you hear about what's been happening down south. A lot of them . . . think the south is like hard core, they are more tough than the people from the north, like there are gangs and stuff." On the other hand, the South Bay Filipino community, owing to its longer history, continues to be perceived—especially by second-generation Filipinos—as the Filipino "cultural center" of San Diego: "The people from the south are more Filipino because they are more exposed to the Filipino culture than the north. Some of them speak Tagalog, and a lot of them understand it."

Alex Camino's and Pablo Gutierrez's involvement in the Philippine Medical Association and the labor union respectively reveals yet another point of divergence: professional and working-class immigrants belong to separate associations that cater primarily to their particular class interests and needs.[42] At the same time, their experiences also foretell unexpected convergences, with the newly arrived physicians assisting the old-timers; with the working-class immigrants socializing with the Navy families; and with workers of different races watching out for each other's interests and safety. Alex's and Pablo's lives thus instruct us that even as a community becomes more diverse, its members do manage to find each other; to create new social relations that cut across class, generational, and even racial boundaries; and to tend to each other's physical and emotional needs—all home-making efforts undertaken to root themselves to their locality. This is not to say that all Filipinos become involved in their local communities. Many from both ends of the class spectrum opt out of community affairs because of a lack of interest, financial resources, and/or time. I found that parents, especially mothers, of young children, are most pressed for time and seldom attend community affairs or join community organizations. Working-class immigrants, because of their long and irregular work hours and limited financial resources, are also less able to participate. However, even when Filipinos do not participate in voluntary associations, they are not "totally out of touch" with the community. Paz Jensen, a community college professor, did not belong to any community organizations but managed to stay connected with the Filipino community through telephone contacts and informal get-togethers with close friends. When she wanted more news about the community, she would visit her Filipino hairdresser and Filipino stores in National City and "just listen." "I just listen to gossip without being involved, without being in the middle," she confided. She also regularly reads the local Filipino newspapers to find out "what is going on in the community." Paz Jensen's strategies confirm Rick Bonus's findings that Filipino stores, community centers, and community newspapers serve as vital public spaces within which Filipinos in the United States reconfigure and recreate ethnic identities, citizenship, and community.[43]

UNITY AND DIVISIONS: FILIPINO COMMUNITY ORGANIZATIONS IN SAN DIEGO

Filipino community life in San Diego is thriving, or at least growing, as Filipinos create ever-newer organizations to meet their needs and desires. As the number of Filipinos in San Diego grew, so did the number of community organizations. By the late 1990s, according to my estimate and that of those I interviewed, the number of Filipino American community organizations in San Diego County had risen to between 150 and 175—an exponential increase from the handful that existed prior to 1970.[44] The majority are hometown or provincial organizations, some of which have been started anew, while others have been revived by the influx of new immigrants from their hometown. The proliferation of community organizations in San Diego—and elsewhere—is commonly perceived by Filipinos as evidence of divisiveness and disunity within their community. But this is an inaccurate, or at least an incomplete, assessment of the workings of these associations. For one, most associations are not restrictive, often extending membership to the spouses of members who are not from the same hometown and honorary membership to officers of other associations.[45] Association officers are also expected to sell fund-raising tickets for each other and to attend each other's social functions and are maligned when they fail to do so. Indeed, many of the social affairs that I attended drew Filipinos (and a few non-Filipinos) from all over San Diego County and even from nearby counties who may or may not originate from the community in question. As such, these organizations—through their activities—more often than not build linkages rather than erecting divisions within the Filipino American community.

As Jonathan Okamura correctly observes, the divisions that exist are often internal to the same hometown association.[46] Although hometown associations purport to bring together all the various segments of a given community, the promise of regional/hometown solidarity often breaks down most visibly along social status and class lines. Even as hometown associations (re)connect people who share similar memories and histories, they also function as venues for status competition. Association members vigorously vie for leadership positions, stage elaborate officer-installation ceremonies, and have their pictures displayed prominently in community newspapers, leading to the often-heard complaint that officers (mis)use the association for their personal glorification—to assert their own prestige and to distinguish themselves from the general membership. Ruth Abad expressed her disdain in the following way: "We cannot unite the Filipinos. This has always been a problem, because everybody wants to be president. No one wants to give in. They love power. It's in their blood." At the association-sponsored social events, members compete to see and be seen and to broadcast their, and especially their children's, latest achievements. Moreover, these events are often elegant affairs that are prohibitively expensive for the economically struggling members of their community. Living "at a very minimal level," Maricela Rebaya and her family felt like "outcasts" whenever they attended the social functions of their hometown association: "When we go there, they do nothing but brag of what they have, how many jewelries, how much money they have in their banks. They would throw it at you in passing and we would have nothing to say. So we'd better not go."

But this intragroup status competition needs to be understood within the larger history of enforced "homelessness" outlined thus far in this book. Ruth Estrada, when asked why she belonged to a Filipino American organization, explained, "For the same reason, you know, because you cannot get into an American organization. Because they would take one look at you and they always think, 'Oh, she's a foreigner.' You know, they immediately put you down because of your skin color. Because of your accent."

Since leadership positions in the wider San Diego society are generally denied to most Filipino immigrants, those seeking social recognition and prestige can best do so by holding office in a hometown association. Partly for this reason, most hometown associations have a multitude of elective and appointive offices, in order to recognize as many members as possible. For example, the 1992 slate of elected officers of the Calasiao Sr. Divino Tesero of San Diego, California, includes one president, two vice presidents, two secretaries, three treasurers, two auditors, nine sergeant-at-arms, nine board directors, two business managers, and three advisors: thirty-two positions in all. And since persistent social exclusion provides so few public spaces for Filipinos to shine, those who wish to shore up their self-image can do so by "outdoing" each other at the community social events. As discussed in chapter 4, making organized donations to their hometowns in the Philippines is a way for members to contribute substantially to the development of their home communities and thereby to gain recognition and prestige as civic-minded and economically successful individuals. Viewed within this larger context, these status-seeking practices may be better conceptualized as acts of status reclamation, and not only of status competition. Coming from a small hometown where "everybody knows everybody," Marcella Rebaya had expected "an instant bonding" with her town mates now living in San Diego and was disappointed when "all they wanted to talk about was money and cars." But it is precisely because "everybody knows everybody" that the reclamation or proclamation of status is most prevalent within hometown associations, where the opinions of those who knew them once become the principal yardstick by which to measure their "progress" in the United States and ultimately to validate their reasons for leaving their hometown in the first place.

In 1971, at the urging of visiting officials from the Philippines and the more activist-minded second-generation Filipinos, a group of community leaders founded the Council of Pilipino American Organizations of San Diego County (COPAO) to serve as the umbrella organization for all the local social, political, and professional organizations. Unlike the regional and hometown associations, COPAO is a coalition meant to unify Filipinos from diverse regional and class origins. As an "organization of organizations," COPAO has had some successes. It brings together approximately 80 to 85 percent of the local organizations; its meetings are well-attended, drawing delegates from organizations across the county; and it is well recognized as *the* representative of the San Diego Filipino community. It has also advanced the interests of the community, through collective projects that address the health and well-being of senior citizens, the social welfare of the youth, and the civil and political rights of all Filipinos. In this sense, COPAO provides a space where Filipino Americans can "organize themselves and build networks of mutual support outside of the traditional or mainstream political venues that usually exclude or marginalize them."[47] At the same time, COPAO, like many of the regional/hometown associations, is plagued by tenacious internal discord and personal entanglements. These squabbles—over matters ranging from financial mishandling to election results to lack of support for member organizations to "discourteous behavior"—are publicly fought: most often at COPAO public meetings, but also at various community events and in community newspapers, especially in lengthy letters to the editor. But Bonus correctly reminds us that these fights are not particular to Filipinos but are inescapable parts of the political process. As one of Bonus's respondents stated, "It's like that in American *din* [too]. American politicians are also dirty."[48] Still, we need to trace the possible sources of these cleavages. Generation and class matter. Reflecting the changing class composition of the community, the battles for top positions often occur between the Navy longtimers and the more recent professional immigrants. The former often characterize the latter as "arrogant" newcomers who "do not know the community" but who insist on "telling us what to do." For their part, professional immigrants are impatient with what they perceive to be the longtimers' lack of leadership experience and abilities. As Roz Alano, a Filipina physician, complained:

> There is always a friction there between the professionals and the Navy. The present president of COPAO was in the Navy. He's not very articulate. He has a hard time holding a meeting. So here is this person who is supposed to be the chairman and out there are the members of the board, some of them are professors and doctors, they are very articulate people. So these people are annoyed that the president can't run a decent meeting.

Despite these divisions, COPAO continues to exist. Regardless of their assessment of COPAO, all my respondents agree that the goal of unity is important; and COPAO is one means, however imperfect, to accomplish it. Leo Sicat's comment is typical: "We want to unify because we want to be a stronger force. It's important because we want to be involved in this country; that's part of being a U.S. citizen. If we are unified and we are strong, then perhaps we will be able to either vote for a Filipino who will look after our interests or at least vote for someone who will listen to us." Leo's call for unity draws attention to the "differential inclusion" of Filipinos: Even as U.S. citizens, Filipinos have had little political representation, and thus no one to listen to their claims and to look after their interests. Leo historicizes and contextualizes this need for unity when he concludes that "if Filipinos are not strong politically or if we are not unified, nobody is going to talk to us."

◆ ◆ ◆

The point of this chapter has not been to determine whether the Filipino American community in San Diego is cohesive or fragmented. As we have seen, it is *both*. Instead, I have tried to emphasize that the community is fraught with contradictions, comprising both instances of progressive collective endeavors *and* moments of horrific interpersonal fights. This is so not only because there is a lot at stake, for the community as well as the individual, but also because the complexities of the community and its people cannot be contained within the constructed boundaries of any one organization. As Bonus suggests, the proliferation of regional and hometown associations can be aptly read as resistance to homogenization: that of being lumped into an undifferentiated and unified Filipino American category.[49] I also want to underscore the importance of understanding the process of community formation—that is, the act of home making—as historically specific and socially situated. The cultural, economic, and political relationships between the Philippines and the United States have provided and continue to provide the historical context within which Filipino construct their identities and form their communities. It is the interaction between this binational history and the local San Diego space(s) and individual needs and desires that a community is made. In the next chapter, I move my discussion from community to household politics, focusing on the impact that the process of "differential inclusion" has had on gender relations among Filipino immigrants.

CHAPTER 6

Home, Sweet Home

Work and Changing Family Relations

There is no such thing as a private sphere for people of color except that which they manage to create and protect in an otherwise hostile environment.

Aida Hurtado, "Relating to Privilege"

During the first year when I first arrived, Mom had the daytime job working for the county hospital as a nurse while Dad watched over me. That's how I got to be Daddy's girl. And then when Mom would come home, Dad would get ready to go to work at his janitor job. That's how we started off.

Sara Santos, Filipino American daughter

One of the significant outcomes of U.S. colonialism in the Philippines is the creation of particularly gendered migration opportunities.[1] This chapter presents a comparative analysis of the male-dominated migration of Navy stewards and the female-dominated migration of health-care professionals from the Philippines to the United States. I am interested in these two groups because they represent an inversion of the idealized gendered division of labor, with the Navy men migrating as domestic workers and the health-care women migrating as professionals. This inversion is but one example of how the material existence of immigrant women and men of color has historically contradicted the traditional construction of "man" and "woman."[2] As detailed in chapter 2, the Navy and health-care labor flows are inextricably linked to early-twentieth-century U.S. imperialism and colonization of the Philippines and to the changing needs of these two nation-states throughout the twentieth century. Reflecting this history, the Filipino Navy men and the

Filipina health-care professionals are overrepresented in the Filipino community in San Diego. The 1992 CILS survey of approximately eight hundred Filipino students in San Diego found that more than 50 percent of the respondents' fathers worked for or were retired from the U.S. Navy; and close to a quarter of the respondents' mothers worked in the field of health care, about half of whom were registered nurses.[3]

Labor arrangements are often at the core of race, class, and gender inequalities. Accordingly, I examine in this chapter how migration processes, labor recruitment practices, and employment conditions have reconfigured family relations for Navy enlistees and health-care professionals. As discussed in chapter 3, Filipino migrants have historically been denied the right to form families in the United States through both law and social practice.[4] In this hostile environment, the act of establishing and maintaining families—that is, of *home making*—is itself a form of resistance. However, as feminist scholars of color have documented, the family is not only a "unity, bound by interdependence in the fight for survival," but also a "segmented institution in which men and women struggl[e] over power, resources, and labor."[5] That is, home is simultaneously a place of nurture, comfort, and protection and a site of patriarchal hierarchy and gendered self-identity.[6] It is this tension—between the desire for "home" and the perils that accompany that desire—that I hope to capture in this chapter.

FILIPINO NAVY MEN: DOMESTIC WORK, MASCULINITY, AND FAMILY RELATIONS

The constructions of masculinities and femininities along racially differentiated lines provide ideological justification for race, gender, and class oppression.[7] Like other men of color, Asian American men have been largely excluded from white-based cultural notions of the masculine. Whereas white men are depicted as both virile and as protectors of women, Asian men have been characterized both as asexual *and* as threats to white women. It is important to note the historical contexts of these seemingly divergent representations of Asian American manhood. As I have argued elsewhere,[8] racist depictions of Asian men as lascivious and predatory were especially pronounced during the nativist movement against Asians at the turn of the century. The exclusion of Asian women from the United States, the subsequent establishment of bachelor societies, and the relegation of Asian men to "women's work" eventually reversed the construction of Asian masculinity from "hypersexual" to "asexual" and "homosexual." The contemporary model-minority stereotype further emasculates Asian American men as passive and malleable. Although an apparent disjunction, both the hypermasculinization and the feminization of Asian men serve to define and confirm the white man's virility and superiority.[9]

Like other Asian American men, Filipino men have been cast both as hypermasculine and as feminine. As discussed in chapter 3, Filipino men, in the United States and in the Philippines, have been depicted as a sexual danger to white middle-class women. At the same time, racialized and gendered immigration laws, labor recruitment policies, and employment conditions have emasculated heterosexual Filipino men, forcing them into womanless communities and into the sector of the labor force that performed "feminized" work. In this section, I examine the racialized and gendered experiences of Filipino Navy stewards who performed domestic work for the naval officers and their wives, paying particular attention to the men's efforts to reclaim their masculinity in both the private and public spheres.

A "Brown-Skinned Servant Force": Stewards in the U.S. Navy

Feminist scholars have argued accurately that domestic service involves a three-way relationship between privileged white men, privileged white women, and poor women of color.[10] The experiences of Asian immigrant men call attention to yet another form of racial and gender subjugation of domestic workers: one involving Asian men and white men and women. Prior to World War II, many Asian men were forced into "women's work" such as domestic service, laundry work, and food preparation. Because of their noncitizen status, the closed labor market, and the shortage of women, Asian immigrant men, first Chinese and later Japanese, Korean, and Filipino men substituted to some extent for female labor in the early-twentieth-century American West. As domestic servants, Asian men became subordinate not only to privileged white men but also to privileged white women. Their experiences thus demonstrate that not all men benefit equally from patriarchy. Depending on their race and class, men experience gender differently. For Asian American male domestic workers, economic and social discrimination locked them into an unequal relationship not only with privileged white men but also with privileged white women.[11]

The Filipino Navy stewards whom I interviewed clearly felt stigmatized by their "feminized" work. Vicente Rodriquez deplored his tasks:

"I didn't like my job: washing dishes, making coffee, cooking, cleaning the officers' quarters, shining shoes. . . . I wanted to be a mechanic." He felt humiliated: "In the Philippines, it's macho. . . . Guys, they either be mechanics or do some manual jobs. Only girls cook. . . . And I didn't want to do girls' work." J. J. Cruz also detested doing "women's work," likening the work of stewards to that of cleaning ladies:

> Stewards were like cleaning ladies, like if you were in a hotel, make up the beds, clean the laundry, and even put this clean laundry in the respective places and even shine [the officer's] shoes. Can you imagine us shining shoes? I was poor in the Philippines, but I never shined my own shoes. Somehow I could afford to pay a shine boy to shine my shoes. But when I came in the Navy I was shining somebody else's shoes. I had to learn very fast how to shine shoes so I could do it. I was good learning how to shine shoes. But that was very, very demeaning.

J. J. Cruz and his friends were so ashamed of their steward status that they hid their Navy uniforms whenever they went on liberty:

> I remember right here in San Diego, where we went to steward school, we were required to wear these symbols on our uniform that say we were stewards. So we would take these off when we went out. But every morning we had to wear a uniform, we'd have to sew them back on so we learned how to sew quickly. Or we rented a locker at the Y.M.C.A. and we would hide our uniforms there and put on our civilian clothes.

He also resented the oversimplified training that they received in steward school:

> In steward school, the books they gave us, I think were not even one hundred pages and they're all pictures. I mean, they're pictures, the whole page, and they would tell us in one sentence a description of the picture. I think it was insulting because even in the first grade where I went, there were about six sentences and one little picture and now, it's one big picture and one sentence.

For college-educated Leo Sicat, the work of a steward was "insulting" because it was so incommensurate with his training as a chemical engineer. As he explained:

> At steward school, we were taught how to cook and bake, how to set the table, and how to position the silverware, and the glass and the cup. They taught us the job of a waitress. Personally, I was so insulted. I felt bad when I saw the job of being a steward. What do you expect from me? I am almost a chemical engineer and I came to the United States just to become a steward.

The humiliation was most acute when Filipino stewards were assigned to be the personal servants for the officers' wives. Reynaldo Cablay related how he resented working for the wife of an admiral: "I was first working for the admiral in his office, but then they transferred me to work for the admiral's wife in the house: being a butler, washing the car, walking the dog, drive the wife to the store, make their beds and wash their clothes. That was the bottom line for me. I had enough of it."

Adding to the indignities of the job was the racial harassment that Filipino Navy enlistees received from other sailors. Luella Barcenas remembered how other Navy men used to heckle her Filipino father:

> Part of my father's story is that he worked as a Navy steward and it was a very, very prejudiced time [the 1950s and 1960s]. . . . I can still remember, when I was a little kid, standing on the peer with my mother waving goodbye to him . . . and seeing that the white sailors, you know, were making fun of him, criticizing him and looking down at us and heckling and that kind of stuff.

Another Navy daughter, Rose Dumlao, decried the mistreatment that her father received from his commanding officer:

> It took my dad a long time to make chief because he had to deal with a lot of discrimination in the Navy. . . . His commanding officer was racist. It was really, really blatant. I saw it myself because [my dad] used to take me to work with him when I was little. . . . My dad was the only minority in the whole office. And I would watch how his boss treated my dad so rudely in comparison to the other people in the office. His tone of voice was different; and the way he addressed them was different.

The experiences of these Navy men underscore the fact that for many immigrants, the experience of migration is most often a compromise: although their wages may be higher, their status is not, and their dignity suffers.

The relegation of Filipino men to "feminized" work illustrates the interconnections of race and gender in that the racialization directed at them takes the form of sexism. That is, the indignities braved by these men are similar to those endured by women who traditionally perform both paid and unpaid domestic work. Because these Filipino men have been "feminized," they could choose to attest to and fight against patriarchal oppression that has long denied all women male privilege. However, many choose instead to distance themselves from the perceived indignities of "women's work" and to reclaim their masculinity in other spheres.

The majority of the Filipino Navy stewards I interviewed opted to reclaim their masculinity in a transnational context. As established in chapter 4, in the Philippine context, to be a U.S. Navy enlistee is a marker of success and high status; thus for many of these men, it is in returning "home" that they can best reconstruct themselves as able economic providers and desirable sexual partners. Vicente Rodriquez's account of his migration and its meaning illustrates how some Filipino Navy men have negotiated and manipulated their differential status in the Philippines and in the United States. On finishing high school, Vicente labored as a jeepney driver on the hot and dusty streets of Angeles City. Seeing no future for himself in the Philippines, he resolved to leave for the United States. He was deeply influenced by the apparent success of those who had gone abroad, especially the ones who had joined the U.S. Navy:

> In our town, whoever go abroad, when they come back, it seems like they're rich. They got plenty of money! Especially the sailors that have been joining the U.S. Navy. A Filipino sailor got it all. He got all the girls . . . the prettiest girl in town. He got all the money. He got everything! He's looked up to. He's got good clothes. He's got good shoes. He's got good everything. And then I say, "Damn, I like to be like him." I like to be like that guy. . . . And I would like to get away from this kind of job . . . driving jeepney, it's hot, it's dusty. And I cannot see in the future for me that I'm gonna have a son, and my son is going to be where I am . . . be like me. I don't want that. So I set my mind on going abroad.

Implicit in this statement is Vicente's gender-based concern that if he stayed in the Philippines, he would not be considered a desirable sexual partner and adequate economic provider for his family. In 1967, at the age of twenty, he successfully enlisted in the U.S. Navy and began his naval career as a steward. As related earlier, Vicente bitterly resented doing "housekeeping type of jobs" and experienced "lots of racism" from other sailors. Even so, he felt satisfied because he was earning good money: "I don't care what kind of job I do as long as they pay me. I liked the money." This statement must be understood in its proper transnational context. Vicente "liked the money" not for what it could provide him personally in the United States but for what it allowed him to accomplish "back home": to provide for his widowed mother and younger sister; to gain the respect and envy of his town mates; and to attract the "prettiest girls in town"—all of which enable him to shore up his masculinity.

As someone who could not afford a college education, Vicente Rodriquez was proud that his earnings as a steward had surpassed those of the college graduates in his town: "My pay as an E-3 is more than the people I know from home who are lawyers and doctors. More. A lot more. I know somebody in our town, he was a doctor. I know I make more than him." And he was thrilled by the attention he received from the young women in his town: "When I relocated to Subic, I had me a 1973 Pontiac Firebird. And I'm the only one who has a Pontiac Firebird in the whole Philippines! And I drive it in Angeles City, and everybody looks at it. And then, those pretty girls they are all over me, see?" In 1976, Vicente married one of these "pretty girls" and brought her back to the United States. That Vicente, a Navy steward, was able to earn more than college-educated Filipinos and to own an American sports car attests to the enduring legacy of colonialism—one that prescribes the differential between what Filipinos can earn in the United States as opposed to in the Philippines. That he used his earning prowess and his coveted Pontiac Firebird to attract the "pretty girls" attests to the continuing appeal of patriarchy—one that encourages men to use ownership of women's bodies to reassert their lost patriarchal power.

Shouldering the Burdens: Navy Wives and Children

Prior to the passage of the 1965 Immigration and Naturalization Act, exclusion laws and gender-based labor recruiting patterns skewed the sex ratio of Asian American communities and truncated the development of conjugal families. Unable to send for wives and legally prohibited from marrying white women, most heterosexual Asian men were lonely bachelors or absentee husbands, destined for a harsh life without families.[12] Filipino Navy men, especially before the influx of the post-1965 immigrants from the Philippines, had to adjust to the shortage of Filipinas in the United States—yet another assault on their manhood. Given their small numbers, single Filipinas were highly prized as sexual and marital partners. In the 1930s, the few Filipinas already in the United States commanded attention from the single Filipino sailors. "Back in the 1930s," recalled Julia de Leon, who then lived in Virginia, "lots of Filipinos came through the Navy on the ships to North Virginia. I was just like gold because I was the only Filipina in town. I had thirty to thirty-five men wanting to marry me." Thirty years later, the situation remained relatively unchanged. Maria Rafael, who came to San Diego in 1965 as a high school exchange student, related how she and her friend had to fend off the aggressive and unwanted attention from the young Filipino sailors:

> My first contact with Filipinos in San Diego were with Navy people. There were just so many Navy people. Every time there was a Filipino function, Strela and I would go and the Navy people would be there. They always managed to get our names and phone numbers. It was just a big thing for them to see Filipinas. Everyone wanted to meet us. We tried to be nice; we gave them our names and the phone never stopped ringing. . . . We were just trying to be friendly; we didn't know that they were going to pursue us all the way here and all the way back [to the Philippines]. We didn't know they were going to harass us to the point where they would always call us and want to go out. You almost had to be mean to them.

Given the shortage of Filipinas in the United States, the majority of Filipino sailors, like Vicente Rodriquez, returned to their hometowns to marry.[13] For many of these young brides, the transition to the United States was difficult as they confronted language barriers, cultural differences, limited economic resources, and the sheer pressure of daily survival. Ron Villa, who joined the U.S. Navy in 1953, returned to his hometown of San Carlos in 1955 to marry his longtime sweetheart, Felicia. Even though Felicia was excited about moving to the United States, her first year in southern California was a "struggle":

> When we first arrived in Santa Ana, there's no Filipinos. It was terrible. I cannot find what I want to eat. I did not know where to buy Filipino food and all that. I had a hard time . . . really hard. I didn't know how to drive and my husband just learned how to drive. We didn't go anywhere for a long time. We just didn't know what to do. . . . And then you live here, you don't know your neighbors unless you are brought up with them. And I didn't know that much English. I worried that people might not understand what I say.

For Penelope Reyes, who married her Navy husband in 1967, coming to the United States was a "shock" because she had not anticipated their poor living conditions. She was "disgusted" by the dilapidated state of their first apartment:

> My husband, being in the military, had a limited income at the time. My shock when I first came was that the money wasn't there. I came to San Diego, to one of those really old apartments there in Point Loma. It was terrible. Given what I heard about the U.S. and being a movie-goer, I was always on top of everything, like fashion and style. Then I came into this apartment, ya know, where the carpeting probably has never been replaced. Everything was just disgusting to me. The bed was missing one post, one leg. Two bricks . . . big blocks were holding the bed up. That was terrible. I thought I want to go back. I said, "This is not the United States." This is worse than the poor areas in the Philippines.

To ease the transition to the United States, some brides opted to remain in the Philippines until their husbands became more established in the U.S. Navy. As an example, Cynthia and Simon Flores married in 1959, but Cynthia and their four small children did not come to the United States until 1965. By then, Simon was a third-class petty officer with an adequate income; he was also assigned to his first shore duty. Cynthia had insisted on shore duty: "Everybody say, you know, you marry a Navy man and you'll be here, and he'll be there. That's a very hard thing. So I tell my husband, 'Don't pick me up until you got shore duty.' " Even so, Cynthia was overwhelmed by her new life. For the first time in her married life, Cynthia was left alone to care for her four young children, who ranged in age from one to six. In the Philippines, there was always someone to help: her mother, her sisters, her maid. But in the States, she had no one. Moreover, not knowing how to drive added to her burdens:

> I had to get my oldest son to school. I didn't drive, so I had to get a taxi each time. And then I had nobody to watch the younger kids. So I had to take them with me every time. All five of us, every day. . . . It was very, very hard. . . . My husband was at work . . . I had nobody. I used to cry every day. I wanted to go back home.

Filipino Navy wives also had to cope with the constant moving that typifies military families. Lisa Hernandez's husband was transferred so often that their five children were born at five different naval stations: in Ohio, Hawaii, Virginia, the Philippines, and Japan. My interviews indicate that when the children reach school age, most women put a stop to the moving. As Rose Castillo related, "When I started fourth grade, my mom told my dad that she didn't want to travel with him anymore. So she made him buy a house here in San Diego, and she stayed with us kids while he went overseas." Eleanor Ocampo, another Navy daughter, remembered how much she resented the moving: "That was very difficult on all of us, especially on us kids, because when you are living in one place for six months or only a year, you never learn to develop healthy friendships." Eleanor's mother must have sensed her children's anguish because she stopped the moving. "Around the time I was in the sixth grade, my mom said, 'This has to stop,' " recalled Eleanor. "I think she saw what it was doing to us in terms of the instabilities of our lives. So she told my father he really needed to start moving toward retirement because the children can't take it anymore. They are getting too old. They need to stay at the same school. And she said, 'If you are deployed, I won't take them. We won't follow you anymore.' "

Besides placing a strain on the children, the frequent relocations also limited the women's ability to find and keep jobs. Owing to their husbands' limited incomes, many Filipino Navy wives have had to engage in paid labor to supplement the family income. Even when husbands preferred that their wives stayed home, they understood the value of an added income. As Reynaldo Cablay explained to his daughter, "I don't mind Mom working, though. The money she made was money we needed. I really didn't want her to work, but I figured if we were going to get ahead in this ball game here, one income isn't sufficient. Her money was vital to our well-being. Without it, we couldn't have qualified for the home loans or anything like that."[14] Not only do Navy wives have to fit their work schedules to their domestic responsibilities, they also have to make do with temporary jobs that often change from one naval post to another. Annette Gamboa's work history provides an example. When the family was in Guam, Gamboa waited until her youngest child was in preschool to start her first job as a part-time cashier for the Navy commissary. When the family moved to Hawaii, she worked as a lunch supervisor at her children's elementary school. Finally, when the family settled in San Diego, she worked full-time as an electronics assembler for General Dynamics, where "most of the workers were Filipino."

The work interruption was especially difficult for women with professional training, many of whom have had to forgo their career plans. For Agnes Cruz, it meant working as a data processor instead of an accountant: "Because we moved seven times in twelve years, I just had to stick with doing keypunch work. But I always wanted to be an accountant." For Cecile Flores's mother, it meant working as a baby-sitter instead of as a nurse. "When we would get to a new station, Mom would look for work in a hospital," remembered Cecile. "If she couldn't find work as a nurse, she would baby-sit, because we lived in naval housing and a lot of them had children. Mom worked to help supplement the income because there are four of us kids." For Romeo Morales's mother, the burden of being a Navy wife and a mother of four children crushed her dream of becoming a doctor. A smart and ambitious woman, Romeo's mother graduated from the University of the Philippines at the top of her class. She enrolled in medical school but quit after two years when she married and relocated to the United States with her Navy husband. She had various temporary jobs and was employed as an assembly worker at the time of the interview. According to

Romeo, his mother regretted that she had to subordinate her career to that of her husband's:

> I know she regrets not becoming a doctor. It came up a lot of times, like sometimes we see their yearbooks and we see that my mom was a much better student than my dad in school because in her yearbook she was up at the top of her class. And on her picture, there was a caption that says everyone's ambition and hers says that she wants to be a doctor. And when I saw that I was just so sad because I see the way she works sometimes, nine to five. Sometimes she would work a part-time job in addition to her full-time job to help out the family.

Jovy Lopez's mother, a teacher in the Philippines, also toiled in "jobs that no white Americans would want":

> My mom had jobs that occupied the older minority women, the Filipinas, Hispanics, and some blacks, but hardly any white. First she worked for an electronics firm. And then she quit because it was too hard on her eyes to have to see such small parts. And then she took a job at the cannery, and it got so bad that she'd come home smelling like fish every night. Her next job was bagging groceries at the Navy Commissary.

According to Jovy, these were jobs that other Navy moms also did: "I used to be embarrassed that my mom worked in a cannery because it was just like, oh, she cleans fish guts . . . and I would never want to tell my friends where she worked. And I found out later that a lot of my mom's friends worked at the same place. So it was one of those things that as a kid we never discussed."

Racial and anti-immigrant discrimination added to the indignities of these women's work. Romeo Morales recalled how upset his mother was when a promised promotion went instead to a "Caucasian" woman:

> My mom was so upset about that promotion that she said to us kids, "That's why you have to finish school because I want them to see that it is not just your color, you could show them that . . . this is my degree. I just want you guys to . . . have something to show so that you won't have to work like this."

Jovy Flores also became sensitized to discrimination as she watched how others mistreated her mother:

> One thing that really makes me mad is that the minority women doing these jobs that no one else wants to do, they got treated really badly. . . . They treated a lot of the women like, excuse my language, like crap. . . .

> Like when my mom worked at the Commissary, you have to have a military ID card to shop there. This man, my mom asked him to please show his ID card, he put it straight in front of her face and said, "Can't you read English?" And another time, my mom worked at the express line. And this man had like a whole cart full of food and my mother told him to go to another line. And then he started yelling at her saying, "Go back to your own country!" It's very insulting, but my mom had to take it.

Like other military wives, Filipino Navy wives also *work* at promoting their husband's naval careers—yet another example of their unpaid labor. Teri Guillermo insisted that her assistance was indispensable to her husband's successful career in the U.S. Navy. A U.S.-born Filipina, Teri helped her Philippine-born husband with his English and coached him on his written assignments:

> I helped him study. I helped him write his work. So throughout our beginning, I used to write all of his work for him, and I used to coach him and everything, so much so that we would study together and so that every time he would be up for a promotion, and there were some words that he didn't understand, I would coach him on it. So that every time that there was a promotion, it was because of me.

Teri also organized and participated in local activities, which raised her husband's standing within the naval community. She explained her contribution in the following way:

> It was through my participation with the Fleet Reserve that he went up the ranks pretty fast. Then wherever we went, like when we went to Guam, I would create the activities, Little League with the kids, and he would be the administrator of the League, and I would be the cheerleader and we would raise money and all this. I also went through the educational system and participating in the PTAs and stuff like that. . . . So naturally with all that, the people of the base would know who we were, and he was recognized for all the achievements.

Because Teri's husband was among the first Filipinos to become an officer in the Navy, Teri was among the first Filipinas to join the ranks of the officer's wives. Her presence disturbed some of the wives who were more accustomed to seeing Filipino women in servile positions. Teri related one racist incident: "I remember sitting at this table for the officers' wives and everybody was looking at me. One of the wives said, 'Oh, we were stationed in the Philippines and the natives there do not know how to use their silverwares.' Well, everybody turns and looks at me." But Teri was confident; her father, who served as a Navy steward for twenty years, had always insisted on "proper" dining etiquettes. As Teri proudly recounted,

> You got to know that my father was a steward . . . and so we always ate at home with placemats, and our forks and knives. . . . We had to eat properly. Our plates were always set. So these women were watching me to see if I knew how to cut my meat, butter the bread, and I knew all of that.

This incident is just one of the many ironies of immigrant life: the father's training as a Navy steward helped to prepare the daughter to pass the etiquette "test" of being an officer's wife.

As indicated above, women often put a stop to the moving to provide more stability for their children and for their own employment situation. However, being separated from the husband had its costs: it loaded all the household work and responsibilities on the wives and children who stayed behind. Most of the Navy children I interviewed reported that their father was frequently absent during their formative years: "I did not see my dad full time until I was ten years old"; "My dad was away often when we were younger"; "I remember when I was growing up, he was gone a lot 'till I was about nine"; "I hardly ever saw him"; "My father wasn't there growing up"; and "My father was away for quite a bit. Maybe six months at a time." In the husband/father's absence, the family relied heavily on the assistance of family friends, most often other Navy families. When her husband was deployed, Cynthia Flores called on old friends to ease her burdens: "I had four children so it was really, really hard on me. I relied on a lot of my friends . . . like the other Navy wives who also had kids . . . to help me as far as looking in on the children and to keep me company." Similarly, Antoinette Reyes related that family friends "were a big help" to her mother: "When my dad was away, my mom managed by relying on family friends. As a matter of fact, my godfather, a Navy friend of my dad, was the guy that took my mom to the hospital when she was having me."

Family friends notwithstanding, the bulk of the work fell on the wives' shoulders. Eleanor Dizon described her heavy workload: "I have always held the family together especially since my husband wasn't there when the children were growing up. I had to do everything in and out: the money, the kids, the shopping, teacher conferences, the medical, and driving. I do all that. And I do the traditional things of cooking and cleaning and taking care of the children as well as working." Prolonged family separation can spawn marital conflict, as wives hold their husbands responsible for their overburdened lives. Rose Dumlao's formative years were marked by her father's frequent absence and her mother's incessant complaints about her unfair workload:

> It made my mom upset because she kind of had to take the burden of everything, the whole entire house. Like, my dad loves to plant and she would have to come home late at night and water all the plants and everything like that. I remember my dad coming back one time and, like, one of the trees had died and he was really mad. My mom was like, "What do you think I am? Your maid?"

Disappointed with her life in the United States, Rose's mother talked often about returning to the Philippines: "My mother always said that she would have liked to live in the Philippines because life there would have been so much easier. She could have had maids; she could have had more children and she wouldn't have had to be working as much as she's doing now." This longing is common among immigrants: in times of disappointment and disillusionment, the country of origin assumes a curative, revitalizing role—never mind the things that led to their leaving in the first place.[15]

Children also have to do more to compensate for their fathers' absence. As Roz Verano related:

> We were more relaxed when my dad was home. I guess because he did a lot of things when he is home, like cook, do the grocery shopping. When he wasn't there it's like, you have to clean this, clean that because my mom was alone. And we had to help her out. And when he's here it was like, "Here, dad, you can help mom."

When mothers worked outside the home, the workload that the children had to bear could be overwhelming. Many of the Navy children whom I interviewed confided that they were "latchkey kids" at a young age and that some had to "mother" younger siblings because of their mothers' long work hours. Rose Dumlao's account provides an example. When Rose was nine years old, her nurse mother was working two jobs and her father was stationed in another state. For about four years, she and her younger brother hardly saw their parents. Even though her mother lived with them, she would come home late at night and leave again early the next morning. Rose detailed the adult responsibilities that she had to assume as a nine-year-old:

> My mom would drop me and my younger brother off at school and then she would go to work and then we would get off of school at three and then we would walk home by ourselves. . . . We would come home and

> then I would make my brother change. Then I would have to make him do his homework and then fix him a snack or something, and then I would start doing my homework. And then I would make him dinner and then I would have to check his homework. My mom wanted me to check his homework so that when she came home, she didn't have to do it. Then I would put him to sleep and then I would eat dinner. After everything was done, then I would go to sleep.

Looking back, Rose remembered feeling resentment toward both her parents. "I didn't have a childhood," Rose concluded. "I never got to go out and play like all the other kids. After school, we were never allowed to go outside because my mom didn't want anyone to know that we were home by ourselves. . . . We weren't even allowed to answer the phone." Rose also resented the fact that her parents were not there to protect her and her brother from possible harm. She remembered one incident in particular:

> I used to hate walking home by ourselves because we would have to pass all these kids from public school and we would be in our Catholic school uniforms. . . . They would come up to us and they would try to start picking fights. I actually got into a fight with a girl once because she came up to me and she called me a "chink" and she was starting to jump my brother. And it made me so mad and we got into a fight and I remember going home and I was really upset but I didn't tell my mom about it. And she never found out about it. But ever since then, I guess, I was like, "Well, if anybody else pushes me around, I can take care of myself."

Her resentment affected her relationship with her mother:

> Because my mom was so stressed, she would take it out on me. She'd be like complaining to me and I felt like saying, "Why are you complaining to me? I'm the one that's doing everything. I'm the one that comes home. I'm the one that takes care of David, and I'm the one that makes him dinner, puts him to sleep. So why are you complaining to me? I should be the one complaining to you. I am only nine years old."

When Rose turned thirteen, the strain on the family had become so unbearable that her father, at her mother's insistence, agreed to request a transfer back to San Diego.

Reconfiguring Family Relations: Making It Work

Navy life, with its mandated absences, transformed the balance of power in Filipino American families in some fundamental ways. As argued above, the prolonged absence of their husbands saddled most women with a disproportionate share of household tasks as well as a life without the company and assistance of their husbands. Yet this arrangement simultaneously gave the women more independence and increased their authority over family governance.[16] With long stretches of time away from home, Filipino Navy men had to cede some of their decision-making power to their wives, especially over budgetary matters. Juanita Cablay beamed with pride when she stated that it was she who purchased their family home: "My husband leaves me the decision when he's away. I bought our house when he was deployed. I just asked him for the power of attorney and I did everything. I was really nervous, but I did it." Their husbands' absence also compelled the women to master an expanded number of tasks such as driving, fixing cars, hiring repairmen, and balancing checkbooks. Rose Dumlao reported that during her father's absence, her mother "became more and more independent. She has her own checkbook now. And she also learned how to drive."

Filipino Navy men also risk losing some of their power over their children. Prolonged separation often exacts a toll on the father-child relationship: it widens the generational distance and decreases the fathers' authority to discipline their children. When the father returns home after a long absence, the reintegration process requires adjustments from all family members. Eleanor Ocampo confided that the only time she was able to date was when her strict father was away from home. But when her father returned, she had to readjust to his rules: "He just said, 'It's over. It's gonna stop.' And it was sad because when my father came back, I wasn't allowed to see my boyfriend anymore, and we broke up a short time after that." Although Eleanor abided by her father's rules, she resented what she characterized as his "intrusion" into her life. Not all fathers are able to integrate back into the family. For Amanda Flores, her father was a "stranger" who wielded little authority over the family:

> When I was growing up, my father wasn't around a lot. So I can't say we were very close with him at that time because he was always out at sea. And my brothers and I grew up without him there. And so when we did see him, during those days, he tended to be strict because he wasn't involved with the family on a daily basis. When he would come home, it was very different for him, I am sure. I guess he had a shorter level of tolerance, kids running around him, so he tended to get more easily upset. He was more

> strict on us so we were more fearful because he was more like a stranger. So the way we saw him as we were growing up was he was more the breadwinner and my mom was the one who was always there for us, who took care of us, who raised us since my dad wasn't around much.

As evident in this case, parental authority, once lost, is not easily recoverable. According to Amanda, her father remained a marginal member of the family, even after he had retired from the U.S. Navy:

> Even after my dad retired, he was still unable to fit into the family easily, because we were already grown and it was hard for us to see him as a father figure who could place restrictions on us and tell us what to do. It was hard for us to receive that kind of feedback from him. So he kinda kept his distance. So my mom would place the restrictions on us and enforce them. . . . My dad didn't have a say because I think he just felt so detached.

Not only do Navy fathers risk losing their children's respect, they also risk losing their children's affection. Many Filipino Navy children I interviewed expressed that they did not have a close relationship with their fathers. Pablo Barcenas's response is typical: "Because of the situation of the Navy, I think that kind of disrupted the communication between my dad and me. We don't talk very much. We pretty much do our own thing. I feel I could talk to my mom more easily than to my dad." Many Navy fathers are pained by this estrangement. In the following exchange between a Navy father and his daughter,[17] the father told her how painful it was for him to be separated from the family, especially from the children:

Daughter: When you were stationed in Seattle, how did you visit us?

Father: Every weekend for eight months, I took a military flight down to San Diego. . . . It was the first time as a family we were separated.

Daughter: Was that hard?

Father: Well, before I left, every time you got hurt, you would cry, "Daddy." Then, when I got back, you would cry for your mom instead. It was hard, but it was my job. I felt I was the breadwinner of the family. . . . I should have pursued my education more, my college and better myself, so I could have provided all the same things for the family without having to leave so much like I did and putting up with the military discipline.

Daughter: Do you think everything worked out pretty well?

Father: Yes, well, the only thing is that by the time I'm ready to retire,

> you girls are already grown up and gone. Retirement is supposed to be a time to spend with your family.

This exchange—and numerous other untold exchanges—reminds us that the cost of institutional oppression is palpable not only in blocked opportunities but also in stunted relationships.[18]

Then again, in an illustration of the intimate relationship between agency and structure, some Navy families actively created strategies to make their families work. When possible, fathers and mothers coordinated their work schedules to provide around-the-clock care for their children. For example, when Reynaldo Cablay had shore duty, he volunteered for the night shift so that he could care for the children during the day while his wife was at work. As he told his daughter:

> I worked at night so your mom could work in the day. I took care of you kids in the day. It was hard taking care of you, especially since after that I had to go to work at night. And I helped around the house! I always helped, you know that! I can sew buttons, fix your hair.

Rose Dumlao's father likewise rearranged his work schedule so that he could pick the children up from school:

> Once my dad was transferred back to San Diego, he would leave work in the middle of the afternoon and go pick us up from school. . . . Then he would take us back to his work and we would be there for another two hours until he got off his shift. And we'd just be like running around the base. At least, you know, we got to spend a little bit more time with our dad.

Migration-related challenges also forced Navy men to participate more in household tasks. Juanita Cablay relates,

> My experience is that most of the Navy men, they help their wives. They work in the house, they do the laundry, they do the cooking, everything. Not like in the Philippines. There, if the men are working, that's it. They don't do anything else. And it's easy for us to hire maids in the Philippines, not like here. We have to help each other here. I think it's because we cannot afford to get help, like do the housework, and that's why they help us. Because they know that the wife is also working.

Luis Ones, a retired Navy man, agreed that men needed to do their share: "You have to help one another, you know, because here you both have to be working. So, I mop the floor, I clean the kitchen, I cook, I baby-sit. Nope. It doesn't bother me. You cannot use your macho macho here. No, here you cannot be that way." Some Navy stewards also brought home the domestic skills they learned on the job. Anamaria Labao Cabato related that her Filipino father, who spent twenty-eight years in the navy as a steward, is "one of the best cooks around." Rene Cruz heaped the same praise on her father: "My dad is not the macho kind of guy where the woman does this and that only. . . . In terms of cooking for big parties and stuff, he is really good at cooking large meals, because, you know, in the Navy he had to cook for hundreds of people." Rene's father concurred: "I cook most of the time since I am an expert in the 'food industry.' " These men's willingness to put to use their domestic skills suggests that the denigration of women is only one response to the stripping of male privilege. Another is to institute a revised domestic division of labor and gender relations in the family.

FEMALE-FIRST MIGRATION: THE HEALTH-CARE PROFESSIONALS

In contrast to pre–Word War II immigration from Asia, which consisted mostly of men, the contemporary flow is dominated by women. Women comprise the clear majority among U.S. immigrants from nations in Asia but also from those in Central America and South America, the Caribbean, and Europe.[19] During the 1960s, two thirds of all immigrants from the Philippines to the United States were women.[20] The dual goals of the 1965 Immigration Act—to facilitate family reunification and, secondarily, to admit workers with special job skills—have produced a female-dominated flow. Since 1965, most visas have been allocated to relatives of U.S. residents. Women who came as wives, daughters, or mothers of U.S. permanent residents and citizens comprise the primary component of change.[21] The dominance of women immigrants also reflects the growth of female-intensive industries in the United States, particularly in the service, microelectronics, apparel manufacturing, and health-care industries.[22]

The growth of female-intensive industries has produced a new trend in international migration: female-first migration in which women migrate abroad before or without their spouses and other family members. Whereas the first half of this chapter focused on the male-first migration of Navy enlistees, this second half will explore the impact of the female-first migration of health-care professionals on gender and family relations. The Philippines is the largest supplier of health professionals to the United States, sending nearly twenty-five thousand nurses to this country between 1966 and 1985 and another ten thousand between 1989 and

1991. A U.S. General Accounting Office report indicated that in 1989, Filipino nurses comprised the overwhelming majority (73 percent) of foreign nurse graduates in the United States.[23] As indicated in chapter 2, Filipina health-care professionals entered the United States through two major avenues: the Exchange Visitor Program and the new occupational preference categories of the 1965 Immigration Act. The few studies that have investigated the female-first labor migrant experiences concluded that this type of migration had created new opportunities for these women and disrupted their traditional familial and societal roles. While most of the authors focused on domestic workers,[24] I explore here the female-first migration of highly educated and professional women to the United States.

"We Were Young and We Wanted to See the World": Migration of Single Women

Rose Ocampo grew up in Cavite among four sisters and three brothers as the fourth of eight children. Her father, who worked for an American engineering firm, earned enough money to send all eight children to college. Rose decided to become a nurse because "it was a trend": "All my friends were going into nursing, so I went ahead and went into nursing too." Rose came to the United States in 1961 under the auspices of the U.S. Exchange Visitor Program (EVP).[25] She explained that she and a friend wanted to visit the United States "to see the country." "It wasn't for the money," she said quickly. "The stipend was only a hundred dollars a month and they worked you forty-eight hours a week." What the two young women wanted was "a new environment, for adventure. We were young and we wanted to see the world." Rose was sent to a small town in Minnesota, where she befriended other EVP Filipino nurses who helped her to integrate into her new community. When her exchange visa expired at the end of two years,[26] Rose wanted to extend her stay because "my friends and I still wanted to go around the world." Instead of returning to the Philippines, she exited the United States by going to Canada, where she worked for a year. However, just before she left for Canada, she befriended a Filipino American man who followed her to Canada. The two married a year later, allowing Rose to officially immigrate to the United States.

Juanita Boado grew up in Manila as the fourth daughter of nine children. Her family belonged to the upper stratum of the Philippines: her father was a prominent judge, and her mother a physician. After graduating from medical school in 1965, Juanita applied to come to the United States via the Exchange Visitor Program. When I asked Juanita why she wanted to come to the United States, her first response was: "For adventure, to meet Americans, to know their customs and traditions." Then she added:

> For prestige also. When you come to the United States, and you train in the United States, it's like a move forward . . . really, professional growth. And when you come back to the Philippines to practice, you almost can be assured that you will have a good practice . . . because the people in the Philippines, if they hear you're U.S.-trained . . . then they automatically think that you're a good doctor.

As many as half of her classmates had already left for the United States; this fact motivated her to go abroad: "It's not really professionally fulfilling to stay in the Philippines knowing that some of my friends are in the States, and they are doing their training already. . . . They write to me and tell me to come." She had yet one more reason for leaving: to join her boyfriend of five years who was already interning at a hospital in New York under the auspices of the EVP. Although Juanita wanted to join him in New York, she did not feel the need to work at the same hospital: "He was writing to me to come to his hospital. I didn't feel like I need to go to the same hospital he's working at. I could try another hospital." But the executive secretary at that hospital, on learning of Juanita's impending arrival, sent a letter inviting her to join their staff. In June of 1966, Juanita traveled to New York City to reunite with her boyfriend and to begin her internship as an exchange physician. Six months after she arrived in New York, she and her boyfriend married. Shortly after, the two decided to apply for permanent resident status. Because both had job offers from local hospitals, their applications were quickly approved.

Rose and Juanita's experiences illustrate the power of gender in shaping migration. First, they show that migration opportunities are circumscribed by gender-based transnational social networks.[27] While Navy men relied on the resources and connections of other men, women health-care professionals migrated to and settled in the United States with the help of other women. Through letters, phone calls, and return visits, Filipino nurses and physicians who had gone abroad created new expectations, goals, and desires among young Filipino women still in the Philippines. According to Luz Latus, her nursing friends' and colleagues' decisions to apply for U.S. visas influenced her own decision to emigrate:

> After I graduated, I decided to come here. I thought, "Well, it seems like everybody wants to go there." So I thought I'd try. Why not, you know? There is always a farewell party for so-and-so. She's leaving for the U.S. to do this and that. Well, somehow, a whole bunch of us, we decided, let's go ahead and apply. You know how when you were young, I mean . . . you know, you're really, just want to experience this. What is this thing they're talking about? America.

In the process of relocating and settling in the United States, Filipino health-care migrants also created new transnational networks of support, helping each other to adjust to their new occupational, social, economic, and cultural settings.[28]

Second, Rose and Juanita's experiences reveal that men and women differ in their reasons for migrating.[29] In my analysis of Navy men above, I argued that their motivations for joining the U.S. Navy were gendered: to better represent themselves as able economic providers and desirable sexual partners. In contrast, Rose and Juanita had other desires and ambitions: to see the world and experience untried ways of living. The Exchange Visitor Program, and the new occupational preference categories of the 1965 Immigration Act, created opportunities for Filipino women health professionals to enter the United States on their own accord. Indeed, the majority of the nurses that I interviewed came to the United States initially as single women, a fact corroborated by other studies of Filipino nurses.[30] In the interviews, many of these nurses represented their decision to come to the United States as an effort to push gender roles, especially to unshackle themselves from family discipline, which hindered their individual development.[31] For example, Cecilia Bonus (profiled in chapter 2) explained why she had applied to study in the United States: "My family was just so protective. I just kind of wanted to get away and be independent." Being away from home enabled many young women to free themselves temporarily from strict parental control on their activities and movements. In the United States, they traveled freely, socialized widely, lived in their own apartments, and stayed out late at night.[32]

Perhaps most important, Filipino health-care professionals reveled in their newfound freedom to befriend and date men. Carmen Reynila described how she and her fellow exchange nurses enjoyed the company of the Filipino sailors:

> There used to be lots of Filipino gatherings around. So you got to meet each other, and then the sailors, you know, they would come to our apartments,

> and then, you know, we would go out with them, but then always in a group [laughter]. Because I would say there is safety in numbers [laughter].

In Juanita Boado's case, if it were not for the Exchange Visitor Program, her desire to follow her boyfriend to the United States would have been construed as improper and probably prohibited. Rose and Juanita's experiences also suggest that many women seize their newfound freedom to make more independent choices about marriage. Both women elected to marry in the United States, partly to mute any possible objections from their parents. As Juanita related, "We decided to get married in New York because we kinda knew that if we go back home, my parents would tell us to wait at least a year or two more." In another example, Rosie Roxas, who met her Filipino Navy husband while in San Diego, explained why she did not return to the Philippines to marry: "My parents would not have approved of him. Their background . . . it would have been very difficult. . . . They wanted me to marry a professional. . . . He would not have passed." In her seminal study of Filipino nurses, Catherine Choy reports that Philippine government health officials and nursing leaders used a rhetoric of spirituality and morality to criticize the new lifestyles of Filipino exchange nurses abroad.[33] These critics charged that some Filipino exchanges nurses had become morally corrupt and associated the nurses' new lifestyles in the United States with licentiousness. Choy accurately interprets these charges as efforts to persuade Filipino nurses to return to work in the Philippines. However, in light of the women's newfound independence, I believe these charges must also be viewed as retaliating moves to reassert patriarchal control over the bodies of these women.

Negotiating Changing Gender Roles: The Migration of Married Women

When the women are married, a female-first migration stream can have enormous ramifications for both family relations and domestic roles. In a reversal of historical patterns of migration, many married women health professionals enter the United States as primary immigrants, with their husbands and children following as dependents. Take Cecile Garcia's story, for example. Cecile had always dreamed of "America," and going abroad figured prominently in her decision to select a nursing career. In 1973, married with two young children, she left for the United States under the auspices of the Exchange Visitor

Program. Although both she and her mechanic husband shared a desire to move the family to the United States, it was her profession that allowed them to do so. As an exchange nurse, she came alone; her husband stayed behind to care for their two young daughters. Eighteen months later, when she had successfully adjusted her status from exchange visitor to permanent resident, she petitioned for her family to join her. But the temporary separation from the children had its costs:

> My daughter, who was two when I left, didn't even know me when I went back to get them. She would not come to me. I stayed there for three weeks when I picked them up . . . still she would not come to me. I was very hurt by that. I was like a stranger . . . and that really struck me. I don't want to not be known by my children.

These separations, even when temporary, can leave lifelong scars. At the age of twenty-one, Melanie Villa still harbored unresolved grief over her mother's decision to leave for the United States during her first two years of life: "Sometimes, I still think about it . . . like the fact that I was never breast-fed like my sister, who was born here. . . . It doesn't seem fair, you know. . . . And I wonder if it had affected my relationship with my mother." These experiences of transnational motherhood, albeit temporary, continue a long historical legacy of people of color being incorporated into the United States through restrictive systems of labor that do not recognize the workers' family needs and rights.[34]

A female-first migration stream also affects traditional gender roles. In many instances, men who immigrate as their wives' dependents experience downward occupational mobility in the United States, while their wives maintain their professional status. Pyong Gap Min reports that among Korean immigrant families in New York, while Korean nurses hold stable jobs, many of their educated husbands are unemployed or underemployed.[35] Gender role reversals—wives' increased economic role and husbands' reduced economic role—challenge men's sense of well-being and place undue stress on the family. For example, Elizabeth Mayor, a Filipino medical technologist, entered the United States in 1965 through the Exchange Visitor Program, leaving behind her husband and two sons. One year later, Elizabeth changed her status to permanent resident and petitioned for her family. Elizabeth's husband, who had a degree in criminology, could not find work in the United States comparable to his education and training. Elizabeth described their differential access to suitable employment:

> For me, since I had the training in Michigan, and had my license as a med tech, I was able to work in the medical profession in the laboratory. I had no problems finding a job. But for him, it was difficult. He had to work odd jobs, anything that was available there. That was a minus for him. . . . My husband was more dependent on me because I had a stable job.

Her husband was bitter about this role reversal: "He had a big problem. His self-esteem was really low. When he first came, he worked as a janitor, then as a dishwasher. He was working all the time, but in blue-collar jobs. It took a lot out of his self-esteem, as far as that goes." Because of this loss of status, Elizabeth's husband—for the duration of their thirteen-year stay in Michigan—repeatedly expressed his desire to return to the Philippines. In 1989, Elizabeth's sister urged them to leave Detroit and join the family business in San Diego. Although Elizabeth had a "good job" in Detroit, she decided to accept her sister's invitation, in part because it included a job offer for her husband. At the time of our interview in 1994, Elizabeth reported that her husband's self-esteem has been restored: "My husband is happy now. That was the first steady job he'd held since he came to the United States." In contrast, Elizabeth had difficulty finding a stable job and instead worked part-time for a local company. But Elizabeth expressed that she was content with her new life: "So it is just the opposite here. He has a steady job and now I work part-time. Which I like too. . . . As an Oriental, my upbringing is . . . usually the husband is the bread earner back home. So that worked perfect for me. It's a lot better for him here than back East. So I am happy."

Elizabeth's account of her family experiences calls attention to the dissimilar structure of opportunities that many immigrant men and women encounter in contemporary United States.[36] The dynamics of the U.S. economy, in this case the shortage of medical personnel, gives many women an increased access to paid work, whereas their male peers do not fare as well. At the same time, Elizabeth's experience challenges the relative resource models, which predict that as women's earnings rise relative to their husbands', their authority and status in the family will correspondingly rise. Elizabeth's story suggests that the labor market advantage does not automatically or uniformly lead to more egalitarian relations in the family. Instead, perceived cultural ideals about gender and spousal relations that were held in the Philippines, such as the belief that the men should be the primary economic provider and head of the household, continue to influence the outcomes of the changing balance of resources in the new country.

Working at Family Life

A primary theme in gender and immigration research concerns the impact of immigrant women's employment on gender equality in the family. Like other case studies on gender relations among salaried professionals, my research on women health professionals indicates that women's employment has led to greater male involvement in household labor.[37] However, this more equitable household division of labor is not due to women's earning power, but rather to the women's demanding job schedules and to the couple's recognition that at least two incomes are needed to "make it" in this country. As in the case of the Navy men, the health-care professionals' success requires the work of the whole family, with husbands and children at times having to assume tasks not usually expected of them.

A survey of Filipino nurses in Los Angeles County reveals that these women, to increase their incomes, tend to work double shifts or the higher-paying evening and night shifts.[38] Given the long hours and the graveyard shifts that typify a nurse's work schedule, many husbands have had to assume more child-care and other household responsibilities in their wives' absences. Like the Navy fathers, some nurses have elected to work the night shift, not only because of the higher pay, but also because they can leave the children with their husbands instead of with paid child-care providers. Cecilia Bonus related, "I work mostly at night. So my husband takes care of the kids. . . . He's pretty good at helping when I have to work. . . . He's pretty understanding as far as that goes." Maricela Rebaya's mother took pride in the fact that she never left her children with baby-sitters:

> We never had baby-sitters. Oh, my mom is the toughest person in the world. She just managed. When she was in nursing, she would work at night. And my dad would take care of us when she was at work. So, like, in the morning, when she gets home, she makes breakfast for the kids, and then my dad drives us to school, and then she would go to sleep.

In her research on shift work and dual-earner spouses with children, Harriet Pressner finds that the husbands of night-shift workers do a significant part of child care; in most cases, it was the husbands who supervised the often-rushed routines of getting their children up and off to school or to child care.[39] In the same way, women physicians rely on their husbands' assistance with child care, especially during the hectic years of residency. Juanita Boado described how she and her physician husband managed their residency years: "We had two children at that time. We just alternated between my husband, myself, and sometimes baby-sitters. We alternated our weekends. Weekend that he was on, I was off. Weekend that I was on, he was off. That's how we did it."

When wives and/or husbands are unable to manage around-the-clock care for their children, they tend to rely on the eldest child to shoulder the responsibility. When Maria Galang turned fifteen, both her parents worked the night shift: her mother as a nurse at the local hospital and her father as a janitor at the local mall. Maria was forced to take care of her younger sister during her parents' absence:

> Because mom and dad worked so much, I had to assume the role of mother hen. And it was a strain especially at that point when I hit high school. They figure that I was old enough now. I remember frequent nights when my sister would cry and she wanted Mom. What could I do? While Mom and Dad provided that financial support, we needed that emotional support as well, which was often lacking.

This arrangement can take a toll on family relations: a child who has grown up without the mother's presence may no longer respond to her authority.[40] As we learned above, for five years, Rose Dumlao "mothered" her younger brother while her Navy father was away at sea and her nurse mother was working long hours at the hospital. As a result, Rose's brother channeled his affection and respect to Rose, his "other mother," instead of to his mother:

> I think the reason why my brother doesn't really respect my mom the way he should is because he never really saw my mom as the caretaker because she was never around. So even now, whenever my parents want my brother to do something, like if they have to talk to him, I have to be either in the room or I have to be the one that's talking to him because he's not going to listen to them. Because I spent more time with him.

Even when there are no younger siblings to care for, the parents' absence still pains their children. Gabriela Garcia, whose parents divorced when she was nine years old, recounted how she managed when her mother worked the graveyard shift:

> After my parents divorced, my mother was working two shifts. She would work basically from three in the afternoon till seven in the morning. She

> would be gone by the time I had come home from school. And then I was by myself. . . . So I slept by myself. I had to have the radio, the TV, and the light on because I was so scared sometimes.

Research on gender relations among salaried professionals indicates that gains in gender equality have been uneven. Even when there is greater male involvement in child care in these families, women continue to perform more of the household labor than their husbands do.[41] Moreover, Pesquera reports that, for the most part, the only way women have altered the distribution of household labor has been through conflict and confrontation, suggesting that ideologically most men continue to view housework as women's work.[42] These findings remind us that professional women, like most other working women, have to juggle full-time work outside the home with the responsibilities of child care and housework. Cecilia Bonus, a nurse and mother of three young children, confided that she felt overwhelmed by the never-ending chores: "Here you have to work so hard. You have to do everything. You have to wash the dishes, you have to do laundry, you have to clean the house, you have to take care of the kids. It's just endless." Although Cecilia's husband took care of the children when she worked the night shifts, she wished that he would do more:

> The husbands should help out more, I think . . . as far as the children go, and the housework. . . . That's one thing I like about Western culture. They have more liberty as a female and the rights that men have. It's not just a one-way thing where women have to do everything. Men should do things like chores at home, too, you know.

Cecilia, who came from a middle-class family in the Philippines, confided that she missed the "helpers" that she had in the Philippines. "Over there, you have maids to help you," she said. "You don't have to do the chores. You have one maid for each child. Life is so much easier there. Every little thing is offered to you, even a glass of water. I just wished I had a helper here." Like Cecilia, the majority of the women in my study longed for the "helpers" that they once had or would have had, had they stayed in the Philippines. Instead of enlisting their husbands' help with the housework, these women chose to "solve" their "double-day syndrome" by forcing it on other less privileged women. This solution raises a challenge to the feminist notion of "universal sisterhood." As Mary Romero correctly observes, "Domestic service accentuates the contradiction of race and class in feminism, with privileged women of one class using the labor of another woman to escape aspects of sexism."[43]

In a disturbingly familiar pattern, when both wives and husbands are professionals, it is often the woman who has to subordinate her career to that of her husband. Juanita Boado's account of her married and professional lives reveals a string of compromises on her part to accommodate her husband's career choices. Although both were physicians, it was she, and not her husband, who switched her specialization, from obstetrics to pediatrics, to better accommodate a family life with young children. As Juanita explained,

> Before I came to New York, I was determined to specialize in OB because I enjoyed delivering babies when I was an intern [in the Philippines.] But when I got married, I realize it's not an easy job because . . . pregnant women . . . they deliver any time of the day or night. If you're already on your own and you have a family, it's not an easy job. So I switched to pediatrics.

In 1974, her husband moved the family from New York City to a small town in Michigan because he wanted to start a private practice. Juanita was ambivalent about moving to this town of 3,200 people, especially since the invitation to be the town physician was extended only to her husband. As she explained, "He was the primary person. The move is so that he can practice there. I didn't particularly want to go. A that time, I moved because my husband moved. The Filipino culture is you stick to your husband for better or for worse." Although Juanita was not officially invited to be the town physician, the townspeople welcomed her expertise in pediatrics. From this shaky beginning, Juanita worked hard to build a thriving practice, eventually extending it to an adjacent town. Juanita was proud of her success: "I was able to build up my practice. I enjoyed my practice. Nice people. I was welcomed. The people were just happy to have a pediatrician there." However, after four years, her husband, a trained surgeon, became tired of working as a family practitioner. In 1978, after a trip to San Diego to attend a surgical convention, her husband announced that the family would be moving to San Diego. Once again, Juanita had little say in the decision:

> Again, it was a passive move for me. My husband moved, so I moved with him. I was carried by my husband. I would have settled in Michigan. I had no complaint. I was happy with my practice. I built the practice for four years, and then only to leave the practice, it was traumatic for me . . . to leave my practice, my patients, and everybody there.

Because it was "traumatic" for her to leave her practice, Juanita vowed that she will never start another private practice, saying, "I don't know what he's gonna do next." Instead, she found work at a local clinic, helping the underserved populations of San Diego. Juanita summed up the power differential in the spousal relationship: "It's always been that way. He's the major decision maker. He makes major decisions . . . moving from one state to the next . . . selling the house . . . buying another house. And I just have to deal with these decisions." In another example, Ofelia Velasco, herself a physician, did not practice medicine but worked instead as an office manager at her husband's private practice: "I take care of my husband's practice. My husband, as a man, he expects me as his wife, to hire and fire, to give salaries to the employees, to make sure that we have enough stocks of medicine—all those dirty jobs. He just practices."

◆ ◆ ◆

The experiences of these immigrant families underscore just how much work it takes for immigrants of color to try to "make it" in the United States. In their pursuit of the "American dream," Filipino Navy men and Filipina health-care professionals need the paid and unpaid labor of their entire family. Thus the American mythology of the rugged individualist pulling himself up by his own bootstraps is just that: a myth. These life accounts also tell us that the pursuit of the American dream, even when "successful," entails physical and psychic costs, the majority of which are borne by the wives and children of these families. Among the costs are a string of broken dreams along the way—of missed family time, deferred careers, and shortened childhood. In the best scenario, responding to migration-related challenges, both husbands and wives have become more interdependent and equal as they are forced to rely on each other and on the traditional family for economic security and emotional support. However, entrenched cultural perceptions, such as the belief that the male should be the head of the household and the primary economic provider, continue to dominate despite the changing economic contributions of women. As I will argue in chapter 7, in the context of migration, the desire to preserve the traditional family system is one attempt by migrant Filipinas to assert their cultural "authenticity" and to claim moral distinctiveness for their community within the larger society.

CHAPTER 7

"We Don't Sleep Around Like White Girls Do"

The Politics of Home and Location

I want my daughters to be Filipino especially on sex. I always emphasize to them that they should not participate in sex if they are not married. We are also Catholic. We are raised so that we don't engage in going out with men while we are not married. And I don't like it to happen to my daughters as if they have no values. I don't like them to grow up that way, like the American girls.

Rosa Lopez, Filipino immigrant mother

I found that a lot of the Asian American friends of mine, we don't date like white girls date. We don't sleep around like white girls do. Everyone is really mellow at dating, because your parents were constraining and restrictive.

Maria Ricasa, second-generation Filipino daughter

In this chapter, I continue my discussion of "home" as a domestic space by focusing on the relationship between Filipino immigrant parents and their daughters. I argue that gender is a key to immigrant identity and a vehicle for racialized immigrants to assert cultural superiority over the dominant group. In immigrant communities, culture takes on a special significance: not only does it form a lifeline to the home country and a basis for group identity in a new country, it also serves as a base from which immigrants stake their political and sociocultural claims on their new country.[1] For Filipino immigrants who come from a homeland that was once a U.S. colony, cultural reconstruction has been especially critical in the assertion of their presence in the United States—a way to counter the cultural Americanization of the Philippines, to resist the assimilative and alienating demands of U.S. society, and to reaffirm for themselves their self-worth in the face of colonial, racial, class, and gendered subordination. As discussed in chapter 3, although Filipinos have been in the United States since the middle of the 1700s and Americans have been in the Philippines since at least the late 1800s, U.S. Filipinos—as racialized nationals, immigrants, and citizens—"are still practically an invisible and silent minority."[2] This chapter explores the ways racialized immigrants claim through gender the power denied them by racism. My major concern in this chapter is to understand the politics of location—how immigrants use literal or symbolic ties to the homeland as a form of resistance to places and practices in the host country that are patently "not home."[3]

The epigraphs, quotations of a Filipino immigrant mother and a second-generation Filipino daughter, suggest that the virtuous Filipino daughter is partially constructed on the conceptualization of white women as sexually immoral. This juxtaposition underscores the fact that femininity is a relational category, one that is coconstructed with other racial and cultural categories. These narratives also reveal that women's sexuality and their enforced "morality" are fundamental to the structuring of social inequalities. Historically, the sexuality of racialized women has been systematically demonized and denigrated by dominant or oppressor groups to justify and bolster nationalist movements, colonialism, and/or racism. But as these narratives indicate, racialized groups also look down on the morality of white women as a strategy of resistance—a means of asserting a morally superior public face to the dominant society.

By exploring how Filipino immigrants characterize white families and white women, I hope to contribute to a neglected area of research: how the "margins" imagine and construct the "mainstream" in order to assert superiority over the latter. This strategy reminds us that those at the margins "may read their marginality as positive, even superior, stance from which to experience the modern nation."[4] But this strategy is not without costs. The elevation of Filipina chastity (particularly that of young women) has the effect of reinforcing masculinist and patriarchal power in the name of a greater ideal of national and ethnic self-respect. Because controlling women is one of the principal means of asserting moral superiority, young women in immigrant families face numerous restrictions on their autonomy, mobility, and personal decision making.

"AMERICAN" AND WHITENESS: "TO ME, AMERICAN MEANS WHITE"

In U.S. racial discourse and practices, unless otherwise specified, "Americans" means "whites."[5] In the case of Asian Americans, U.S. immigration exclusion acts, naturalization laws, and national culture have simultaneously marked Asians as the inassimilable aliens and whites as the quintessential Americans.[6] Excluded from the collective memory of who constitutes a "real" American, Asians in the United States, even as citizens, remain the "foreigner-within"—the "non-American." In a study of third- and later-generation Chinese and Japanese Americans, Mia Tuan concludes that despite being longtime Americans, Asians—as racialized ethnics—are often assumed to be foreign unless proven otherwise.[7] As discussed in chapter 3, in the case of Filipinos who emigrated from a former U.S. colony, their formation as racialized minorities does not begin in the United States but rather in a "homeland" already affected by U.S. economic, social, and cultural influences.[8]

Cognizant of this racialized history, my Filipino respondents seldom identify themselves as American. As will be evident in the discussion below, they equate *American* with *white* and often use these two terms interchangeably. For example, Paz Johnson, who is married to a white American, refers to her husband as "American" but to her African American and Filipino American brothers-in-law as "black" and "Filipino" respectively. Others speak about "American ways," "American culture," or "American lifestyle" when they really mean *white* American ways, culture, and lifestyle. Dante Gomez, who has lived in the United States for thirty years, explained why he still did not identify himself as American: "I don't see myself just as an American because I cannot hide the fact that my skin is brown. To me, American means white." Genelle Calderon, a second-generation Filipina, recounted this following story when asked if she defined herself as American:

> I went to an all-white school. I knew I was different. I wasn't American. See, you are not taught that you're American because you are not white. When I was in the tenth grade, our English teacher asked us what our nationality was, and she goes, how many of you are Mexican, how many of you are Filipino, and how many of you are Samoan and things like that. And when she asked how many of you are American, just the white people raised their hands.

Other Asian Americans have also conflated *American* and *white*. In an ethnographic study of Asian American high school students, Stacey Lee reports that Korean immigrant parents often instructed their children to socialize only with Koreans and "Americans."[9] When asked to define the term *American,* the Korean students responded in unison with, "White! Korean parents like white." Tuan found the same practice among later-generation Chinese and Japanese Americans: the majority use the term *American* to refer to whites.[10]

CONSTRUCTING THE DOMINANT GROUP: THE MORAL FLAWS OF WHITE AMERICANS

Morality is an important technology for "disciplining and regulating the social."[11] Given the centrality of moral themes in popular discussions on racial differences, Michele Lamont has suggested that morality is a crucial site for studying the cultural mechanisms of the reproduction of racial inequality.[12] While much has been written on how whites have represented the (im)morality of people of color,[13] less critical attention has been paid to how people of color have represented whites.[14] Shifting attention from the "otherness" of the subordinate group (as dictated by the "mainstream") to the "otherness" of the dominant group (as constructed by the "margins"), this section focuses on the alternative frames of meaning that racially subordinate groups mobilize to (re)define their status in relation to the dominant group. I argue that female morality—defined as women's dedication to their families and sexual restraint—is one of the few sites where economically and politically dominated groups can construct the dominant group as other and themselves as superior. Because womanhood is idealized as the repository of tradition, the norms that regulate women's behaviors become a means of determining and defining group status and boundaries. As a consequence, the burdens and complexities of cultural representation fall most heavily on immigrant women and their daughters. Below, I show that Filipino immigrants claim moral distinctiveness for their community by representing "Americans" as morally flawed, themselves as family-oriented model minorities, and their wives and daughters as paragons of morality.

Family-Oriented Model Minorities: "White Women Will Leave You"

In his work on Italian immigrant parents and children in the 1930s, Robert Anthony Orsi reports that the parents invented a virtuous Italy (based on memories of their childhood) that they then used to criticize the immorality of the United States and of their U.S.-born or -raised children.[15] In a similar way, many of my respondents constructed their "ethnic" culture as principled and the "American" culture as deviant. Most often, this morality narrative revolves around family life and family relations. When asked what set Filipinos apart from other Americans, my respondents—of all ages and class backgrounds—repeatedly contrasted the close-knit Filipino families to what they perceived to be the more impersonal quality of U.S. family relations.[16] In the following narratives, both immigrant and U.S.-born Filipinos characterize "Americans" as lacking in strong family ties and collective identity, less willing to do the work of family and cultural maintenance, and less willing to abide by patriarchal norms in husband-wife relations:

> American society lacks caring. The American way of life is more individual rather than collective. The American way is to say I want to have my own way.
>
> Filipina immigrant, fifty-four years old

> Our [Filipino] culture is different. We are more close-knit. We tend to help one another. Americans, ya know, they are all right, but they don't help each other that much. As a matter of fact, if the parents are old, they take them to a convalescent home and let them rot there. We would never do that in our culture. We would nurse them; we would help them until the very end.
>
> Filipino immigrant, sixty years old

> Our [Filipino] culture is very communal. You know that your family will always be there, that you don't have to work when you turn eighteen, you don't have to pay rent when you are eighteen, which is the American way of thinking. You also know that if things don't work out in the outside world, you can always come home, and mommy and daddy will always take you and your children in.
>
> Second-generation Filipina, thirty-three-years old

> We are staying with my husband's parents right now because they have just gone through heart surgery. They are not able to take care of the house on their own. And they have room for us, so we are willing to help. One of my Caucasian friends, when she heard that I was going to be living with my in-laws, she was like, "Are you crazy? You need to be out on your own." Which is fine, but I think in the Filipino culture, the family values are much stronger. You feel obligated to be there to help. You can't just turn your back on your relatives.
>
> Second-generation Filipina, twenty-five years old

Implicit in the negative depiction of U.S. families—as uncaring, selfish, and distant—is the allegation that white women are not as dedicated to their families as Filipino women are to theirs. Several Filipino men who married white women recalled being warned by their parents and relatives that "white women will leave you." As David Davila related, "My mother said to me, 'Well, you know, don't marry a white person, because they would take everything that you own and leave you.' " For some Filipino men, perceived differences in attitudes about women's roles between Filipino and non-Filipino women influenced their marital choice. Jose Melegrito, a U.S.-born Filipino American navy man, explained why he went to the Philippines to look for a wife:

> My goal was to marry a Filipina. I requested to be stationed in the Philippines to get married to a Filipina. I'd seen the women here, and basically they are spoiled. They have a tendency of not going along together with their husband. They behave differently. They chase the male, instead of the male, the normal way, the traditional way, is for the male to go after the female. They have sex without marrying. They want to do their own things. So my idea was to go back home and marry somebody who has never been here. I tell my son the same thing: if he does what I did and finds himself a good lady there, he will be in good hands.

In another example, Daniel Gruta, who had dated mostly white women in high school, recounted that when it came time for him to marry, he "looked for the kind of women" that he met while in the Philippines: "I hate to sound chauvinistic about marriages, but Filipinas have a way of making you feel like you are a king. They also have that tenderness, that elegance. And we share the same values about family, education, religion, and raising children."

The claims of family closeness are not unique to Filipino immigrants. For example, when asked what makes their group distinctive, Italian Americans, Vietnamese Americans, South Asian Americans, and African Americans all point proudly to the close-knit character of their family.[17] Although it is difficult to know whether these claims are actual perceptions or self-legitimating answers, it is nevertheless important to note the gender implications of these claims.[18] That is, while both men and women identify the family system as a tremendous source of cultural pride, it is women—through their unpaid housework and kin work—who shoulder the primary responsibility for maintaining family closeness. As the organizers of family rituals, transmitters of homeland folklores, and socializers of young children, women's labors have been crucial to the maintenance of family ties and cultural traditions. In a study of kinship, class, and gender among California Italian Americans, di Leonardo argues that women's kin work, "the work of knitting households together into 'close, extended families,' " maintains the family networks that give ethnicity meaning.[19]

Because the moral status of the community rests on women's labor, women, as wives and daughters, are expected to dedicate themselves to the family. Writing on the constructed image of ethnic family and gender, di Leonardo argues that "a large part of stressing ethnic identity amounts to burdening women with increased responsibilities for preparing special foods, planning rituals, and enforcing 'ethnic' socialization of children."[20] Amanda Flores, a twenty-three-year-old Filipina, spoke about the reproductive work that her mother performed and expected her to learn:

> In my family, I was the only girl, so my mom expected a lot from me. She wanted me to help her to take care of the household. I felt like there was a lot of pressure on me. It's very important to my mom to have the house in order: to wash the dishes, to keep the kitchen in order, vacuuming, and dusting and things like that. She wants me to be a perfect housewife. It's difficult. I have been married now for about four months, and my mother asks me every now and then what have I cooked for my husband. My mom is also very strict about families getting together on holidays, and I would always help her to organize that. Each holiday, I would try to decorate the house for her, to make it more special.

The burden of unpaid reproductive and kin work is particularly stressful for women who work outside the home. In the following narrative, Rose Ocampo, a wife and mother of three teenagers, describes the pulls of family and work that she experienced when she went back to school to pursue a doctoral degree in nursing:

> The Filipinos, we are very collective, very connected. Going through the doctoral program, sometimes I think it is better just to forget about my relatives and just concentrate on school. All that connectedness, it steals parts of myself because all of my energies are devoted to my family. And that is the reason why I think Americans are successful. The majority of the American people they can do what they want. They don't feel guilty because they only have a few people to relate to. For us Filipinos, it's like roots under the tree; you have all these connections. The Americans are more like the trunk. I am still trying to go up to the trunk of the tree, but it is too hard. I want to be more independent, more like the Americans. I want to be good to my family, but what about me? And all the things that I am doing. It's hard. It's always a struggle.

It is important to note that this Filipina only interprets her exclusion and added responsibilities as racial when they are also gendered. For example, when she says, "the American people, they can do what they want," she ignores the differences in the lives of white men and white women—the fact that most white women experience similar pulls of family, education, and work.

Racialized Sexuality and (Im)Morality: "In America, Sex Is Nothing"

In her work on the postcolonial state in Trinidad and Tobag and its regulation of black women's sexuality, Jacqui Alexander calls attention to the link between morality and sexuality: "To be moral is to be asexual, (hetero)sexual, or sexual in ways that presumably carry the weight of the 'natural.' "[21] Sexuality, then, as a core aspect of social identity, is fundamental to the structuring of gender inequality. Sexuality is also a salient marker of otherness and has figured prominently in racist and colonialist ideologies.[22] Historically, the sexuality of subordinate groups—particularly that of racialized women—has been systematically and subversively portrayed by the dominant groups.[23] As Alexander establishes, attempts to manage sexuality through morality are bound to colonial rule: "The very identity and authority of the colonial project rested upon the racialization and sexualization of morality."[24] At stake in these stereotypes is the construction of women of color as morally lacking in the areas of sexual restraints and traditional morality. Asian women—both in Asia and in the United States—have been racialized as sexually immoral, and the "Orient"—and its women—has long served as a site of European male-power fantasies, replete with lurid images of sexual license, gynecological aberrations, and general perversion.[25] In colonial Asia in the nineteenth and early twentieth centuries, for example, female sexuality was a site for colonial rulers to assert their moral superiority and thus their natural and legitimate right to rule. The colonial rhetoric of moral superiority was based on the construction of colonized Asian women as subjects of sexual desire and fulfillment and European colonial women as the paragons of virtue and the bearers of a redefined colonial morality.[26] The discourse of morality has also been used to mark the "unassimilability" of Asians in the United States. At the turn of the twentieth century, the public perception of Chinese women as disease-ridden, drug-addicted prostitutes served to underline the depravity of the "Orientals" and played a decisive role in the eventual passage of exclusion laws against all Asians. The stereotypical view that all Asian women were prostitutes, first formed in the 1850s, persisted. Contemporary American popular culture continues to endow Asian women with an excess of "womanhood," sexualizing them but also impugning their sexuality.[27]

Filipinas—both in the Philippines and in the United States—have been marked as desirable but dangerous "prostitutes" and/or submissive "mail-order brides."[28] These stereotypes emerged out of the colonial process, especially the extensive U.S. military presence in the Philippines. As discussed earlier, until the early 1990s, the Philippines housed some of the United States' largest overseas air force and naval bases. Many Filipino nationalists have charged that the "prostitution problem" in the Philippines stemmed from U.S. and Philippine government policies that promoted a sex industry—brothels, bars, and massage parlors—for servicemen stationed or on leave in the Philippines. During the Vietnam War, the Philippines was known as the "rest and recreation" center of Asia, hosting approximately ten thousand U.S. servicemen daily.[29] In this context, *all* Filipinas were racialized as sexual commodities, usable and expendable. U.S.-born Connie Tirona recounted the sexual harassment she faced while visiting Subic Bay Naval Station in Olongapo City:

> One day, I went to the base dispensary. . . . I was dressed nicely, and as I walked by the fire station, I heard catcalls and snide remarks being made by some of the firemen. . . . I was fuming inside. The next thing I heard was, "How much do you charge?" I kept on walking. "Hey, are you deaf or something? How much do you charge? You have a good body." That was an incident that I will never forget.

The sexualized racialization of Filipinas is also captured in Marianne Vilanueva's short story "Opportunity."[30] As the protagonist Nina, a "mail-order bride" from the Philippines, enters the hotel lobby to meet her American fiancé, the bellboys snicker and whisper *puta,* whore: a reminder that U.S. economic and cultural colonization in the Philippines always forms a backdrop to any relations between Filipinos and Americans.[31]

Cognizant of the pervasive hypersexualization of Filipino women, my respondents, especially women who grew up near the military bases, were quick to denounce prostitution, to denigrate sex laborers, and to declare (unasked) that they themselves did not frequent "that part of town." As Mona Ampon said:

> Growing up [in the Philippines], I could never date an American, because my dad's concept of a friendship with an American is with a GI. The only

reason why my dad wouldn't let us date an American is that people will think that the only way you met was because of the base. I have never seen the inside of any of the bases because we were just forbidden to go there.

Many of my respondents also distanced themselves culturally from the Filipinas who serviced U.S. soldiers by branding them "more Americanized" and "more Westernized."[32] In other words, these women were sexually promiscuous because they had assumed the sexual mores of white women. This characterization allows my respondents to symbolically disown the Filipina "bad girl" and, in so doing, to uphold the narrative of Filipina sexual virtuosity and white female sexual promiscuity. In the following narrative, Ruth Abad, who came to the United States in her thirties, contrasted the controlled sexuality of Filipinas in the Philippines with the perceived promiscuity of white women in the United States:

In the Philippines, we always have chaperons when we go out. When we go to dances, we have our uncle, our grandfather, and auntie all behind us to make sure that we behave in the dance hall. Nobody goes necking outside. You don't even let a man put his hand on your shoulders. When you were brought up in a conservative country, it is hard to come here and see that it is all freedom of speech and freedom of action. Sex was never mentioned in our generation. I was thirty already when I learned about sex. But to the young generation in America, sex is nothing.

Similarly, Ofelia Velasco criticized the way young American women are raised: "Americans are so liberated. They allow their children, their girls, to go out even when they are still so young." In contrast, she stated that "the Filipino way, it is very important, the value of the woman, that she is a virgin when she gets married."

The discourse of "American" female sexual promiscuity has even been directed at U.S.-born and -raised Filipinas. This lumping together can have tragic consequences. In 1961, at eighteen years old, Belinda Alegado reluctantly left her home in Seattle to attend college in the Philippines. Belinda's parents insisted on the move because they wanted her eventually to marry a Filipino. Belinda was unprepared for the attention that she received from her classmates in Manila: "At school, they made me into a celebrity because that was the first time that they saw somebody 'from abroad,' as they would say." This unwanted attention turned violent one evening when a group of young Filipino men sexually molested Belinda. Belinda linked the attack to her perceived "Americanness": "I think the people there, my age group, felt that because I was from the States that I was supposed to be so Americanized, to be free and loose and stuff like that. And I was taken advantage of seriously."

The ideal "Filipina," then, is partially constructed out of the community's conceptualization of white women. She is everything that they are not: she is sexually modest and dedicated to her family; they are sexually promiscuous and uncaring. Within the context of the dominant culture's pervasive hypersexualization of Filipina women, the construction of the "ideal" Filipina—as family oriented and chaste—can be read as an effort to reclaim the morality of the community. This effort erases the Filipina "bad girl," ignores competing sexual practices in the Filipino communities, and uncritically embraces the myth of "Oriental femininity." Cast as the embodiment of perfect womanhood and genuine exotic femininity, Filipinas (and other Asian women) in recent years have been idealized in U.S. popular culture as more truly "feminine" (that is, devoted, dependent, domestic) and therefore more desirable than their more modern, emancipated white sisters. Capitalizing on this image of the "superfemme," mail-order bride agencies market Filipinas as " 'exotic, subservient wife imports' for sale and as alternatives for men sick of independent 'liberal' Western women."[33]

Embodying the moral integrity of the idealized ethnic community, immigrant women, particularly young daughters, are expected to comply with male-defined criteria of what constitutes "ideal" feminine virtues. While the sexual behavior of adult women is confined to a monogamous, heterosexual context, that of young women is denied completely.[34] In the next section, I detail the ways Filipino immigrant parents, under the rubric of "cultural preservation," police their daughters' behaviors in order to safeguard their sexual innocence and virginity.[35] These attempts at policing generate hierarchies and tensions within immigrant families—between parents and children and between brothers and sisters.

THE CONSTRUCTION(S) OF THE "IDEAL" FILIPINA: "BOYS ARE BOYS AND GIRLS ARE DIFFERENT"

As the designated "keepers of the culture,"[36] immigrant women and their behavior come under intensive scrutiny from both men and women of their own groups and from U.S.-born Americans.[37] In a study of the Italian Harlem community from 1880 to 1950, Orsi reports that "all the community's fears for the reputation and integrity of the domus came to focus on the behavior of young women."[38] Because women's moral and sexual loyalties were deemed central to the maintenance of group status, changes in female behavior, especially that of growing daughters, were interpreted as signs of moral decay and ethnic suicide and were carefully monitored and sanctioned.[39]

Although details vary, young women across groups, space, and time—for example, second-generation Chinese women in San Francisco in the 1920s, U.S.-born Italian women in East Harlem in the 1930s, young Mexican women in the Southwest during the interwar years, and daughters of Caribbean and Asian Indian immigrants on the East Coast in the 1990s—have all identified strict parental control on their activities and movements as the primary source of intergenerational conflict.[40] Recent studies of immigrant families also have identified gender as a significant determinant of parent-child conflict, with daughters more likely than sons to be involved in such conflicts and instances of parental derogation.[41]

Although immigrant families have always been preoccupied with passing on culture, language, and traditions to both male and female children, it is daughters who bear the unequal burden of protecting and preserving the family name. Because sons do not have to conform to the image of an "ideal" ethnic subject as daughters do, they often receive special day-to-day privileges denied to daughter.[42] This is not to say that immigrant parents do not have unreasonable expectations of their sons; it is rather that these expectations do not pivot around the sons' sexuality or dating choices. In contrast, parental control over the movement and action of daughters begins the moment she is perceived as a young adult and sexually vulnerable. It regularly consists of monitoring her whereabouts and forbidding dating.[43] For example, the immigrant parents I interviewed seldom allowed their daughters to date, to stay out late, to spend the night at a friend's house, or to take an out-of-town trip.

Many of the second-generation women I spoke to complained bitterly about these parental restrictions. Debra Ragaza railed against her parents' constant surveillance:

> I couldn't get along with my family, especially my father . . . because of the experience of being the girl . . . the surveillance. I would get in so much trouble because they wouldn't let me go out, not even to the front yard even, let alone going to a dance or going out with my girlfriends, or just friends in general. And they just say, "No!" That's it. And I'm like: "Why? Why? Why? Is it because I'm a girl?" They wouldn't let me out, and I hated them for that.

These young women particularly resented what they saw as gender inequity in their families: the fact that their parents placed far more restrictions on their activities than on their brothers' activities. Maricela Rebaya talks about this double standard: "My parents are very strict. I guess I grew up shy because of them being strict. I don't go out at all normally. They put a guilt trip on you. It's more like the guys can do anything. Boy, oh boy, they can brag about girls and my parents won't say anything. But wait till we start talking." Some women decried the fact that even their *younger* brothers had more freedom than they did. Genelle Calderon complained: "It was really hard growing up because my parents would let my younger brothers do what they wanted but I didn't get to do what I wanted even though I was the oldest. I had a curfew and my brothers didn't. I had to ask if I could go places, and they didn't. My parents never even asked my brothers when they were coming home."

Some Filipino American brothers, such as Arturo Caponong, are cognizant of the double standard in their families:

> My sister would always say to me, "It's not fair, just because you are a guy, you can go wherever you want." I think my parents do treat me and my sister differently. Like in high school, maybe 10:30 at night, which is pretty late on a school night, and I say I have to go pick up some notes at my friend's house, my parents wouldn't say anything. But if my sister were to do that, they would be "No way!" Even now, when my sister is in college already, if she wants to leave at midnight to go to a friend's house, they would tell her that she shouldn't do it.

Even though Arturo empathized with his sister's frustration, he still sided with his parents in characterizing his sister's behavior as too "Americanized":

> I think my sister is too Americanized. Like, she sort of follows more of the American culture. She doesn't respect my parents sometimes in the way that I do. Even though she knows about the culture, I don't think she really puts herself in it, you know. Like my parents would tell her like, "You shouldn't go out right now, it's too late and you're a girl." And then instead of, like, maybe just be quiet and accept it or argue in a voice appropriate, she just go and go, "What do you mean? You are so old-fashioned." I mean, in a really high tone like disrespecting them. Like, I know she's got a right to be mad and everything, but I still feel that she shouldn't yell at them like that because she should respect what they are trying to tell her, they're just looking out for her.

In some instances, older brothers actively participate in the policing of their younger sisters. Roberto Pasquil, who described his own childhood as "idyllic" and "carefree," violently restricted his younger sister's actions:

> When my sister was involved with a guy who was a gangster, we were against it, and I dealt with her harshly. I would beat her. One beating was I caught her smoking and I slapped her around real good. Her friends really influenced her. She knew how to play the game. She knew when to get out of school and do the manipulating and not tell Mom what's going on. She was smart, she was streetwise.

When questioned about this double standard, parents such as Ofelia Velasco responded by pointing to the fact that "girls are different":

> I have that Filipino mentality that boys are boys and girls are different. Girls are supposed to be protected, to be clean. In the early years, my daughters have to have chaperons and curfews. And they know that they have to be virgins until they get married. The girls always say that is not fair. What is the difference between their brothers and them? And my answer always is, "In the Philippines, you know, we don't do that. The girls stay home. The boys go out." It was the way that I was raised. I still want to have part of that culture instilled in my children. And I want them to have that to pass on to their children.

Even among self-described Western-educated and "tolerant" parents, many continue to ascribe to the "Filipino way" when it comes to raising daughters. As Pedro Gonzales, a college-educated immigrant father, explained,

> Because of my Western education, I don't raise my children the way my parents raised me. I tended to be a little more tolerant. But at times, especially in certain issues like dating, I find myself more towards the Filipino way in the sense that I have only one daughter so I tended to be a little bit stricter. So the double standard kind of operates: it's alright for the boys to explore the field, but I tended to be overly protective of my daughter. My wife feels the same way because the boys will not lose anything, but the daughter will lose something, their virginity, and it can be also a question of losing face, that kind of thing.

Although many parents generally discourage dating or forbid their daughters to date, they still fully expect these young women to fulfill their traditional roles as women: to marry and have children. Eleonor Ocampo recounted the mixed messages she received from her parents:

> This is the way it is supposed to work. Okay, you go to school. You go to college. You graduate. You find a job. *Then* you find your husband, and you have children. That's the whole time line. *But* my question is, if you are not allowed to date, how are you supposed to find your husband? They say "no" to the whole dating scene because that is secondary to your education, secondary to your family. They do push marriage, but at a later date. So basically my parents are telling me that I should get married and I should have children but that I should not date.

In an important study of second-generation Filipino Americans in Northern California, Wolf reports the same pattern of parental pressures: parents expect daughters to remain virgins until marriage, to have a career, *and* to combine their work lives with marriage and children.[44]

The restrictions on girls' movement sometimes spill over to the realms of academics. Dasgupta and DasGupta recount that in the Indian American community, while young men were expected to attend faraway competitive colleges, many of their female peers were encouraged by their parents to go to the local colleges so that they could live at or close to home.[45] Similarly, Wolf reports that some Filipino parents pursued contradictory tactics with their children, particularly their daughter, by pushing them to achieve academic excellence in high school, but then "pulling the emergency brake" when they contemplated college by expecting them to stay at home, even if it meant going to a less competitive college, or not going at all.[46] In the following account, Eleonor Ocampo related that her parents' desire to "protect" her surpassed their concerns for her academic preparation:

> My brother [was] given a lot more opportunity educationally. He was given the opportunity to go to Miller High School[47] that has a renowned college preparatory program but which [in order to attend] you have to be bussed out of our area. I've come from a college prep program in junior high and I was asked to apply for the program at Miller. But my parents said, "No, absolutely not." This was even during the time, too, when Southside [the neighborhood high school] had one of the lowest test scores in the state of California. So it was like, "You know, Mom, I'll get a better chance at Miller." "No, no, you're going to Southside. There is no ifs, ands, or buts. Miller is too far. What if something happens to you?" But two years later, when my brother got ready to go on to high school, he was allowed to go

to Miller. My sister and I were like, "Obviously, whose education do you value more? If you're telling us that education is important, why do we see a double standard?"

The above narratives suggest that the process of parenting is gendered in that immigrant parents tend to restrict the autonomy, mobility, and personal decision making of their daughters more than that of their sons. I argue that these parental restrictions are attempts to construct a model of Filipino womanhood that is chaste, modest, nurturing, and family-oriented. Women are seen as responsible for holding the cultural line, maintaining racial boundaries, and marking cultural difference. This is not to say that parent-daughter conflicts exist in all Filipino immigrant families. Certainly, Filipino parents do not respond in a uniform way to the challenges of being racial-ethnic minorities, and I met parents who have had to change some of their ideas and practices in response to their inability to control their children's movements and choices. The following statements provide a sample:

I have three girls and one boy. I used to think that I wouldn't allow my daughters to go dating and things like that, but there is no way I could do that. I can't stop it. It's the way of life here in America. Sometimes you kind of question yourself, if you are doing what is right. It is hard to accept but you got to accept it. That's the way they are here.

Immigrant father

My children are born and raised here, so they do pretty much what they want. They think they know everything. I can only do so much as a parent. . . . When I try to teach my kids things, they tell me that I sound like an old record. They even talk back to me sometimes. . . . The first time my daughter brought her boyfriend to the house, she was eighteen years old. I almost passed away, knocked out. Lord, tell me what to do?

Immigrant mother

My children grew up here and they are Americanized. They know the American way of living. So you cannot really interject what you are used to in the Philippines because they were not raised in the Philippines.

Immigrant father

In the Philippines, I had a chaperon, even when I was engaged already to my husband. But it's really different here. We tried [to be strict] with our oldest daughter, and I think it caused more problems. It didn't work. So it was tough but we learned from her. With the next one, we didn't interfere.

Immigrant mother

These narratives call attention to the shifts in the generational power caused by the migration process and to the possible gap between what parents say they want for their children and their ability to control them.[48] However, the interview data do suggest that intergenerational conflicts are socially recognized occurrences in the Filipino communities. Even when respondents themselves had not experienced intergenerational tensions, they could always recall a cousin, a girlfriend, or a friend's daughter who had.

SANCTIONS AND REACTIONS: "THAT IS NOT WHAT A DECENT FILIPINO GIRL SHOULD DO"

I do not wish to suggest that immigrant communities are the only ones that regulate their daughter's mobility and sexuality. Feminist scholars have long documented the construction, containment, and exploitation of women's sexuality in various societies.[49] We also know that the cultural anxiety over unbounded female sexuality is most apparent with regard to adolescent girls.[50] The difference is in the ways that immigrant and nonimmigrant families sanction girls' sexuality. To control sexually assertive girls nonimmigrant parents rely on the gender-based good girl–bad girl dichotomy in which "good girls" are passive, threatened sexual objects while "bad girls" are active, desiring sexual agents.[51] Dasgupta and DasGupta write, "[T]he two most pervasive images of women across cultures are the goddess and whore, the good and bad women."[52] This good girl–bad girl cultural story conflates femininity with sexuality, increases women's vulnerability to sexual coercion, and justifies women's containment in the domestic sphere.

Immigrant families, though, have an additional strategy: they can discipline their daughters as racial/national subjects as well as gendered ones. That is, as self-appointed guardians of "authentic" cultural memory, immigrant parents can attempt to regulate their daughters' independent choices by linking them to cultural ignorance or betrayal. As both parents and children recounted, young women who disobeyed parental strictures were often branded "nonethnic," "untraditional," "radical," "selfish," and not "caring about the family." Female sexual choices were also linked to moral degeneracy defined in relation to a narrative of a hegemonic white norm. Parents were quick to warn their daughters about "bad" Filipinas who had become pregnant outside of marriage.[53] As in the case of "bar girls" in the Philippines, Filipina Americans who veered from acceptable behaviors were deemed "Americanized"—women who have adopted the sexual mores and practices of white women. As one Filipino immigrant father described the "Americanized" Filipinas: "They are spoiled because they have seen the American way. They go out at night. Late at night. They go out on dates. Smoking. They have sex without marrying."

To the second-generation daughters, these charges are stinging. The young women I interviewed were visibly pained—with many breaking down and crying—when they recounted their parents' charges. This deep pain, stemming in part from their desire to be validated as Filipinas, existed even among the more "rebellious" daughters. As twenty-four-year-old Amanda Flores explained:

> My mom is very traditional. She wants to follow the Filipino customs, just really adhere to them, like what is proper for a girl, what she can and can't do, and what other people are going to think of her if she doesn't follow that way. When I pushed these restrictions, when I rebelled and stayed out later than allowed, my mom would always say, "That is not what a decent Filipino girl should do. You should come home at a decent hour. What are people going to think of you?" And that would get me really upset, you know, because I think that my character is very much the way it should be for a Filipina. I wear my hair long, I wear decent makeup. I dress properly, conservative. I am family oriented. It hurts me that she doesn't see that I am decent, that I am proper, and that I am not going to bring shame to the family or anything like that.

Debra Ragaza expressed a similar sentiment:

> When I lived with my parents, I was going out all the time . . . just hanging out with my girlfriends. And they didn't like that because I was coming home at two in the morning. But I try to tell them [that] we're not doing anything bad . . . that was my defense growing up. "I'm not doing anything bad. Jut because I'm out doesn't mean I'm bad."

These narratives suggest that even when parents are unable to control their children's behavior, their (dis)approval remains powerful in shaping the emotional lives of their daughters.[54] Even as she rebelled against her parents' restrictions, Debra Ragaza continued to seek their approval: "I was just really in a rebellious stage. . . . But I would never want my parents to find out that I was dating behind their back. I'd do anything to cover up. Any notes that I got I would hide them in a box under my bed, you know, any kind of evidence, just get rid of it so that I would have my parents believing that I was paying attention to them and not disobeying them." Although better-off parents can and do exert greater controls over their children's behaviors than poorer parents, I would argue that *all* immigrant parents—regardless of class backgrounds—possess this emotional hold on their children. Therein lies the source of their power: as immigrant parents, they have the authority to determine if their daughters are "authentic" members of their racial-ethnic community. Largely unacquainted with the "home" country, U.S.-born children depend on their parents' tutelage to craft and affirm their ethnic self and thus are particularly vulnerable to charges of cultural ignorance and/or betrayal.[55] Since U.S.-born Filipinas are also excluded from full American membership (see chapter 8), the parental accusation of "you are not Filipina enough" essentially strips the second generation of all meaningful identity, rendering them doubly "homeless." Thus the emotional hold that immigrant parents have on their children is their unique ability to strip them of identity in what might, in nonimmigrant family quarrels, be no more than a heated exchange about curfew violations by a teenager.[56]

Despite the emotional pain, many young Filipinas I interviewed contest and negotiate parental restrictions in their daily lives. Faced with parental restrictions on their mobility, young Filipinas struggle to gain some control over their social lives, particularly over dating. In many cases, daughters simply misinform their parents of their whereabouts or date without their parents' knowledge. Mona Ampon listed the strategies that she used as a teenager to escape her parents' surveillance:

> [In high school,] I was very policed by my parents, like I couldn't have a boyfriend. They kept saying, "You can't date. You can't have a boyfriend until you finish college." I thought it was unfair because I saw other people had boyfriends in high school and being able to date. So I would have to resort to, you know, doing it behind my parents' back. Like, I would sneak out when my parents are away out of town, I would go on dates. . . . Like, I would say I am going over to a friend's house to spend the night and then I would go out on a date . . . or I would tell my mom that I was going out with a bunch of girls . . . and then just like after school, just hanging out with my boyfriend until when my parents were supposed to be home and then I would take off for my house. I was bad!

Amanda Flores said that she had to "rebel" to "experience life":

> I mean, when I look back on it now, if I could call them my rebellious years, but I think if I hadn't done that, I would have been very sheltered. I felt like I had to be rebellious in order for me to experience life to that extent. Otherwise, I would just be home and help with the dishes and cleaning and

> cleaning and that would have been my life. And I wouldn't have experienced anything outside of that.

Other women rebel by vowing to remain fiercely independent and/or to create more egalitarian relationships with their own husbands and children. Wary of losing her independence, Anne Sotelo vowed to remain unmarried as long as possible:

> I don't see myself as married, period. I think marriage is a beautiful thing for other people but I am terrified of it for me. And I am afraid of losing my individuality. Now that I finally reach the point where I am my own person and I am just terrified of having my identity taken away from me, ya know, to go from being Anne Sotelo to being someone's wife and then to become someone's mother and someday progresses to grandmother.

Genelle Calderon, who is married to a white American, explained why she chose to marry a non-Filipino:

> In high school, I dated mostly Mexican and Filipino. It never occurred to me to date a white or black guy. I was not attracted to them. But as I kept growing up and my father and I were having all these conflicts, I knew that if I married a Mexican or a Filipino, they would be exactly like my father. And so I tried to date anyone that would not remind me of my dad. A lot of my Filipina friends that I grew up with had similar experiences. So I knew that it wasn't only me. I was determined to marry a white person because he would treat me as an individual.[57]

Rose Dumlao developed a feminist consciousness in reaction to her father's overbearing chauvinism: "I think that's why I'm so feminist in my views because my dad's so chauvinistic. He gives my brother everything and I have to do like ten times as much to get the same kind of respect that my brother does." Eleonor Ocampo who was labeled "radical" by her parents indicated that she would be more open-minded in raising her own children: "I see myself as very traditional in upbringing but I don't see myself as constricting on my children one day, and I wouldn't put the gender roles on them. I wouldn't lock them into any particular way of behaving." It is important to note that even as these Filipinas desired new gender norms and practices for their own families, the majority hoped that their children would remain connected to Filipino culture. Debra Ragaza, as bitter as she was about her relationship with her parents, still professed that "if I had children, I'd want them to grow up with my family and my relatives and not be cut off from the family and the Filipino culture like I was."

My respondents also reported more serious reactions to parental restrictions, recalling incidents of someone they knew who had run away, joined gangs, or attempted suicide. Maria Gomez, a Filipina high school counselor, reported that most of the Filipinas with whom she worked "are really scared because a lot of them know friends that are pregnant and they all pretty much know girls who have attempted suicide." Mona Ampon poignantly described the "pressure" that led some second-generation Filipinas to contemplate suicide:

> I think it's the whole Filipino upbringing of their kids was so strict that you can't confide in your parents . . . when it comes to identity. I couldn't relate to my parents . . . and also they grew up in the Philippines so they didn't understand what it was for me growing up in the U.S., how hard it was for me. . . . And so it was a problem too with all my other Filipino friends that, you know, we were like, had long discussions on the phone at night, and they would tell me that they were contemplating to commit suicide, that kind of thing, because they were just so unhappy. And I think that pressure of having to be a certain way and then always being policed in a certain way, it really drives you to, you know, where you're really scattered. You're not happy because you know you have to satisfy your parents and living up to all these expectations that are placed upon the Filipino daughter. She has all these duties that she has to fulfill. And then having to also want to live that mainstream experience, 'cuz that's what everybody else is doing. And wanting to be accepted and not being able to do that. And then having nobody to confide in.

A 1995 random survey of San Diego public high schools conducted by the Federal Centers for Disease Control and Prevention (CDC) found that, in comparison to other ethnic groups, Filipino female students had the highest rates of seriously considering suicide (45.6 percent) as well as the highest rates of actually attempting suicide (23 percent) in the year preceding the survey. In comparison, 33.4 percent of Latinas, 26.2 percent of white women, and 25.3 percent of black women surveyed said they had suicidal thoughts.[58]

◆ ◆ ◆

Mainstream American society defines white middle-class culture as the norm and whiteness as the unmarked marker of others' differentness.[59] In this chapter, I have shown how idealized descriptions of the virtue of immigrant daughters allow aggrieved groups to turn negative ascription into affirmation, and to attribute their own marginalization to the deficient morality of their oppressors. Like other immigrant groups, Filipino immigrants use the largely gendered discourse of morality as one strategy to mark and decenter whiteness and to locate themselves above the dominant group, demonizing it in the process. In particular, they criticize

American family life, American individualism, and American women.[60] In so doing, they racialize whiteness by marking it as sexually and morally deviant. Enforced by distorting powers of memory and nostalgia, this rhetoric of moral superiority often leads to patriarchal calls for cultural "authenticity," which locates family honor and national integrity in its female members. Because the policing of women's bodies is one of the main means of asserting moral superiority, young women face numerous restrictions on their autonomy, mobility, and personal decision making. This practice of cultural (re)construction reveals how deeply the conduct of private life can be tied to larger social structures.

The construction of white Americans as the "other" and American culture as deviant serves a dual purpose: it allows immigrant communities to reinforce patriarchy through the sanctioning of women's (mis)behavior *and* to present an unblemished, if not morally superior, public face to the dominant society. Strong in family values, heterosexual morality, and a hierarchical family structure, this public face erases the Filipina "bad girl" and ignores competing (im)moral practices in the Filipino communities. Through the oppression of Filipino women and the criticism of white women's immorality, the immigrant community attempts to exert its moral superiority over the dominant Western culture and to reaffirm to itself its self-worth in the face of economic, social, political, and legal subordination. In other words, Filipino families forge cultural resistance against racial oppression by stressing female chastity and sacrifice, yet they reinforce patriarchal power and gendered oppression by hinging ethnic and racial pride on the performance of gender subordination. This form of cultural resistance severely restricts women's lives, particularly those of the second generation, and casts the family as a site of potentially the most intense conflict and oppressive demands in immigrant lives. In the next chapter, I discuss some of the public sites within which second-generation Filipino Americans have constructed home for themselves.

CHAPTER 8

"What of the Children?"

Emerging Homes and Identities

Cultural identity is a matter of "becoming" as well as of "being." It belongs to the future as much as to the past. It is not something which already exists, transcending place, time, history and culture. Cultural identities come from somewhere, have histories. But, like everything which is historical, they undergo constant transformation.

Stuart Hall, "Cultural Identity and Diaspora"

I think being Filipino American is being constantly at odds with who you are as opposed to being a white American pretty much knowing where everything fits in for you.

Rose Camacho, second-generation Filipina American

When asked why they chose to move their families from the Philippines to the United States, Filipino immigrant parents would say, "We did it for the children." In the United States, they believe, their children would have better health care, education, and job opportunities. As we learned in chapter 4, even when immigrant parents desired to return to the Philippines permanently, their children's welfare often mandated against such a move. This chapter discusses what it is like to grow up as young Filipinos in San Diego, paying particular attention to contestations over terms of inclusion, to instances of cross-group alliances, and to the constant transformation of ethnic identities. The point of my analysis is not to determine the extent to which second-generation Filipino Americans have retained their "original" culture or adopted the "American" culture. To do so would be to accept the essentialist position that identity is bipolar as suggested by the assimilationist and pluralist schools, that is, that one gravitates toward either the pole of assimilation or the pole of nativism.[1] Rather, my interest is in the strategies these Filipino Americans have used to construct distinct new cultures and subcultures and to rework dominant ideologies about their place in the United States. As Renato Rosaldo points out, immigrants and their children are not positioned in a singular unified manner but rather "live at the intersection of multiple subject positions."[2] In addition to my interview data, this chapter draws on quantitative data from the Children of Immigrants Longitudinal Study (CILS) conducted in San Diego in 1992 and again in 1995.

GROWING UP FILIPINO: "I DIDN'T FIT IN"

The CILS data indicate that of the approximately eight hundred Filipino high school students surveyed in 1995, close to two-thirds reported that they had experienced racial and ethnic discrimination. Among those suffering discrimination, it is important to note, their own race or nationality were the overwhelming forces perceived to account for that unfair treatment (66.8 percent of boys and 73.3 percent of girls).[3] My interviews with forty children of Filipino immigrants, ranging in age from seventeen to thirty-five, corroborate these findings: the majority related that they were ignored, teased, harassed, or ostracized by their peers because of their perceived racial difference. At the same time, reflecting the complexities of identities and identifications in contemporary United States, many Filipino San Diegans have ongoing relations—both cooperative and antagonistic—with multiple racial and ethnic groups. According to the 1995 CILS data, about 90 percent of the students surveyed stated that they had Filipino friends. But their circle of friends also included other racial and ethnic groups: more than 40 percent reported having (non-Filipino) Asian friends; about a quarter had Latino friends; 18 percent had white friends; and close to 4 percent had African American friends.[4] These data suggest that white American culture, while still prominent, is no longer the only point of reference from which young Filipino Americans construct their identities. To understand the complexity of young Filipino lives, in this section I examine their interaction with the local groups in their communities. Not surprisingly, the family's choice of residence and school plays a major role in structuring the children's friendship patterns.

Multiracial Neighborhoods

Reflecting the long history of racial and class segregation in San Diego, multiracial neighborhoods house primarily working-class families, including a high number of Navy families.[5] According to the 1992 CILS data, 43 percent of the respondent's fathers and 28 percent of the mothers were in either blue-collar or low-wage service jobs, and more than 50 percent of the fathers worked for or were retired from the U.S. Navy.[6] In these neighborhoods, Filipino youngsters mingle and collide with other Filipinos as well as with those in other groups of color. Arturo Caponong, son of a U.S. Navy steward, had fond memories of his tight-knit Filipino neighborhood in National City, where he lived until he was thirteen: "All my friends were Filipino. We were a close community. It was almost like that one street, you know, maybe a strip of eight to ten houses, it was like a gigantic family. . . . All my friends' parents, I would call aunt or uncle. And they would know like each other's parents." As discussed in chapter 5, what bonded these families was their shared military experience:

> Five out of those eight or ten houses were Navy people. The reason why I know who the ones are in the military is because the fathers were even more close because, you know, in terms of ranking, they would always know when someone went up, and got promoted, and they would have a party to celebrate, and everyone would know the other person's father. I don't think we could ever have a party without like a whole bunch of military people because so many Filipinos were in the Navy.

In Arturo's neighborhood, many of the mothers also had the same jobs, providing yet another bond for these families: "And the moms, they had this carpool thing going from National City to the job. . . . They all worked in assembly line–type jobs. They all carpool together, and they eat their lunch together. They would all come over when we have a birthday party or some celebration." These Filipino Navy families also shared other rituals, such as weekly trips to church and the commissary. According to Jovy Lopez, "It used to be a joke; most of the Filipinos are Catholics so we'd go to church and then after church you would see the same families at the commissary and the Navy Exchange and you would see them and they would look at you and acknowledge you."

These Filipino events pull the second generation into a Filipino-centered universe in which they can "hang out" with other Filipinos, eat

Filipino food, enjoy Filipino music, and listen to spoken Tagalog, even if they themselves cannot speak it. Ella Labao, an active community organizer, attributed her activism to her early socialization at these Filipino community affairs:

> Our whole family is involved in the community. So . . . all my life practically, I have been going to Filipino functions. I remember when I went to my first dinner and dance with [my parents]. I was maybe eight years old, and I danced with my dad and it was really fun, you know, and then after going to all those different functions, I'd meet all my parents' friends and then all of a sudden, I'd have a lot of aunties and uncles. That's why I started getting involved with the Filipino community when I was maybe sixteen years old. It was just something I knew that I wanted to get involved with.

For many young Filipinas, these get-togethers provided a meaningful space to discuss their lives as daughters of immigrant parents. Mona Ampon cherished the times that she shared with other Filipinas: "There was really a comfortable feeling because you ate the same food and you stay up late and watch videos and talk . . . because you know your parents are playing mah-jongg and socializing with their friends." These late-night talks invariably pivoted around the young women's often-stormy relationships with their parents—a forum to vent their frustrations over the numerous restrictions on their autonomy and mobility. For Mona, "trading stories" with like-minded Filipinas helped her to weather the difficult teen years:

> I was just really in a rebellious stage, you know, and I just thought that my parents were being really unfair. I was very policed by my parents. That was one thing that was good about having other Filipino women, you know, when we had these little get-togethers, we always talked about these kinds of stuff. You know, things like "if my parents ever found out this and that, this is what they would do. . . . " Talking about those kinds of things and sharing our upbringing. That really helped.

As these narratives suggest, the family and community get-togethers thrive because they nurture and reinforce Filipino claims to "community" and "home." But as Karin Aguilar-San Juan reminds us, evocations of home and community—as a claim to truth, originary places, and authenticating devices—are often problematic because they signal who is "in" but also who is not.[7] For example, Grace Espartero, a multiracial Filipina, did not feel "at home" at these Filipino get-togethers. Grace's father was a Filipino immigrant and her mother a third-generation white American. Her paternal grandparents disapproved of the interracial marriage and often slighted Grace's mother at family functions. As the following excerpt indicates, Grace felt excluded because she was perceived to be "not Filipino enough":

> I hated going to my father's side. I saw them not real often, like Easter, Christmas, and there are a whole bunch of birthdays. . . . It was always uncomfortable because . . . I wasn't that close like everybody else who would go there all the time. Most of my cousins, I don't know who they are. They all knew each other. . . . I felt uncomfortable because I was half white too 'cuz I could see how they treated my mom, and her reactions were like a fight, and then I'd see that and I'd feel like they were doing that to me, too. I think also because I didn't understand what they were saying 'cuz they had very heavy accents, and it used to make me uncomfortable because I didn't know how to answer them. Just the fact that I didn't know all the cultures . . . and I thought if I did something wrong they would get really mad.

Henry Aguilar, who is gay, also felt uneasy at Filipino functions because his gayness often collided with the group's notion of what constituted Filipinoness:

> It's really hard. I'm still finding it hard to go out to a Filipino gathering knowing that a lot of people would probably reject me if they find out that I am gay, because there aren't too many liberal-minded Filipinos out there. I mean, I can tell because when I go to my sister's party, a lot of Filipino guys who gather around drinking and talking about girls and all that and I can very much tell that if I say something about my lover, they will just stop the conversation or talk about something else.

Tension also emerged between Philippine-born and U.S.-born Filipinos. Dario Villa, who immigrated to San Diego at the age of seventeen, reported that he faced "overt racism" from the local Filipino Americans:

> When we arrived in San Diego in 1976, I attended Montgomery High School in South San Diego. I was happy to be there because I saw many Filipino faces that reminded me of home. . . . To my surprise, I offended many Filipinos because I was an "FOB"—"fresh off the boat." I was ridiculed because my accent reminded them of their parents. It was their shame coming out at my expense. I was a reminder of the image they hate, part of themselves. The overt racism from the Filipino Americans broke my heart. . . . So I had very few Filipino friends in high school, not because I didn't want to be friends with them, but because they didn't want to be friends with somebody who was their own but not really theirs.

U.S.-born Eleonor Ocampo admitted that in her quest to fit in with the high school crowds, she would harass the recently immigrated Filipinos:

> In high school, we were at an age where we didn't want to be seen as the FOB, fresh-off-the-boat type of stereotype. And we were so bad that we would tease people who recently immigrated who had an accent. They would be, like, speaking the language and we would be, like, walking down the hall, "Why don't you guys learn English?" We would be as rude as that.

Joseph Gonzalez likewise acknowledged that he and his friends used to snub the "FOBs": "The people who were fresh from the Philippines, we did not hang around them at all. I had this unfortunate belief that the newcomers were not as good as the people who were born here: they talked weird; they didn't understand the language; they dressed differently." Grace, Henry, and Dario's vexed relationships with other Filipino Americans underscore the larger argument that I wish to make in this book: home, however nurturing and comforting, is by definition a place that is established as the exclusive domain of a few. In these cases, Filipinoness is defined as the exclusive domain of monoracial, heterosexual, and English-speaking Filipinos; all others, by definition, are constructed to be outside these carefully drawn and maintained boundaries.

Some young Filipinos have expanded their notion of home by building cross-racial relationships. Upon arrival in San Diego in 1988, Maricela Rebaya was thrust into the ninth grade of an underresourced school, where most of her classmates were African American, Laotian, Vietnamese, or Mexican. This new situation brought forth new understandings: "I became aware of different cultures, different races in America. I saw for myself how blacks are being discriminated against and things like that. Like, I was in R.O.T.C., and every time we would go to other campuses, we were the only ones that were minorities. The other schools were all white." It also produced new friendship patterns: "So most of my friends were black. And every time I am with my black friends, I notice how the cops are always all over the place. I really had a good idea then, you know, of how society works, that I couldn't get anywhere else." Coming from a working-class immigrant family, Maricela soon discovered that she had more in common with other working-class African Americans than she did with middle-class Filipinos:

> Some Filipinos . . . are so materialistic. Instead of supporting you, trying to help you get used to the place, they took advantage of you because you looked so different. They talk about you, and when they see you in swap meets, they say, "Oh, God, look where you shop!" Very materialistic. So it

> was a bad experience that I had with Filipinos my age. I didn't experience that with my black friends, I guess, because we are all poor. So they didn't bother us about what we wore.

Nicholas Santos likewise found that his African American friends were more accepting of his immigrant background than were his Filipino American classmates:

> It was weird because normally Filipinos will bond together, but I had more in common with my black friends than Filipino Americans who were born here. At that time, I felt that there was this mocking of anything Filipino by Filipino Americans who were born here and raised here. My best friend was black. He didn't mind my parents' accent, and he loved coming to the house and eating my mom's cooking.

In the same way, mocked by his Filipino American peers, Dario Villa "found comfort in the company of Mexicans, other FOBs, open-minded Filipinos, and others who accepted me unconditionally."

Other Filipino Americans built cross-racial friendships because they grew up alongside other groups of color. Jovy Lopez related that she felt "comfortable" in her "largely Hispanic and Filipino" neighborhood in Southeast San Diego:

> I always felt comfortable in junior high and high school growing up because there were other people just like us. I never went through stuff that some of my other friends that grew up in those kinds of neighborhoods where they were the only ones. . . . Growing up, there were always other Filipino kids in the neighborhood and other races. It was cool learning different words in Spanish from my friends and eating different foods and just knowing different things. After school, I had friends that were Mexican that I would just hang out with and we would just play together and ride bikes and go to each other's house and I would do that with my Filipino friends too. I didn't really have that many white friends; in fact some kids had to be bussed to my old elementary school to make it more diverse.

In the same way, Rose Dumblao recounted that many of her high school friends were Mexican and Puerto Rican: "I was hanging out with, like, all these Mexicans and Puerto Ricans. And I felt very comfortable because, you know, I knew how to associate with them. I mean, I knew what they call their 'lingo.' The way they spoke and what they said and what means what. So I didn't feel awkward at all." For Mona Ampon, Mexican culture was so prominent in her community that she grew up thinking that she *was* Mexican:

> There was a lot of Mexicans in our town so that was just part of the culture. . . . When I was growing up, I actually spoke Spanish because when I was three years old, when my mom was working the two jobs, she asked my neighbor to take care of me and she only spoke Spanish. So I learned Spanish. . . . And I grew up with the Mexican girls. I would have the braids, you know, with the loop braids and things like that. . . . I was even in the classes where they did the *folklorico* dancing.

These cross-racial friendships suggest that migration—and a shared class location—often bring forth new social relations and conditions. These new social relations, in turn, "bring new social subjects into being, and these subjects out of necessity create new epistemologies, ideas, and identities."[8] These new epistemologies, ideas, and identities have at times propelled interethnic struggles for social change. Paul Ambo participated in such a struggle. When Paul moved from Washington, D.C., to San Diego in 1968 at the age of twenty, he did not meet many Filipinos around his age. So he befriended Chicanos and dated Chicanas. His involvement in the Chicano community eventually brought him to City Hall to demonstrate for housing rights for Chicano migrant workers. He concluded his story by remarking wryly, "So I guess I was a Chicano activist." Paul's experience underscores the centrality of coalition work in contemporary political organizing. As Angela Davis points out, we can accomplish important things in the struggle for social justice if we focus on the creation of "unpredictable or unlikely coalitions grounded in political projects."[9]

But not all cross-racial encounters end in friendships. Mary Doria was taunted by her Mexican and African American classmates:

> I went to school in El Centro. It was, like, mostly black kids and Mexican. Just the teachers were white. The only other Filipinos in the school were my brother and my neighbors. Oh, God! I didn't like it at all. A lot of the kids would call us Chinese. They would come up and slant their eyes and say, "Chinese go home." And of course that hurt because no one had ever treated us like that before, and we didn't know why they were doing that because we weren't Chinese. We're Filipino.

Cecilia Pasallo endured similar mistreatment when her family moved from Hawaii to San Diego:

> When we moved here, I was discriminated against because I didn't fit in. I didn't dress like they did. I had very long hair, part in the middle. I was quiet. I kept to myself a lot and I read a lot. And I didn't wear makeup. And this was a low-income area and even though everybody was dressed poorly,

> if you weren't dressed like them, you weren't accepted. I got picked on by a lot of African Americans, I guess because I looked different and I didn't talk like they did. So most of my friends were Anglo American and Mexican American.

At the same time, some Filipino Americans espoused antiblack and anti-Latino rhetorics. Growing up along the U.S-Mexico border, Eleonor Ocampo witnessed many anti-Latino incidents:

> Where I grew up, it's a war zone down there with the border. So relations with Latinos and Mexican Americans were very negative. I remember people would say "wetback" around me, and I didn't understand what it meant. And so me and my schoolmates would use the phrase so flippantly. Through high school, the issue of undocumented workers, it was us and them, why don't they just leave our country and this and that. They were perceived as invaders to our home.

In the same way, the majority of the young Filipinos I interviewed, especially the women, reported that their parents forbade them to befriend African Americans. Eleonor Ocampo confided, "It's like an understood silence in my family; don't ever cross the line and marry an African American. It just saddens me because of the perception that my parents have of African Americans as being on welfare and lazy and crimes and gangs."

The above narratives suggest the following: all-Filipino and cross-racial friendships emerged in part out of shared experiences within the racial economy of the United States. Although personal affinities drew young people together, it was their families' racial and economic subordination that landed them in the same neighborhoods and schools. But the narratives also indicate that shared experiences with subordination do not always produce meaningful friendships and alliances. As George Lipsitz points out, "persecuted people often seek the subordination of others to win material advantages and psychic consolation for themselves."[10] Thus some Filipinos adopt anti-black and anti-Latino racism in an effort to secure ethnic inclusion for themselves. For their part, U.S.-born Filipinos, African Americans, and Mexican Americans taunt Dario, Nicholas, Mary, and Cecilia in part because they have internalized the anti-Asian and anti-immigrant rhetorics and practices that characterize so much of the culture and social structure in the United States.

White-Dominated Neighborhoods

A sizeable proportion of the post-1965 Filipino immigrants in San Diego are college-educated professionals who end up in the U.S. middle class. Of the students sampled for CILS, 30 percent of their fathers and almost 50 percent of their mothers had at least a college degree or more. The proportion of parents in white-collar occupations matches closely their educational attainment, with almost 60 percent of the mothers and 40 percent of the fathers in white-collar positions. Additionally, almost 75 percent of those sampled come from families that own their home, a strong indicator of middle-class status.[11]

Like other highly trained immigrants, professional Filipino immigrants are dispersed among and within metropolitan regions and thus seldom form tight-knit ethnic communities.[12] The majority live in white-dominated suburban neighborhoods, where they often are the lone Filipino family.[13] This is not to say that Filipino suburbanites are wholly isolated from other Filipinos. Although they may not live in immigrant neighborhoods, many actively maintain social ties with friends and kin through membership in various professional and alumni organizations and through family get-togethers in both the United States and the Philippines. However, from the perspective of the second generation, these "ethnic events" are periodic, brief, and disconnected from their otherwise white-dominated environment. As Armando Alvarez explained, "Being Filipino was an event, it was going to a party on the weekend with my parents and eating Filipino food; that's when I was a Filipino. It was periodic and external. . . . We only associated with Filipinos, mostly my parents' friends, two, three, or maybe four times a year. The rest of the year, it didn't come into play."

In this largely white environment, young Filipinos reported that they were often teased, harassed, or excluded from social cliques and events. Pablo Barcenas remembered that he had to learn early on to fend off racial insults:

> I grew up in a neighborhood that was primarily white. I went to an all-white school. They always made fun of me and this other Chinese kid. It was really stereotypical jokes. I guess at the time, I just kinda had to play it off just like a survival thing because, you know, I was just by myself. But the jokes, when you're a kid, they hurt. Like my eyes aren't even slanted, but they'd always give the Japanese eye thing, they'd always called me a "Nip" or a "Chink" or something.

Elaine Reyes, who grew up in a North San Diego suburb, where "all the people in the popular group at school were white and blond" remembered being snubbed by her white schoolmates: "When I was growing up . . . the other kids snub me. I realize now that it wasn't because I wasn't fun to play with; it was because I wasn't white. Like not being able to spend the night at some girl's house because her parents were too uptight about race. At the time, I thought there was something wrong with me." Elaine's most painful memory was of being rejected by her boyfriend's parents in high school: "I was dating this white guy in high school. His parents basically forced him to stop going out with me because I wasn't white. They didn't even know that I was Filipino. They thought I was Chinese. It broke my heart. I was pissed."

But not all Filipinos who live in middle-class suburban neighborhoods are well-educated professionals. I met Filipinos who toiled in blue-collar or low-wage service jobs but who—through "pinching pennies," pooling incomes, and working multiple jobs—managed to own homes in middle-class communities. For example, Rosita Layug's parents were determined to move to a middle-class neighborhood, even if it meant taking on second jobs at a nearby ballpark, selling beer and nachos at night and on weekends. Like most other parents, Filipino immigrant parents covet these neighborhoods because of the "reputation of the school district." But for many of the second-generation children, moving from a largely immigrant, multiracial neighborhood to a predominantly white neighborhood entailed numerous social costs. As an example, Joseph Gonzalez grew up in a working-class community in southeast San Diego where there were "lots of blacks, lots of Filipinos, lots of Mexicans." His best friend was black; and most of his good friends were either Filipino or Mexican. When he turned twelve, his parents had saved enough money to move the family to a predominantly white neighborhood. For Joseph, it was a culture shock:

> At the time we moved there it was all white, probably 90 percent white. I remember distinctly the difference between the Anglos and the people who are of ethnicity where I used to live. Like music. We listened to heavy soul, whereas the people at my new place, they listened to rock and roll. I was like, "God, no one listens to rock and roll." And I was very proud that I listened to that soul music and I let people know that . . . so I got into some fights because of it. And I dressed differently. I talked differently. So I just didn't fit in.

In high school, not fitting in extended to dating. "I was attracted, I remember, to white girls," said Joseph. "But the Anglo girls really didn't accept me. That was what started my feelings of lower self-esteem. I was small and I was not white. So the girls were not attracted to me. That was a big issue for me."

Jo Laguda met with violence when his family moved to a predominantly white neighborhood: "When we first moved to Penasquitos in the seventies, we were among the first group of Filipinos to move in. I remember there were racial fights in front of my house between Filipinos and whites. And a very close friend who lived up the street had his house spray painted "Flips Go Home." I saw my brothers fighting in front of the house." Eleonor Ocampo likewise encountered blatant racism in her new neighborhood:

> When we first arrived, and I still remember it vividly, I remember we got out of the car and we looked at the house . . . and the neighborhood kids there, they started gathering around us and they were running away and they said, "Oh, gosh, niggers have moved in to the neighborhood." You know, you're standing there, and I remember I was in the fifth grade and I'm like, first of all, I am Filipino American; second of all, the term *nigger* was so derogatory. We were never accepted in that neighborhood, never. There would always be fights that were started by the other children against us, and that's when my brothers, my sister and I really pulled together because we had to protect each other.

To counter the social costs of being racially different, many young Filipino Americans strove to be "average American teenagers": to speak only English, to date and associate primarily with whites, and to slight Filipino culture. Joseph Gonzalez detailed his efforts "to be white":

> I tried whatever I could to assimilate like the other Anglos. I did a lot of Anglo things like surfing, skiing, and I listened to not real Filipino-type music. I did a lot of things that were almost anti-Filipino. I didn't hang around Filipinos. I didn't join Filipino organizations. And I really missed out. I really did, because I didn't have any real, real, true friends that could understand my culture. I was just setting myself up for being left out. And even the types of girls that I would go after were not the ones that would be attracted to me.

When Mona Ampon moved to the other side of town and attended a white-majority high school, she too developed an "identity crisis": "I had this identity crisis where I just wanted to be white. I guess the feeling of just wanting to be accepted. I started to recognize that, you know, people who were white who had blond hair and blue eyes were popular.

And that's what you want to be, you want that attention." Mona plotted to join the popular groups:

> What you had to do to be popular was basically you had to hang out with people who were white and they were usually wealthy, like they lived in the gated community. And they were the ones who threw the parties. So I joined the tennis team. Going through the tennis team, I met those girls and because I was playing really well, they wanted to practice with me. And that's where I started to be invited to parties. I remember trying to wear all the same brand-name clothes and stuff like that. I feel so sorry for my parents because, like, we used to go to these outlet stores and I made them wait, like, in these three-hour lines to get into the stores to buy me those clothes.

Even though Mona was invited to the parties, she never felt included: "During my senior year, I just got tired of the social scene because I was always getting hurt, you know, because I would think that these people were my friends and then they would talk behind my back." Rosita Layug also tried hard to fit in, with mixed results:

> The girls at my high school, they weren't mean to me, but I didn't really feel like a team player. I felt like I was some tagalong and I did almost anything to be friends with white people. Back then, even some of my good friends, they told me that some of the girls were just using me. But I was willing to do anything to be their friends.

A small group of Filipino Americans eventually managed to penetrate the all-white cliques, through honors courses, through sports, or through other school activities such as the school band and yearbook club. But most were forced to set aside their Filipino selves in the process. Raul Calderon related how he lost touch with his Filipino side during high school:

> In high school, most of my friends were white. So, say my friends were having a party, I really couldn't invite my cousins because they are not used to hanging out with white people. And they really couldn't invite me to their parties 'cause I wasn't used to hanging out with Filipinos. So at that point there was kind of a tension between me and some of my cousins. Some of them are very Filipino centered and some have only black friends.

In the same way, Pablo Bacenas felt "out of place" at all-Filipino events:

> When I went to this dance, it was all Filipino. I felt so out of place. I felt really weird. I have never seen so many young Filipinos in my life. It was just a funny feeling. I think I was just making the whole thing really hard

on myself, like, I didn't talk to anyone. I wasn't sure what to say. I guess I must have thought that I was supposed to act this way or something. I felt maybe there was something lacking in what I knew about myself. I stayed the whole dance, but I didn't dance. In my mind, I pictured they could pick me out of the whole crowd that I was different, that I was a little more like whiter, Americanized, or something.

In the following narrative, Joey Laguda details how excruciating it was for U.S.-born Filipinos like himself to strike a balance between the Filipino and white groups:

> I remember in high school I stopped a fight between the Filipinos that just moved to the States and some white people. That was really weird. I remember telling the Filipinos to knock it off. I said, "You make us all look bad" because I worked hard at that time to integrate myself, to make sure that there is no difference between Filipinos and white people. I didn't want to be associated with any negative feedback like, "Oh, Filipinos hate white people." But I saw both sides. I could see that it was hard for the new Filipinos to fit in. I see my brothers [who were born in the Philippines] having a hard time fitting in and having language barriers.

For Joey, being in the middle was more than he could handle:

> Basically, it was so much going back and forth that sometimes I lost myself. What the hell are these Filipinos doing? What the hell are these white people doing? So I was bouncing back and forth, and in trying to understand, I got caught up in a lot of things. . . . Since I wasn't a part of either group, I didn't quite fit in either model. I got really lost and I got involved in alcohol, drugs, and gangs. I just got into it, basically trying to understand what didn't really make much sense.

Although these personal narratives document on the individual level an acceptance of the given rules of U.S. society, they are important because they are part of a dialogue of domination. They reveal that young Filipinos live within and in tension with a racist system that defines white middle-class culture as the norm.[14] This system of domination entices and coerces Filipinos and others to "become simply a mimicry of the White American."[15] But this is not a unilinear process. As I will discuss below, for these young Filipino Americans, repeated encounters with the inequalities of a race-based social world at first puzzled and wounded them but ultimately led them to reconsider their relationship to and understanding of their assigned place in U.S. society—and in so doing, to act.

LANGUAGE AND CULTURE: "NOBODY TALKS ABOUT FILIPINOS"

When Joey Laguda was in elementary school, his friends used to think he was Chinese. When he told them that he was Filipino, they were puzzled: "What is a Filipino?" The invisibility of Filipino Americans in U.S. culture prompts at least one second-generation Filipina to exclaim, "Nobody ever talks about Filipinos." As evident in the accounts of racism above, young Filipinos were repeatedly mistaken for Chinese, Japanese, and even Mexican. Armando Alvarez's experience is typical: "In my high school, they didn't know how to discriminate against me. They called me like Kung Fu. They called me Tojo because of World War II, and they called me VC because of the Vietnam War, and things like that." While these mistakes may reflect genuine ignorance, they also are symptomatic of a society that is racialized and yet indifferent to or contemptuous of the racial differences and hybridization among its peoples.

School curriculum also marginalizes the experiences of U.S. Filipinos. No matter where young Filipinos attended school, whether in underresourced or affluent school districts, they seldom learned about Filipino American or Philippine history in their classes. High school senior Agnes Estrada felt frustrated by the black-white framework of her school curriculum:

> When we were in U.S. history last year, we spent so much time on slavery or on white-people stuff. Then we watched a movie about blacks sitting in the back of the bus and whites in the front and I was like, "Okay, where did we sit? In the middle?" You see, even in the films, just black or white. You never see Filipinos. I always ask my friends but they're just like, "They are working somewhere else. They are in Hawaii."

There was thus little institutional support for young Filipinos interested in learning about the Philippines and Filipino American culture and history. Pablo Barcenas relates:

> I didn't know anything about the Philippines. It seems like these thousand mysterious islands on the map, and I had a big question mark on it. It was never really taught to me in school. You know, it was just the basic geography. That's the Philippines, okay, let's move on. When it got to that point where they would get to the Philippines, they would already have moved on by the time my excitement got up so, you know, I have to go on and look it up in the encyclopedia.

In the same way, high school senior Lisa Graham hungered for more information on the Philippines and Filipino culture:

> I want to learn more about Filipino culture, but I don't know how to go about it. I wish they would teach that kind of stuff in school because it would make things a lot easier. But if you want to learn about the Filipino culture, you have to go do your own research on your own time. In school, they don't really teach us about the Philippines. Once in a while in world history, the teacher will mention the Philippines. That class usually puts me to sleep, but when the teacher says anything about the Philippines, I wake up. I am interested. I want to know more about the Philippines, because it has something to do with me.

Many young Filipinos I interviewed also complained that even in their homes, "nobody talks about Filipinos." The CILS data lend support to this complaint. Although close to three-quarters of the parents surveyed stated that it is very important for their child to know about the Philippines, 57 percent reported that they seldom talked to their child about the Philippines and 72 percent admitted that their family seldom celebrated special days connected with the Philippines.[16] With some bitterness, Armando Alvarez told of what he perceived to be a "cultural void" in his family:

> Not much was going on at my house. Nothing. It wasn't made explicit that Filipino culture is something that we should retain, that we should hold on to, as something that's valuable. There wasn't that sense that we should keep the language. So you don't really get taught, you know. And I found that to be a real common experience among Filipinos my age. Our parents don't realize that we don't know anything about the old country: Who was the first president, when was Independence Day, who was Jose Rizal?

On the issue of language, Filipino children of immigrants are unequivocally moving toward being monolingual, that is, speaking English only. According to the CILS data, only about one in ten indicated that they spoke a Filipino language "very well" and even fewer could read it "very well." In contrast, nearly nine out of ten Filipinos reported speaking and reading English "very well." Indeed, Filipinos were the most linguistically assimilated of all the CILS groups surveyed, with 96 percent of the respondents in 1995 preferring English. But these data do not necessarily indicate a rejection of Filipino languages. Many of the young Filipinos I interviewed deeply regretted their inability to speak a Filipino language. As Agnes Gonzalez stated, "I want to be a Filipina, but I can't really say that I am a true Filipina because I don't know how to speak the language. I wish my parents had taught me." And Lisa Graham reported, "Once in a while, I would ask my mom how to say this and that in Tagalog. I always hear her talking Tagalog on the phone. I wish there were a Tagalog class at school so I could learn."

Armando Alvarez attributed the lack of cultural and linguistic socialization in his and other Filipino families to the influence of U.S. cultural imperialism on his parents' generation:

> They were raised in an environment that valued American and Western things. . . . I've talked to Filipinos who know more about the American Civil War, about George Washington and Abraham Lincoln than they do about their own history. I've got aunts and uncles who were raised on John Wayne, Gary Cooper, Clark Gable. Those were the heroes. So if you have that mind-set, it makes the American culture, the American perspective, more important than the Filipino.

There is some truth to Armando's claim. I interviewed a Filipino journalist who refused to teach his children Tagalog and Filipino history. He said, "I don't see what's the point. The Filipinos haven't made much contribution in terms of the world. Take inventions, for instance, Filipinos are just noncreative." But his is a minority viewpoint. The majority of the immigrant parents I interviewed regretted their decision not to pass on the language to their children. Some parents simply were unable to cram language lessons into their hectic work schedules. But as the following comments indicate, most parents decided against language instruction because they wanted to spare their children from race- and language-based discrimination:

> One thing I was sorry [about] and the children are even sorry [about is] that we did not teach them how to speak Tagalog from the beginning. We were afraid that if we teach them our dialect that they might be behind in their schooling. I was stupid, I should have known better, but I didn't want them to be mistaken for somebody who is an immigrant speaking their Filipino language.
>
> Immigrant father

> When our children were growing up, when they were starting school, the school teacher advised us not to use our language because she said they would get all mixed up.
>
> Immigrant mother

> When I was little, my parents would always talk about the Philippines. Every time our relatives from the Philippines wrote to us, she would make me read it or when they sent pictures, she would want me to look at them.

> But then after a while, after she saw all the problems that I had at school, with all the kids harassing me and stuff, she wanted me to learn American ways because it was so hard for us.
>
> Second-generation Filipino

> My sister was five when we came to the United States, and so she started school. And they actually held her back because she didn't know English very well. And so there was a lot of pressure for me not to learn Tagalog, because basically my parents didn't want me to be held back.
>
> Second-generation Filipina

Partly out of their deep and abiding dissatisfaction with their assigned place in the United States and partly out of their desire to be more "authentically" tied to the "original" culture, some young Filipino Americans look upon the Philippines with "utopian longing, making a complex, colonized, wounded culture bear the weight of their desire."[17] In his quest to become "more Filipino," Pablo Barcenas longed for the Philippines:

> I have been wanting to go to the Philippines really, really bad. I don't know, I feel like if I go back to the Philippines, I am just going to learn so much more or at least that part of me will be answered just to see what's like. I guess as much as people have been telling me about the Philippines here, until I go there, I am not going to be completely satisfied.

Similarly, Maria Galang yearned to visit the Philippines: "I have already lost so much of my Filipino culture." "I feel this need to understand where I came from. To feel a sense of completion," she explained. When I asked Maria why she felt that she had lost a lot of her Filipinoness, she elaborated:

> I don't speak the language enough. I don't listen to Filipino music, folk or popular music from the Philippines. . . . I don't know what being Filipino is. Is it listening to Filipino music or reading or cooking Filipino food and eating Filipino food all the time? I am trying to eat at Filipino eateries all the time, just being in a Filipino atmosphere, just hanging out with Filipino friends who speak Tagalog. I love it because it enables me to be Filipino or just reading about Filipinos and stuff like that and that is another frustrating thing because there is nothing out there.

These personal narratives reveal the complexity of contemporary cultural and identity politics. On the one hand, the narratives challenge simplistic formulas that attribute cultural and linguistic assimilation among immigrant children to a generational decline in interest in the ethnic culture. Instead, they direct our attention to the lack of institutional support for the learning of Filipino/Philippine history and language and to the intense pressure faced by both immigrants and their children to assimilate. At the same time, they point out the degree to which many Filipino Americans have internalized a cultural definition of "Filipinoness" that is tied to "homeland" traditions and represented by a fixed profile of traits such as language and folk music.[18] Indeed, every year, thousands of college-age students stage elaborate and sophisticated Pilipino Cultural Nights (PCN) to packed auditorium of attentive and appreciative young Filipinos. By far the central organizing activity for many Filipino American student groups, the PCNs allow young Filipinos to build community, to educate themselves about Philippine/Filipino American history, and to represent their "culture" through "indigenized" Philippine dances, music, and costumes. In a cogent analysis of PCNs, Theodore S. Gonzalves warns that the PCN is vulnerable to charges of essentialism:

> The tacit assertion being made here is that the Philippines is a sturdy repository of "knowledge," a repository of authentic representations of Philippine life that can be accessed and brought back. The exercising of the "reverse exile" motif refuses to acknowledge the fact of cultural change, indeterminacy, and reconstruction at work in *both* the Philippines and the United States.[19]

This is not to say that the PCNs are not important. Many PCN participants described the event as "life changing." Take Raul Calderon, for example. His participation in a PCN launched him on an earnest and empowering search for his "roots":

> My sophomore year in college, I got involved in the Pilipino Cultural Night. I was so involved, like I really found a passion in it and this started instilling, this is when I really made the connections to the Filipino culture and my culture identity. I really found a passion in learning about myself, and I started checking out the Filipino history books in the library, not Filipino American, but Filipino, the history of the Philippines. I started feeding my brain with all the knowledge. I was never taught any of this before. Never once in the history classes in high school was I ever taught that there was a war between the Filipinos and the Americans. Never once was that mentioned. And I never knew anything about the American colonization. Learning about these things empowered me and it made me want to pursue, I guess, understanding between Filipinos and non-Filipinos.

Given the desire for a Filipino identity that is pure and fixed, of all the young Filipinos I interviewed, the ones who perceived themselves to be the most culturally grounded were those who had lived for significant periods of their lives in both the Philippines and the United States. Bryan Zamora and Melanie Mariano were two Filipino Americans who grew up across borders. Born in 1959 in the Philippines, Bryan immigrated to the United States at age three to join his Navy father. In 1970, when his father was stationed at Subic Bay, Bryan returned to the Philippines and completed his sixth, seventh, and eighth grades there. Bryan credited his biculturalism and bilingualism to his three-year stay in the Philippines:

> A lot of Filipinos who grew up here really don't have a sense of being Filipino. I had the opportunity to live there for a period of time so I was able to appreciate Filipino culture and the customs that come along with that culture. I was able to see the extended family in action. I was able to see how the Filipino value system was enforced in the culture. So to me accepting Filipino culture is not a problem because I have seen it actually happen. I have a reference point. I think a lot of Filipinos here don't have that reference point. Had I not lived there for that period of time, I can honestly say that I don't think I'd have the same sense of being Filipino that I do.

Bryan's transnational experience provided him with a "reference point" from which to challenge U.S. assimilationist ethos:

> I think a lot of people feel that in order to be effective in American society, you can't have two cultures. To me, I think that that's not true. I have no problem being at work and being amongst Caucasians and fitting in there. On the other hand, I have no problem being in a room full with all these Filipinos all speaking Tagalog. I see no reason why an individual can't maintain two cultures. In fact, it puts you in a very unique position of being able to evaluate both cultures and to pick and choose what things you want out of those two cultures.

As an example, Bryan refused to replicate what he perceived as the gender hierarchy embedded in Filipino culture: "I don't believe in the traditional husband and wife relationship. I don't believe that a Filipino wife is meant to serve her husband. I see the husband and wife as equal. So that's a Filipino belief that I can understand . . . but it's something that I choose not to believe in myself."

Whereas Bryan was born in the Philippines but lived most of his life in the United States, Melanie Mariano was born in the United States but grew up in the Philippines. In 1959, Melanie's father and mother left the Philippines for Omaha, Nebraska, as visiting scholars. Melanie was born there two years later. When she was three years old, the family moved back to the Philippines:

> My parents had no desire to stay in the United States. There were a lot of people in my father's class who came over at the same time and my father was one of the few who went back. He had this ideal notion that he wanted to help his people. And they wanted to bring us up in our own culture. We were American citizens by birth. They wanted it to be our choice to come back here if we wanted to.

Melanie did return to the United States, but not until she was twenty-five years old, to pursue a doctorate degree. Although she had no intention of staying, she met and married a Filipino American and settled in San Diego. Melanie considered herself fluent in both Filipino and American culture:

> I grew up in the Philippines. My whole family was lucky in that all of us are graduated with our own careers. So we have a positive experience being Filipino and at the same time, we know what American culture is. We understand all the idiomatic expressions, we can speak English, we can mask our accent, and a lot of Americans are surprised that we can do that because they think we grew up here. We're able to do that probably because we speak English all the time. My parents speak perfect English because they went to school here. And we watched a lot of American movies.

Secure in her bilingualism and biculturalism, Melanie pitied Filipino Americans who seemed confused about their identity: "I can see Filipino Americans struggling and I can sit in my spot and say, 'Oh you poor thing! You don't know what you're giving up, and you don't know what you're looking for, and I have no idea if you'll ever find it.' "

Bryan's and Melanie's self-presentation challenges the conceptualization of identity as bipolar and linear and insists on the merit of syncretic and hybridized identities and cultures. At the same time, their uncritical endorsement of biculturalism and bilingualism reduces the cultural politics of racialized and gendered ethnic subjects to individual will and desire while ignoring the historical processes of material exclusion and differentiation that racially form Asian American subjects in the first place. As Brackette Williams argues, the ethnic aspect of identity formation "must be understood in relation to the societal production of enduring categorical distinctions and not simply in terms of individuals adopting and 'shedding' particular manifestations of those categorical identities."[20] Below, I discuss instances when Filipino Americans have critically fashioned a Filipino American culture and identity, not only through inheriting, modifying, and inventing cultural traditions, but also through active contestations and constructions of racial meanings.

CLAIMING HOME: "I *AM* AMERICAN!"

"You're not American," her friend said. But Grace Espartero defiantly shot back, "I too am. I was born here. I *am* American!" This too-familiar exchange encapsulates the failure of U.S. citizenship to guarantee truly equal rights to all the nation's citizenry. Like other Asian Americans, Filipino Americans—even as U.S. born citizens—continue to be constructed as different from, and as other than, Americans of European origin. Many young Filipinos, like Juanita Domingo, understood full well the bounds of U.S. citizenship:

> You can't really ever be looked upon as completely American just because of what you look like, even though you were born here, even though you grew up here, even though you speak English very well. The first impression a person is going to have is that you don't belong here because of how you look.

For many young Filipinos, then, the making of Filipino American culture is intimately linked to the conceptualization of race as "the material *locus* of differences, intersections, and incommensurabilities."[21] According to Ruby Partido, her racial awareness began in her senior year in high school when an academic counselor discouraged her from applying to the University of California. An active and above-average high school student, Ruby was baffled by the counselor's advice: "I remember coming home crying. My self-confidence was really low." When Ruby asked her friends about their experiences with the same counselor, she discovered that while her white friends received ample information on colleges and scholarships, her Filipino friends were advised against applying to prestigious universities—even though they had higher grades. "It started clicking in my head. They are picking us out just because we are not white. This was the first time that I ever started getting any sense of awareness, or consciousness, that I am different." For Leah Dullas, anti-Filipino racism targeted her body:

> One time, I was walking with a friend of mine and it was late, getting kind of dark, and there were these couple of guys and you could tell they had been drinking whatever, and so we walked by and they were like, "I hear Oriental girls give a good time," and I was just like, "Oh, my God!" I was ready just to blow up, but I was also so scared so we just walked away and ignored them. It was so sexist and so racist.

The ability to name racism provides young Filipinos with a frame of reference not only for understanding contemporary incidents but also for reinterpreting childhood episodes. Noting that the experience of racism is cumulative, Armando Alvarez revealed, "My personal understanding of things in the present has allowed me to give names and labels to my experiences in the past. Before, I could only describe it as a 'weird experience.' I didn't understand why they didn't like me, why they kept calling me Jap or Gook when I am Filipino."

The culture, politics, and philosophy of other groups of color have offered Filipino Americans "vital resources for understanding their own racialization, political marginalization, and class exploitation in North America."[22] Mindful that outsiders generally lump all Asians together, many Filipino American activists herald their common fate to build political unity with other Asian Americans. Nicholas Santos described the impact on his identity of lumping all Asians together:

> Growing up, I never saw myself as Asian. When I thought of Asian, it was like the Chinese, Japanese, you know. But eventually, I think my experiences sort of helped me to understand that I have this racial uniform. I've been called, ya know, Chink, Jap. Most of the times I have been called a Chink. So I would look in the mirror and say, "Humph, maybe I do look Chinese! Maybe I do look Asian!"

Similarly, Ella Labao recounted how she developed her Asian American consciousness:

> Not until I became a freshman at San Diego State did I really get involved in the Asian American Student Alliance. I met some friends in some of my classes and we got to be really good friends. A lot of them are Japanese descent. We went to a statewide Asian American Conference, and it was a really good experience. I learned a lot about being Asian American. Just to put it bluntly, we all are going through the same thing and we are all Asian American; we are all minorities here. You know, we're all striving for the same thing. Just because you're Filipino American, Chinese American, Japanese American, whatever, we're all Asian American.

Other Filipino Americans attributed their racial consciousness to their friendships with Latinos and African Americans. As Maria Galang put it, "I think my racial consciousness was raised because I hung around more with blacks in high school." Jovy Lopez attributed her current commitment to racial justice to her early friendships with Latino neighbors and classmates: "I guess it made me more culturally aware and sensitive than some people who only grew up among one race." In the same way, Nicholas Santos credited his African American friends with sharpening his racial awareness: "In some ways they were demything me.

Like, one time, I told a black friend, 'Larry, I want to be a doctor or an astronaut.' And he said, 'You believe that shit? I mean, how do you know that white America is not putting something on you?' And I certainly got a lot out of that. To be careful of trusting the establishment." Nicholas identified the organic links between Filipino Americans and African Americans:

> I realized that what it is to be Filipino American was closer to the African American experience. I think it was Kareem Adbul Jabar who wrote that he refused to join the Olympic team to represent America because he didn't want to play for a country that was not his country. But then his mentor told him, "Don't you ever say that America is not your country because your forefathers' sweat, blood, and tears went into this land, into making it what it is now." So now when people tell me, "Go back to where you came from," I always think to myself, "Wait a minute, who planted the fields of Hawaii? Who built the canneries in Alaska? Filipinos did. So don't tell me that I can't stay here. I have a stake here." So there were those parallel experiences that I felt comfortable in claiming or understanding. I can never be black, but it is comforting to know that I am not alone.

African American history of racial struggles was thus central to Nicholas's claim for full citizenship rights for him and his children:

> I want my [future] children to realize that this is their country, that historically the Filipinos, the *manongs,* the field workers . . . helped build America and that is our heritage. Nobody can tell me to go back to where I came from because as far as I am concerned, this is my home. I have a stake in this country in that I like to see it get better, get more humane, get more kind.

As Nicholas suggested, to stake a claim in the United States, one must fight for a "better, more humane, and more kind" society. Many young Filipino activists did just that. Equal opportunities for education topped their agenda as they tutored and organized "college days" for underrepresented high school students, fought for the admission and retention of students of color on college campuses, and demanded an education that was more relevant and accessible to their communities. For Ruby Partido, working for the Student Affirmative Action/Economic Opportunity Program (SAA/EOP) on her college campus sensitized her to issues of student retention and multiculturalism and helped forge her identity as a student of color: "I was out there on the front line, you know, helping students of color pass classes and talk out their problems." Samantha Reyes attributed her activism to her relationship with her African American roommate and to the racially charged atmosphere of her college campus:

> It was gradual, my becoming active. My roommate, she is an African American, and I learned a lot from her about the civil rights movement, about the things that she learned in high school that I didn't learn. I felt so dumb compared to her because she was so much more aware. And I started taking classes, and we discussed issues of race in terms of what teachers are teaching, the lack of offerings in African American classes, Asian American Studies classes. I really wanted to become involved. It was something I needed to claim for myself. So I got involved. And we wanted to make sure that there was more hiring of women professors and more hiring of professors to teach ethnic studies courses or just to have more Asian American and African American professors, Hispanic professors, more gay and lesbian professors.

In 1995, when the University of California Board of Regents passed two measures, SP1 and SP2, banning affirmative action programs in student admission, faculty hiring, and contracting, Filipino American students at the University of California, San Diego, as leaders and members of the interethnic antiracist No Retreat! coalition, fought vigorously for the repeal of these unjust policies. Participation in a social movement often leads to other commitments. For Mona Ampon, her involvement in the No Retreat! coalition propelled her to join other existing struggles for social justice. For example, she campaigned with low-wage workers to demand an end to employer exploitation and worked with the local youth movement to battle against police harassment and unjust incarceration of working-class youth of color.

As young Filipino activists fought for social justice in the United States, their thoughts often turned to the Philippines, with how to help with the social struggles there. Eleonor Ocampo described the strong responsibility she felt toward the Philippines:

> I would say that the Philippines has a special place in my heart because that's where my roots are. I think there is a stronger sense of hurt when I see, like, when I saw a film in an urban planning class about the development of the international workforce, it has a segment on the Philippines, and you know, I saw what they did to the women workers. And I was ready to cry because, you know, I am fighting for so much here, for Asian Americans in America, but yet there is a sense of helplessness that I can't go back and make a difference for my people, the Filipino people. So, I would

> jockey back and forth between . . . Asian American issues versus Asian and Filipino issues. Do I stay within the confines of North America, or do I take a second look at what's going in the government back home and the people back home? Where can I best be of help? I don't really know much about the Philippines, a land that is so far away, but yet I know that's where my heart truly is.

Few Filipino Americans took the next step to join the social movements in the Philippines. In the next chapter, I will feature three Filipina Americans who did just that. However, the majority of the Filipino activists I interviewed made peace with themselves by focusing their energy on the local struggles. As Arturo Coponong related, "Two years ago I was leaning toward living in the Philippines. And helping out the people there. But then I realized that I probably could be of better use if I stay here and help out the Filipinos that are here." Even for Maricela Rebaya, who planned to return to the Philippines "to help the people," the move would only be temporary: "When I finish college, one of my goals is to bring something back to the Philippines and maybe work there or something. To help the people. But I probably don't want to live there because I can do more if I am here."

◆ ◆ ◆

The multiple subject positions of second-generation Filipino Americans remind us that identities are not fixed or singular, but multiple, overlapping, and simultaneous and that they reflect events both in the United States as well as in the "home country." Filipino immigrant children thus live with paradoxes. They feel strong symbolic loyalty to the Philippines, but they know very little about it and have little contact with their parents and other adults who might educate them about it. They feel pressured to become like "Americans," but their experiences as racialized subjects leave them with an uneasy relationship with both Filipino and U.S. culture. They display the visible markers of assimilation yet remain ferociously nationalist. Their case thus demonstrates the impossibility both of complete assimilation within U.S. society and of a return to the Philippines for these youths. In the end, for many second-generation Filipino Americans, *here* is home—at least for now. They have claimed this space; it is theirs. As Jovy Lopez exclaimed, "This is the country that I was born in, and it's my country too. It's just as much my country as any one else's. This *is* my home."

CHAPTER 9

Homes, Borders, and Possibilities

When people come together voluntarily to create their own vision, they begin wishing it to come into being with such passion that they begin creating an active path leading to it from the present.

Grace Lee Boggs, *Living for Change*

Through my education in Ethnic Studies, I just became really empowered. I gained the knowledge. And through educational discussions and events organized by the League of Filipino Students (in L.A.) I became informed about the oppressive economic, social, and political situations occurring in the Philippines. . . . I gained the tools to really understand the world around me and to make sense of everything. And then it came to that point where I . . . wanted to apply [these tools]. For me, to do that, I felt that I needed to go back to the Philippines and participate in the liberation struggles there.

Melany de la Cruz, second-generation Filipina

Home making is really border making: it is about deciding who is in as well as who is out. I began this project on Filipino Americans in San Diego at the border—the U.S.-Mexico border. Since the mid-1970s, the militarization of the U.S.-Mexico border region has intensified. From San Diego to the Rio Grande Valley, armed U.S. federal agents patrol key border points to block "illegal" crossers—to keep "them" from invading "our" homes.[1] Since 1994, "Operation Gatekeeper," a high-profile blockade-style operation, has turned the San Diego-Tijuana border region into a war zone, pushing immigrants to attempt more treacherous crossings in the forbidding mountains and deserts east of San Diego. Since Gatekeeper's launch, an average of ninety immigrants have died per year; the most common killers are mountain cold, desert heat, and canal drownings and falls.[2] Anti-immigrant practices targeted virtually all people of "Mexican appearance"; many of my Latino students, colleagues, and friends angrily reported being stopped, harassed, and humiliated as they crossed the border. The political furor over undocumented immigration reached its nadir in 1994 when nearly 60 percent of the California electorate voted in favor of Proposition 187, a measure designed to deny almost all publicly funded social services, including education and health care, to undocumented immigrants and their children. The public relations campaign on behalf of Proposition 187 expressly targeted immigrants crossing the U.S.-Mexico border, blaming them for many of California's social, moral, and economic ills and demonizing them as "reproductive, parasitic, benefit-taking, overrunning-the-nation villains."[3]

As I watched this spectacle of border making, I was reminded of my own border-crossing experience. In 1975, when tens of thousands of Vietnamese refugees, including my own family, arrived in the United States, the majority of Americans did not welcome us. A Harris poll taken in May 1975 indicated that more than 50 percent of the American public felt that Southeast Asian refugees should be excluded; only 26 percent favored their entry. Many seemed to share Congressman Burt Talcott's conclusion that, "Damn it, we have too many Orientals."[4] Five years later, public opinion toward the refugees had not changed. A 1980 poll of American attitudes in nine cities revealed that nearly half of those surveyed believed that the Southeast Asian refugees should have settled in other Asian countries.[5] This poll also found that more than 77 percent of the respondents would disapprove of the marriage of a Southeast Asian refugee into their family and 65 percent would not be willing to have a refugee as a guest in their home.[6] Anti-Southeast Asian sentiment also took violent turns. Refugees from Vietnam, Laos, and Cambodia in many parts of the United States have been attacked and even killed; and their properties have been vandalized, firebombed, or burned.[7] The antirefugee rhetoric was similar to that directed against Latino immigrants: Southeast Asians were morally, culturally, and economically deficient—an invading multitude, unwanted and undeserving.

The rhetoric that demonizes anti-Latino and anti-Asian immigrants is disturbing not only for what it says, but more so for what it does not say.

By portraying immigration to the United States as a matter of desperate individuals seeking opportunities, it completely disregards the aggressive roles that the U.S. government and U.S. corporations have played—through colonialism, imperialist wars and occupations, capital investment and material extraction in Third World countries and through active recruitment of racialized and gendered immigrant labor—in generating out-migration from key sending countries.[8] As Joe Feagin reminds us, "recent immigrants have mostly come from countries that have been substantially influenced by imperialistic efforts by U.S. corporations and by the U.S. government around the globe."[9] This portrayal of immigration stigmatizes the immigrants as desperate, undeserving, and even threatening, and delinks contemporary immigration from past U.S. corporate, military, or governmental actions abroad. It is with a deep concern over the (mis)representation of immigration to the United States—what is stated as well as what is concealed—that I began this book on Filipino Americans.

The production of discourses of immigration, both popular and intellectual, is important because modes of representation are themselves forms of power rather than mere reflections of power.[10] Immigration has become a key symbol in American culture, a central and powerful concept imbued with a multiplicity of myths and meanings, capable of rousing highly charged emotions that culminate in violently unfair practices.[11] In the late twentieth century, politicians, anti-immigrant groups, media agencies, and academic researchers have colluded to create "knowledge" of an everyday "reality" that the U.S. borders are out of control and that immigration is overwhelming U.S. public institutions and threatening U.S. core values and identity.[12] In this book, my goal has been to produce a critical representation of immigration. Instead of presenting immigration (and immigrants) as a *problem* to be solved, I have argued that we need to conceptualize immigration as a technology of racialization and gendering—a crucial site for the reproduction of and resistance to "scattered hegemonies."[13]

TOWARD A CRITICAL IMMIGRATION STUDY

Tayyab Mahmud, writing on the "spectre of the migrant" that haunts the modern world, states that immigration is presented in popular and scholarly debates as a "problem to be solved, a flaw to be corrected, a war to be fought, and a flow to be stopped."[14] Conceptualizing immigration primarily as a problem, the dominant theories in the field of U.S.

immigration studies—theories of assimilation (including segmented assimilation), of amalgamation, of the "melting pot," of cultural pluralism—have focused on immigrant cultural and economic adaptation and incorporation and on responses by native-born Americans to the influx.[15] The debates among immigration scholars have been lively. According to immigration opponents, immigrants incur the wrath of "Americans" because they deplete the country's resources and fragment America's cultural unity.[16] In contrast, immigration proponents argue that immigrants benefit the nation's economy and enrich its cultural fabric.[17] Even as they disagree on the relative costs and benefits of immigration, both sides nevertheless approach immigration as a problem to be solved, focusing their research on the immigrants' social, economic, and cultural integration into the United States. This approach to immigration uncritically accepts U.S. white middle-class culture, viewpoints, and practices as the norm. Instead of questioning the ideological and material power of these normative standards, immigration advocates have at times sought to "prove" that immigrants are just "as hardworking or honest as native-born Americans" and that the majority "assimilate rapidly to the English language and other aspects of Euro-American culture."[18] As an example, an informative edited volume on the post-1965 second generation focuses its discussion on the following theoretical and empirical question: Will today's children of immigrants move into the middle-class mainstream or join the expanded multiethnic underclass?[19] An important question to be sure, it nevertheless leaves uninterrogated the ways in which immigration as a cultural system has constructed the "immigrant" and the "American"—the impact of which has been to *naturalize* unequal patterns of mobility and uneven integration into the nation.

Drawing on the works of ethnic studies scholars[20] such as Jose David Saldivar, David Gutierrez, Lisa Lowe, and George Sanchez, I have argued that we need to study immigration not only for what it tells us about the assimilability of the immigrants but more so for what it says about the racialized and gendered economic, cultural, and political foundations of the United States. That is, we need to conceptualize immigration not as a site for assessing the acceptability of the immigrants, but as a site for critiquing state claims of liberal democracy and cultural inclusion, for studying contestation over definition of citizenship and over terms of inclusion, and for understanding the formation and negotiation of racialized and gendered identities. Throughout the book, I have attempted to address not only the constructions of "the Filipino," which were produced through the colonial encounter in the Philippines and the migration encounter in the United States but also how these constructions and the practices associated with them were experienced and contested by Filipinos themselves. Most immigration studies have privileged U.S.-born American responses to "distant languages and alien cultures" among their midst.[21] To counter this trend, I have relied on Filipino American accounts of their experiences to better understand their subjectivity—how they have created their worlds and made meaning for themselves—and in so doing, to restore, in Amitava Kumar's words, "a certain weight of experience, a stubborn density, a *life* to what we encounter in newspaper columns as abstract, often faceless, figures without histories."[22] In the process, I have pointed out the complexities of Filipino American identities, identifications, and actions. Filipino Americans, like any other group, take up many positions on a continuum between internalization of and overt resistance to oppressive discourses and practices.

Border Is Everywhere

Hovering at the edges of the nation, immigrants call into question implicit assumptions about "fixed identities, unproblematic nationhood, invisible sovereignty, ethnic homogeneity, and exclusive citizenship."[23] As such, immigrants pose a problem to the United States, not because they are economic parasites or cultural aliens but because they reveal the gaps in the promise of liberal democracy and disrupt the fictions of cultural inclusion and homogeneity—fundamental claims of the U.S. modern state.[24] As I have documented in this book, membership to the U.S. nation is regulated by strict rules of exclusion and inclusion. These immigration and citizenship restrictions—enacted to regulate the membership of the national community—send a powerful message that the United States conceives of itself as a singular, predominantly Euro-American, English-speaking culture. As Dorothy Roberts points out, many white Americans assume that "American culture is synonymous with the culture of white people and that the cultures of the new immigrants are inconsistent with a national identity."[25] In such a setting, the question of who is or is not an "American" and anti-immigrant rhetoric become entangled in revealing ways.[26]

The cultural project—the daily reproduction of symbols and myths—of representing the U.S. nation as racially and culturally homogeneous requires the construction of cultures and geographies from which the immigrants come, and therefore the immigrants themselves, as fundamentally foreign and inferior to modern American society and its citizens.[27] As an example, proponents of Proposition 187 charged that the influx of undocumented immigrants would transform California into a Third World nation. This reference to the "Third World" must be seen as a strategic marker that "metaphorically alludes to social evolution and the threat of immigration leading to a de-evolution of 'American civilization.' "[28] In the case of Filipinos, their racial subjugation began not in the United States but in the Philippines—a U.S. colony for more than half a century and a neocolony long after that. The U.S. imperialist drive into the Philippines unleashed a consistent and well-articulated ideology depicting the Philippines and its people as requiring and even beseeching the intervention of white men from the more "civilized" United States. Drawing on ideas about gender, the racist constructions of the Filipinos as uncivilized savages and dependent children bolstered the conviction that Filipinos lacked the *manly* character needed for self-rule and justified the need for U.S. interventions to rectify the Philippine "unnatural" gender order. But as I argued in chapter 3, these racist constructions had less to do with the Filipinos' incapacity for self-rule and more to do with U.S. imperialists' desire to cast themselves as *men* who wielded power—one of the many attempts to restore "proper" gender and racial order in late-nineteenth-century United States. In this sense, the annexation and the colonization of the Philippines must also be understood as subject-constituting projects, fashioning *both* the Filipino and American subjects in ways that were and continue to be mutually implicated in each other.

The imperialist constructions of the Philippines and its people—as inferior, immoral, and incapable—traveled with Filipinos to the United States and prescribed their racialization here. In other words, Filipino immigrant lives are shaped not only by the social location of their group within the United States but also by the position of their home country within the global racial order. In an important essay on culture and U.S. imperialism, Amy Kaplan links the study of ethnicity and immigration inextricably to the study of empire by arguing that imperialism not only contributes to the subjugation of the colonized "other" but also to the consolidation of a dominant imperial culture at home.[29] Lipsitz has made a similar point: U.S. armed conflicts against "enemies" in the Philippines and other Asian countries "functioned culturally to solidify and reinforce a unified U.S. national identity based in part on antagonism toward Asia and Asians."[30] In this sense, imperialism is not only a matter of foreign policy conducted by diplomatic elites or a matter of economic necessity driven by market forces, it is also a way of life.[31] Part of this way of life is the "possessive investment in whiteness" and the corresponding disinvestment in "undeserving" groups. Represented as being at odds with the cultural, racial, and linguistic forms of the U.S. nation, the Filipino immigrant—as a nonwhite, noncivilized body—constitutes "a moving bubble of wilderness in white political space, a node of discontinuity which is necessarily in permanent tension with it."[32] I have argued that this "permanent tension" is the product of *differential inclusion*—a process whereby a group of people is deemed integral to the nation, but integral only or precisely because of their designated subordinate standing. The designation of the Filipino as the "foreigner-within" works to resolve the contradictions between the nation's promise of equal rights and its actual practice of exclusion because it attributes Filipinos' "failed" integration to their own inability or unwillingness to assimilate into the national culture that has been defined as necessarily white.

The process of differential inclusion, then, is not about closing the physical national borders but about creating borders within the nation. In this sense, the border is *everywhere*.[33] These borders within—bolstered by political and cultural mechanisms designed to restrict the membership in the national community—set clear but imaginary boundaries between who is defined as a citizen and who is not.[34] Because Filipino and other Asian Americans are discursively produced as foreign, they carry a figurative border with them. This figurative border marks them as linguistically, culturally, and racially "outside" the national polity, and as targets of nativistic racism. Anti-Asian violence, both symbolic and physical, works to reassure "real" Americans that the national community begins and ends with them and to uphold the fiction of a homogeneous American identity.[35] Nativistic racism thus operates to regulate borders—not only the geopolitical border but the border that is everywhere.

Pushing against Borders

Even though the border is everywhere, Filipino migrants, through their self-made multiple subject positions and transnational connections, repeatedly push against the borders within and between nations. Drawing on historical and oral accounts of Filipino American lives in San Diego, I have documented the multifaceted and shifting experiences of "diasporic" Filipinos as they move across and dwell in the various borders. Most scholars of immigration and transnationalism have approached transnational relations in terms of capital, labor, and political transactions—all of which privilege the activities of adult males. As a departure, I have juxtaposed the "public" world of political economy (the structural reconfigurations that accompany global capitalism) with the more "private" and domestic world of families, women, and children (the social and emotional labor and costs that sustain transnational lives).[36] My goals have been to document the impact of transnationalism on Filipino American everyday life, to understand how their own agencies are implicated in both the unmaking and remaking of the established power structure, and to identify the social relationships and regimes of truth and power in which these agencies are embedded.

I conceptualize border-crossing practices as a disruptive strategy, enacted by the migrants to challenge their differential inclusion in the United States as subordinate subjects. To discipline people under its control, the regime of the nation-state requires the *localization* of its subjects—that people be locatable and confinable, if not actually confined, to the space of the nation.[37] By living their lives across borders, Filipino immigrants, in effect, are challenging the nation-state's attempt to localize them; that is, to mold them into acceptable and "normal" subjects. As such, Filipino transnational activities must be understood in part as an act of resistance: an articulation of their deep dissatisfaction with and anger at the contradictions between official state ideals of equal citizenship and state-sanctioned forms of subordination based on class, race, gender, and sexual orientation.[38] It is also an act of resistance against the violence of globalized capitalism, a personal resolve to provide for themselves and their families even in the wake of the global reorganization of capitalism and to remain stubbornly *Home bound* even as they are flung to the "ends of the earth" in search of work.

Whatever their class background, Filipino immigrants become integrated into the United States as a colonized and racialized people. To contest their enforced homelessness—their political, economic, and/or cultural subordination in the United States—many immigrants look to the Philippines for compensation and protection, producing and maintaining multiple layers of transnational social connections in the process.[39] For the many migrants who have experienced downward economic and social mobility, the "homeland" becomes an important site for establishing a sense of parity—to reclaim, reinforce, or raise their social status. As Pierre Bourdieu points out, "struggles for recognition are a fundamental dimension of social life" and that "what is at stake . . . is the accumulation of a particular form of capital, honor in the sense of reputation and prestige." Applying Bourdieu's insight, we can thus "read" the migrants' conspicuous spending in the home country as an attempt to convert their economic capital into symbolic capital—that is, into status.[40] As I detailed in chapter 4, *balikbayans,* especially hometown association leaders, enjoy lavish welcoming receptions when they visit "home" because of their perceived and actual role as benefactors of the Philippines. Even when Filipino migrants do not physically return home, they can still remit hard-earned money to the Philippines to help an ailing parent, finance a relative's education, or purchase property and build a house there—all actions that work to increase their status "back home" and to blunt the sharpness of life in the United States. In this sense, many Filipino migrants, like the Tongan migrants in Small's study, left the Philippines in order to be better Filipinos—to fulfill their obligations to their families back home and in so doing to raise their own status among other Filipinos.[41] For all these reasons, for many migrants, the "homeland" assumes a larger-than-life role, becoming both a symbolic as well as an actual security net.

At the same time, I do not wish to overstate the frequency of Filipino transnational activities. While significant segments of foreign-born Filipinos regularly engage in transnational activities such as sending remittances or communicating with family members back home, most Filipino migrants I spoke to do not live in transnational "circuits" but are instead settling permanently in San Diego.[42] Their lived reality—their job, their church, their children's school, their social life—is primarily local. As I documented in chapter 5, Filipinos in San Diego have actively built community organizations—more than 150 in all—to address the needs and advance the interests of local Filipinos. But to say that transnational activities are infrequent is not the same as saying that they are not important. True, some Filipino immigrants harbor little desire to stay connected to the Philippines—the place they worked so hard to leave. But they are clearly in the minority. The majority of the immigrants I interviewed spoke longingly and lovingly of their lives in the Philippines and would return home more often if they could. For these Filipinos, maintaining more vigorous transnational ties remains formidable: the prohibitive travel costs, unrelenting work schedules, and relentless household demands all work to minimize their physical connections to the Philippines, however much they desire them. So at least for now, most Filipino immigrants retain transnational ties (through remittances, phone calls, and letters home) but remain quite locally rooted, making do instead with short visits "home," often prompted by emergency situations such as a death or illness in the family.

But transnationalism take places not only at the literal but also at the symbolic level—at the level of imagination, shared memory, and "inventions of traditions."[43] Responding to their enforced "homelessness" in the United States, many Filipino migrants have created a sense of home by memorializing the homeland, inventing traditions, and fortifying familial and hometown bonds. The idealization of the homeland, however, becomes problematic when it elicits a desire among the immigrants to replicate class and gender inequities as a means to buttress their lost status and identities in the United States. In chapter 7, I documented the troubling ways in which immigrant parents, in the name of culture and nationalism, opted to regulate their daughters' independent choices by linking them to cultural ignorance and betrayal. The practice of symbolic transnationalism is perhaps most poignant among U.S.-born Filipinos, many of whom look on the Philippines with "utopian longing"—in part out of their deep dissatisfaction with their marginalized place in the United States.[44] As chapter 8 indicated, given their desire to be more "authentically" tied to the Filipino culture, many young Filipinos have internalized a cultural definition of "Filipinoness" that is tied to "homeland" traditions and represented by a fixed profile of shared traits such as language and folk songs. Such a conception of cultural identity—one that is imbued with stable, unchanging, and continuous frames of reference and meaning—continues to be very powerful because it is directed, in Franz Fanon's words, "by the secret hope of discovering beyond the misery of today, beyond self-contempt, resignation and abjuration, some very beautiful and splendid era whose existence rehabilitates us both in regard to ourselves and in regard to others."[45]

In sum, transnationalism must be understood as a contradictory process—one that has the potential to break down borders and traditions and create new cultures and hybrid ways of life but also to fortify traditional hierarchies, homogenize diverse cultural practices, and obscure intragroup differences and differential relationships. In this sense, as I concluded in chapter 4, transnationalism is at best a compromise—a "choice" made and lived in a context of scarce options.

Self-Making: "Alternative Imaginaries"

Through the lens of popular and academic discourses, we see immigrants objectified as unwanted illegal aliens, welfare dependents, and economic competitors. But what do we know about their complex personhood: their self-identity, their dreams for themselves, their hopes for their children, their "ground of being"? To ask this question is to move the field of immigration studies forward, away from focusing on how immigrants are "being made" to how they are "self-making."[46] As immigrant subjects are "being made" into "minority" subjects, their culture becomes represented as bounded, local, and limited—a reconstruction of that which, outside its relation to the dominant culture, knows no such terms.[47] To engage in the process of self-making, then, is to problematize the very authority and authenticity of the term *cultural identity* (a presumption of liberal discourse), and to assert instead that immigrant subjectivity is a production that is always in process.[48]

In a brilliant essay on diasporic identity, Stuart Hall reminds us that in defining cultural identity, we cannot speak about "one experience" or "one identity" but that we need to acknowledge the deep and significant ruptures and discontinuities that exist within any community and that are subject to the continuous "play" of history, culture, and power. Cultural identities, then, are not an essence but a *positioning:* "the names we give to the different ways we are positioned by, and position ourselves within, the narratives of the past."[49] Other scholars, especially those in ethnic studies, gender studies, cultural studies, and critical anthropology, have likewise established that identities are unstable formations constituted within webs of power relations structured along the lines of gender, race, nationality, subculture, and dominant culture.[50] Because each of these "regimes of truth and power" disciplines people under its control in different ways to form acceptable and normal subjectivities, resistance strategies to undermine the hegemonic views of one regime may have the unintended effect of supporting those of another.[51]

In this book, I have been attentive to the self-activity and subjectivity of Filipino immigrants and their children. Social movement historians have recorded Filipino active engagement in labor struggles over wages, hours, and working conditions.[52] Here I have been more interested in understanding how Filipino immigrants have employed what Nonini and Ong term "alternative imaginaries" to fashion self-identities that evade, move beyond, and even invert the inscriptions and identifications made by state, capitalist, and patriarchal regimes of truth.[53] In particular, I investigate the ways in which Filipino immigrants resist the colonial racial denigration of their culture, community, and women in part by turning the tables of the colonial racial moral calculus against the dominants. In so doing, I shift attention from the otherness of the subordinate group (as dictated by the 'mainstream') to the otherness of the dominant group (as constructed by the "margins). As discussed in chapter 4, Filipinos, both in the Philippines and the United States, construct the United States as a land of unrivaled economic opportunity but one that is marred by licentiousness, unfettered individualism, rampant consumerism, and cultural and spiritual hollowness. In contrast, they insist that the Philippines, though poor, is morally and culturally superior to the United States. In the same way, as detailed in chapter 7, Filipino immigrants claim moral distinctiveness for their community by representing white Americans, especially white women, as morally flawed and themselves as family-oriented models and their women as paragons of morality. Their invocation of family values, loyalty to elders, and female chastity and sacrifice are all pointed critiques of what they perceive as the deficient morality of America and its people. By focusing on the alternative frames of meaning that aggrieved groups employ to invert their status in relation to the dominant group, I have underscored the immigrants' ability to maneuver and manipulate meanings within different domains, especially in the domains of morality and culture, in an effort to counter the fundamental assumption of inevitable white American superiority.

At the same time, I have tried to be attentive not only to cultural and ethnic resistance but also to the limitations of resistance strategies that fail to recognize the "complex *relationality* that shapes our social and political lives."[54] In chapter 7, I showed how idealized descriptions of virtuous immigrant daughters allow Filipinos to resist colonial denigration of their women and culture and to represent themselves as morally superior to the dominant group. But this strategy exemplifies the paradox of immigrant resistance and accommodation and the relation between race, ethnicity, and gender: Filipino families forge cultural resistance against racial oppression by stressing female chastity and sacrifice, and yet they reinforce patriarchal power and gendered oppression by hinging ethnic and racial pride on the performance of female subordination. In so doing, they collapse the heterogeneous and competing (im)moral discourses and practices in the community into a stable and coherent set of collective values and goals. Along the same lines, in chapter 6, I detailed the ways in which Filipino American men resist racist economic exploitation by reclaiming traditional definitions of manhood and sweeping aside the needs and well-being of Filipino American women and children. However, I also pointed out that the denigration of Filipino women and children constitutes only one response to the stripping of male privilege. Another is to institute a revised domestic division of labor and gender relations in the immigrant family. In sum, an alternative frame of meaning is a potent counterforce to existing hegemonies, but one that is not without its own "particular mix of expansive and repressive technologies."[55]

THE *BABAES*: IMAGINING A BETTER WORLD

> We have allowed our imaginations to be so bounded so that we are left with a nation full of borders, borders that too easily become fault lines. We are left with people who live in transit, between their imaginary homelands and the mythic America. But let us not forget the power of imagination. Let us imagine, then a better community.
>
> Robert Chang, "A Meditation on Borders"

In the above passage, critical legal theorist Robert Chang warns us about the dangers of "a nation full of borders" and exhorts us to imagine "a better community." I want to end this book by focusing on three second-generation Filipinas who have heeded this call to transgress borders and to imagine and participate in making a better world. All three were born in the mid-1970s, came of age during the conservative Reagan/Bush years, and attended college (University of California, San Diego) during California's "darkest days," as the state was awash with an anti-immigration and anti–affirmative action fervor.[56] All chose to respond to the urgency of the moment by drawing on their situated knowledges as Pinays[57] to enact a compelling vision of social justice. It is important to note that they understood the relationship between the local and the global—that the injustices, inequities, and indignities endured by California's racialized and gendered groups and by their own families are intimately tied to the historical and contemporary conditions of globalization. To better educate themselves about the workings of transnational capitalism, they left the United States and traveled deep into the Philippines, where they learned from the people there how to visualize alternatives to oppressive conditions and to translate these powerful visions into critical actions. This very act of border crossing is transgressive. By leaving the United States for the Philippines with the expressed intent to obtain "a better education," these young Pinays have in effect redefined what constituted knowledge and education and inverted the racialized hierarchy that privileged the United States as the world's premier center of education.

Melany de la Cruz, Jennifer True, and Strela Cervas call themselves the *babaes,* a Tagalog word for "women," to signal their cultural awareness, their political activism, and their gender consciousness.[58] They view their identities not as represented by a fixed profile of traits but as self-conscious products of political choices and actions. When a former boyfriend's brother charged that "all Filipinos look like monkeys," Melany retaliated by imbuing her identity with political weight: she became immersed in affirmative action, labor, and youth struggles. These panethnic and interethnic social movements introduced her to international labor struggles, including those waged by workers in the Philippines. From her Ethnic Studies and Urban Studies courses, Melany learned about U.S. capitalism, U.S. colonial and neo-colonial modes of development and exploitation in the Philippines, and the post-Fordist imperialism of the International Monetary Fund, the World Bank, and "free" trade. But she wanted to "apply these tools" and to "experience firsthand" the historical and ongoing exploitation of Filipino labor, women, and children. To do that, she believed she "needed to go back to the Philippines and participate in the liberation struggles there." In the summer of 1998, she traveled to the Philippines under the auspices of the Integrate/Exposure Program hosted by the Los Angeles–based League of Filipino Students (LFS). The Integrate/Exposure Program is designed to integrate and expose Americans, especially second-generation Filipino Americans, to different activist sectors of the Philippines, including the peasant, student, small mining community, urban poor, human rights, labor, and religious sectors. The program is thus structured to provide young "Integrationists" and "Exposurists"[59] with examples of already existing activism in the Philippines in the hope that they will inform and energize future struggles.[60]

Like Melany, Jennifer and Strela were drawn to the Integrate/Exposure Program because of its emphasis on activism. "I didn't want to go to the Philippines as a tourist," said Jennifer. "I wanted to see the lives and the struggles of the common Pilipino people . . . and not the megamall or the tourist spots." And Strela wanted to "know exactly what was going in the Philippines"—to concretize what she had learned through her formal and informal education in the United States. As Strela explained,

> After taking some courses on Filipino American history and immigration, I developed a sense of the Filipino population as having a history of exploitation. And . . . I wanted to experience that. I was very interested in "Third Worldism," like why the Third World exists and questions just weren't being answered for me. And then also, I wanted to know exactly why so many Filipinos, like my parents, were immigrating to the United States. I wanted to know what was pushing people out of the country.

In June 1998, Jennifer, along with Melany and another U.C.S.D. student, left for the Philippines for a two-month stay. Inspired by Jennifer and Melany's stories about their experiences in the Philippines, Strela followed suit and left for a six-month stay in the Philippines in January 2000.

Melany, Jennifer, and Strela were deeply affected by their experiences in the Philippines. On a personal level, going "home" brought them face-to-face with their transnational family: they met long-lost relatives, pored over family albums, listened to family stories, and memorized family lores—all of which gave them keener insights into their parents' lives. "I never understood why my father hadn't gone back [to the Philippines] in twenty-five years," stated Melany.

> But when I was in the Philippines, I learned something about my dad. I saw how everybody idolized my father so much because he is the only one in the U.S. My father's family constructed an image of him as someone who "made it." And I think there was pressure for him to come back wealthy, successful, and have this extraordinary ability to financially provide for everybody, no matter what it costs. But my dad was far from wealthy, and so he couldn't go home.

For Jennifer, going to the Philippines empowered her to claim a "sense of ownership" over her Pinay identity. As Jennifer explained,

> I gained a sense of ownership over my identity, a definite tie I could hold on to that I didn't have before. After a decade of refusing to speak Tagalog to my parents 'cuz "I don't need a language no one else around me speaks," and then running across Pilipinos who thought I wasn't Pilipino enough 'cuz I don't speak Tagalog that fluent anymore, I felt a burning sensation in my gut every time I wondered what Pilipino was, what I was 'cuz I tried so hard to be "American" for so long, I had lost my Pilipino identity. Going to the Philippines gave me the perspective, the understanding, and enlightenment I needed to find my identity. I learned the language again. I reclaimed the spirit of what the Philippines was that my parents brought to the U.S. and gave to my brother and I as children, which we lost as we grew up.

Jennifer's connection to the country and its people was so deep that she embraced the Philippines as her motherland, her home:

> Before I went to the Philippines, I saw it not as my *motherland* but as my *mother's land.* I had no ties to that [place] that my parents called home. Their home. The Philippines was just a figment of my imagination, unreal to me as a place I could feel connected to. But after I went there, I now know that it is my land too. My motherland, stretching its loving arms to me and saying "welcome to me, my child." And as its child, with tears in my eyes, in a country strangely foreign yet comforting at the same time, feeling like I am home too.

But Strela cautioned against the romanticized belief that Filipino Americans easily blend into Philippine culture and society:

> It's not always the case that we, as Pil-Ams, can blend in while in the Philippines. In fact, while trying to blend in, we oftentimes feel a sense of alienation because we realize how removed we are from the culture and how privileged we are relative to native Pilipinos. By going to the Philippines, we attempt to reclaim our identity as Pilipinas, but we may never reclaim this identity in its entirety because in some sense, we can never be integrated into the culture entirely.

But the young women were most inspired and awed by the level of activism and political consciousness exhibited by the people and organizations in the Philippines. During their stay there, they met, worked with, and learned from numerous activist groups such as indigenous peoples fighting for scarce resources in the Cordillera, unionized urban workers fighting for a living wage in Manila, and peasant farmers fighting for their land in Hacidena Looc.[61] They learned by doing: they passed out union leaflets in the cities, planted and harvested rice in the provinces, helped organize rallies, and led discussion groups on such topics as landlessness and imperialism. Along the way, they met, befriended, and fell in love with what Jennifer termed the "spirit of the people":

> The spirit of the people [is] so strong. They fight for their land, for their family, for their survival and way of life. No matter how hard life was, they could still laugh, still had hope. The people I met were simple people, they were peasants, organizers, and indigenous peoples, but they were the most inspirational people I had ever met.

Melany, an experienced organizer, was thrilled by the level of activism that she saw in the Philippines: "The things that we participated in [in the Philippines] were things that we never saw here in the U.S., just like the mass amount of people that would protest in the streets, literally in the streets all day, instead of a couple of hours. It was just really powerful to see that kind of opposition." Armed with this collective memory, they felt ready to counter the dominant misrepresentations of the Philippines and its people as "unproductive" and "lazy." As Strela stated, "When I was there, I just saw for myself how hard people worked and how hard they fought for their rights. Especially the people in the provinces, they were just the exact opposite of 'lazy.' " Melany concurred, "Going to the Philippines strengthened me as a person and made me proud that I am a Pinay. It gave me that understanding to now defend myself when it comes to explaining my culture and my history and my people."

To remain connected to the Philippines, all three vowed to continue the social struggles here in the United States. And they have, with all three participating in various organizing efforts including the campaigns for living wage, for immigration rights, and for women's rights. Although they take seriously the power of organic solidarity based on identity, they insist on building coalitions around a common culture of activism. Going to the Philippines introduced them to the possibility of a shared struggle—the notion that people of color everywhere were engaged in a common political struggle against what Charles Mills terms the "racial contract."[62] For example, Melany discovered that the conditions faced by factory workers in the "export processing zones" in the Philippines were similar to those faced by *maquiladora* workers in Tijuana, Mexico—that both constituted the "new" workforce within the global reorganization of capitalism:

> In Manila, I met a woman who took me to the factories where the workers were on strike and exposed me to the working conditions there. I was making connections and I was telling them about how I'd worked with the Support Committee for the *maquiladora* workers in Mexico. I was helping them to see that it was an international thing, by telling them that it was an international, by telling them that I'd seen the same conditions in Mexico.

The ability to "[tell] them that it was an international thing"—that is, to look beyond cultural and national boundaries—is a powerful resource for ordinary people because it enables new forms of "transnational grassroots politics" to emerge in response to the current conditions of transnational capitalism.[63] Such is the power, promise, and possibility of "transnationalism from below": the making of an oppositional culture based on a transformative vision that delineates the violence of global capitalism and calls on the world's people to imagine a new vision and to "create an active path leading to it from the present."[64] Melany, Jennifer, and Strela, and countless other Filipino Americans, have shown us this path. They have instructed us about the creation of new social relations, new social subjects, new connecting ideologies, and new ways of living, seeing, and fighting; these are the tools of home making.

Notes

CHAPTER 1. HOME MAKING

1. I do not use the term *immigrant* to evoke images of permanent uprooting or to suggest a unilinear progression from foreign strangeness to assimilation and citizenship (see Handlin 1973). Instead, following Lisa Lowe (1996), I want to call attention to the ways in which the Filipino immigrant—as colonized national and racially marked minority—constitutes a generative site for critiquing the contradiction between the U.S. promises of inclusion and its practices of exclusion.

2. See Lowe 1996.

3. Michael Peter Smith (2001:6) defines an "agency-oriented theoretical perspective" as one that "concretely connects macro-economic and geopolitical transformations to the micro-networks of social action that people create, move in, and act upon in their daily lives."

4. George 1996:11.

5. George 1996.

6. Gold and Kibria 1993.

7. Grewal and Kaplan 1994:17.

8. Kearney 1995:227–28.

9. See Lipsitz 1999; Clifford 1994; Okamura 1998; Basch, Glick Schiller, and Szanton Blanc 1994; Levitt 2001.

10. See Portes, Guarzino, and Landolt 1999; Glick Schiller 1997.

11. Hondagneu-Sotelo and Avila (1997:549–50) raise the following objection to the transnational perspective: "We object to transnationalism's emphasis on circulation and the inderteminance of settlement. While significant segments of foreign-born Latinos regularly return to their countries for annual fiestas or to visit family members, most Latino immigrants are here to stay, regardless of their initial migration intentions."

12. Portes and Rumbaut 1996.
13. Examples of America-centric works include Archdeacon 1983 and Handlin 1973. For a critique of the America-centric perspective, see Goldberg 1992.
14. Goldberg 1992.
15. Cited in Goldberg 1992:212.
16. Golberg 1992.
17. Smith 1994:16.
18. Guarnizo and Smith 1999; Massey 1999.
19. Massey 1999:43.
20. Grewal and Kaplan 1994; Ong, Bonacich, and Cheng 1994; Abelmann and Lie 1995.
21. Burawoy 1976; Petras 1978; Portes 1978; Zolberg 1986.
22. For example, see Portes 1978.
23. Bonacich and Cheng 1984.
24. See Lowe 1996.
25. Campomanes 1997:534.
26. Lowe 1996:16.
27. Kearney 1995:229.
28. Campomanes 1997; Nguyen 1997.
29. Lowe 1998.
30. San Juan 1998b:12.
31. See Espiritu 1996.
32. Vassanji 1996:112.
33. In her insightful study of Hutu refugees in Tanzania, Malkki (1995:8) similarly argues that the literature on refugees, as well as most asylum states and international agencies dealing with refugees, tend to share the premise that refugees are necessarily a "problem."
34. Goldberg 1992.
35. See Chavez 2001.
36. Moore 1997; Smith and Edmonston, 1997; Suarez- Orozco and Suarez-Orozco, 1995.
37. Hondagneu-Sotelo 1995; Dunn 1996; Chavez 2001.
38. Chavez 2001:260–61.
39. Hondagneu-Sotelo 1995.
40. Chavez 2001:121. It is important to note, however, that even as U.S. national culture represents Asian settlers as model immigrants, it simultaneously locates them outside the cultural and racial boundaries of the nation (Lowe 1996).
41. Ong and Umemoto 1994; Ong 1993; Gold and Kibria 1993.
42. See Portes and Rumbaut 1996:chap. 3.
43. See Kim 2000.
44. Cabezas, Shinagawa, and Kawaguchi 1986–87; Okamura and Agbayani 1997; Foley 1997; Gutierrez 1995.
45. Kim 2000:17.
46. Sanchez 1997:1024.
47. Malkki 1995:8.
48. Hondagneu-Sotelo 1994.
49. Gordon 1997:206.

50. Gordon 1997:206–7.
51. Small 1997; Basch, Glick Schiller, and Szanton Blanc 1994; Rouse 1991.
52. Shukla 1996; Ong 1996; Okamura 1998.
53. Kim 1993:xi.
54. De Manuel 1997:44.
55. Katrak 1996:25. See also Gupta and Ferguson 1992:10.
56. Small 1997:193.
57. Martin and Mohanty 1986:191.
58. Naficy 1999:6, emphasis in original.
59. Santos 1982:11.
60. Katrak 1996:201.
61. Shammas 1996:466.
62. Vince Rafael (1997) raised similar questions about diasporic memory and nostalgia in a proposal for a conference on "Southeast Asian Diasporas."
63. Espiritu 1994.
64. Wolf 1997.
65. Appadurai 1996, 1991.
66. See Lipsitz 1999; Ong 1996; Hondagneu-Sotelo and Avila 1997.
67. Glick Schiller, Basch, and Szanton Blanc 1992:15; Wong 1995:17–18.
68. Ong 1996:738.
69. Guarzino and Smith 1999:12.
70. Foucault 1991; Ong 1996:738.
71. George 1996:2.
72. Lowe 1996.
73. Lipsitz 1998.
74. Saxton 1977:145.
75. Kolko 1976; San Juan 1998a:79.
76. For an analytical summary of these exclusionary practices, see Chan 1991:chap. 3.
77. Wong 1993:6.
78. San Juan 1991:117.
79. Cordova 1983; Cabezas, Shinagawa, and Kawaguchi 1986–87; Penaranda, Syquia, and Tagatac 1974.
80. George 1996:6.
81. Orsi 1985.
82. Gupta and Ferguson 1992:11.
83. Anderson 1983; Smith 1994:18.
84. Das Gupta 1997:574; Guarzino and Smith 1999:23.
85. Kondo 1996:97.
86. George 1996:9.
87. Martin and Mohanty 1986; Khan 1995:98.
88. Kearney 1995: 228.
89. Kearney 1995: 234.
90. Oliver and Johnson 1984; Min 1996.
91. Lipsitz 1998; Saito 2000; Okihiro 1994.
92. George 1996:31.
93. Rumbaut, 1991:220.

94. See Smith 1992:497.
95. Small 1997:203.
96. Personal Narratives Group 1989:261.
97. Sorensen 1999. I am quite aware that this methodology has an obvious limitation. As Arlie Hochschild (1989) found in a study of working parents, what women and men *say* may be quite different from what they actually *do*. Therefore, it is important also to observe what they do. Although I value the participant-observation method, I also want to call attention to the gendered nature of conducting fieldwork, a topic not often addressed in methodology textbooks. As a working mother with young children, I found that I seldom had the uninterrupted time needed to engage in this method "systematically." Most often, I had to squeeze in interviews during my children's school hours and to decline most invitations to community events or home visits that took place during the evening. The participant observation that I was able to conduct was usually at social events where I could bring the children: family birthday parties, church services, picnics, community sports events, and fund-raising activities. However, my participant-observation data were supplemented by ongoing informal conversations and interactions with Filipino American students at the University of California, San Diego, over the last decade and with close Filipino American friends and family members in the San Diego area and elsewhere. Although these Filipino American students and friends are not in my "official" sample and thus do not constitute "data" in the formal sense, their presence in my life—and mine in theirs—has given me keen insights into the more intimate aspects of Filipino American lives.
98. See Personal Narratives Group 1989:4–5.
99. Tapia 1997.
100. Rumbaut 1994.
101. See Morley 1999:152.

CHAPTER 2. LEAVING HOME

1. San Juan 1998a:190. The Philippines is the largest exporter of laborers. By some estimates, 4.5 million Filipinos work abroad, sending home between five and ten billion dollars a year in remittances (Economist 1998:38). Indeed, international migration is so prevalent that in 1997, the Philippine Secretary of Foreign Affairs called for "international migration" to be made a subject for elementary and high school students to prepare them for what he termed the "reality of immigration" (Okamura 1998:5).
2. Okamura 1998.
3. According to the 2000 census, Chinese Americans, at more than 2.4 million, constituted the largest Asian American group in the United States. In California, Chinese Americans, who neared the 1 million mark, also pushed past Filipinos (918,678) to become the state's largest Asian group. Though the Filipino population rose by 31.5 percent nationwide and 25.6 percent statewide, it fell well short of predictions that the 2000 census would crown Filipinos as the largest Asian group in the nation and in California.
4. Hondagneu-Sotelo 1994:6.

5. Hondagneu-Sotelo 1994:34.
6. Hondagneu-Sotelo 1995.
7. Lipsitz 1998:54.
8. See Espiritu (1994) for an elaboration of these arguments.
9. Constantino 1994.
10. Campomanes 1997; dela Cruz 1998.
11. In 1988, for example, there were more than a quarter million U.S. nationals in the Philippines, making it the largest concentration in Asia (Ong and Azores 1994:171).
12. Campomanes 1995:145.
13. dela Cruz 1998:xiv.
14. Lawcock 1975; Posadas and Guyotte 1990.
15. Dorita 1975:11.
16. Espiritu 1995.
17. Espiritu 1995.
18. Bogardus 1930; De Witt 1976.
19. Parrenas 1998.
20. Melendy 1977.
21. Harkavy 1982:17.
22. Cottrell and Hanks 1980:1.
23. Berry 1989; Simbulan 1989.
24. Garcia 1967:55, 92.
25. Drogin 1992.
26. These numbers were derived from the annual reports of the Secretary of the Navy to the U.S. Congress, various years.
27. See Espiritu 1995.
28. The Nationality Act of 1940 and its amendments give aliens who have served three or more years in the U.S. armed forces the opportunity to become U.S. citizens without having to meet the usual requirements such as residence.
29. U.S. House 1973:3.
30. Reza 1992.
31. Melendy 1977:96.
32. U.S. House 1973:15.
33. Lawcock 1975:473.
34. Hayles and Perry 1981:45–46.
35. These ratios were calculated from the annual reports of the Secretary of the Navy to the U.S. Congress, various years.
36. Hayles and Perry 1981:46.
37. Ingram 1970; Quinsaat 1976.
38. *The Nation* 1974.
39. U.S. House 1973:16.
40. Reza 1992.
41. Quinsaat 1976:101.
42. Bouvier and Gardner 1986.
43. Carino, Fawcett, Gardner, and Arnold 1990:2.
44. Liu and Cheng 1994.
45. Chan 1991:149–50.

46. Ruth 1970.
47. Small 1997:191.
48. Berry 1989:168.
49. Steinberg 1990:129–30.
50. Bello and Reyes 1986–87:73–83.
51. Pido 1986; Rumbaut 1991.
52. By 1967, the Philippines sent more nurses to the United States than any other country. In 1967, Filipino nurses received the highest number of U.S. nursing licenses among foreign-trained nurses, 1,521 licensure out of a total of 5,361 (Choy 2003).
53. Ong and Azores 1994.
54. Choy 2003.
55. Choy 2003. The information in the rest of this paragraph is also based on Choy 2003.
56. Carino, Fawcett, Gardner, and Arnold 1990:11–12.
57. See Thomas 1973; Borjas 1990.
58. See Ong, Bonacich, and Cheng 1994.
59. Sawada 1996:177.
60. Gmelch 1992: 26; Jones 1995:108; Perminow 1993; Hondagneu-Sotelo 1994; Sawada 1996; Small 1997.
61. Sawada 1996:177.
62. From the chapter "We Have to Show the Americans that We Can Be as Good as Anybody," interview with A. B. Santos and Juanita Santos, which appears in *Filipino American Lives* by Yen Le Espiritu. Reprinted by permission of Temple University Press.
63. From the chapter "International Medical Graduates Are Tested Every Step of the Way," interview with Edgar Gamboa, which appears in *Filipino American Lives* by Yen Le Espiritu. Reprinted by permission of Temple University Press.
64. Hondagneu-Sotelo 1994.
65. Carino, Fawcett, Gardner, and Arnold 1990.
66. Okamura 1998:110.

CHAPTER 3. "POSITIVELY NO FILIPINOS ALLOWED"

1. Lowe 1996; Gutierrez 1995.
2. Lowe 1996:4.
3. Said 1993.
4. Steinberg 1989.
5. Lipsitz 1998.
6. This sentence and the next two are based on Hobsbawm 1987:57–59.
7. McCormick 1967; Lafeber 1998.
8. Ickstadt 1990:14–15.
9. Lafeber 1998.
10. For example, when the annexation of the Philippines was deliberated in the United States, the *Wall Street Journal* urged the United States to retain enough interest in the Philippines to "assure a coaling station or naval base in Asiatic waters" (cited in Garcia 1967:10).

11. Cited in Palumbo-Liu 1999:19.
12. Cited in Vaughan 1995:307.
13. Lipsitz 1998:2.
14. Said 1993.
15. Said 1993:9.
16. Lowe 1996:5.
17. See Mills, 1997:26.
18. Hoganson, 1998:134–35.
19. As an example, an 1899 article on the Philippines in the popular *Nunsey's Magazine* began with an allegory about a man, a boy, and an apple. The man initially gives the youth a boost to reach for the apple, but then decides to grab the fruit for himself. When the boy fights for the apple, the man gives him a spanking (Vaughan 1995).
20. Vaughan 1995:304.
21. Hoganson 1998:136.
22. Horlacher 1990: 43–44.
23. Cited in Hoganson 1998:134–35.
24. Cited in Perrier 1990:115.
25. Rafael 2000: 21.
26. Anderson 1995.
27. Cited in Anderson 1995:100.
28. Horsman 1981.
29. Hoganson 1998:134–35.
30. Hoganson 1998:135; Vaughan 1995:306.
31. Cited in San Buenaventura 1998:8.
32. Lipsitz 1998:189.
33. Vaughan 1995:309. Unable to penetrate the Filipino "guerrillas," U.S. troops attacked the population at large, burning barrios, destroying storehouses and crops, poisoning wells, slaughtering farm animals, and killing civilians. In the notorious Samar campaign in late September 1901, General "Howlin' Jake" Smith ordered his troops to ravage the province and to kill "everything over ten." Three months later, in another brutal campaign, Major General J. Franklin Bell set out to destroy Batangas. According to statistics compiled by U.S. government officials, by the time Bell was finished, at least one hundred thousand people had been killed or had died as a direct result of the scorched-earth policies. In 1902, through superior military force and the collaboration of the conservative and moneyed Filipinos, the Americans finally put an end to the armed nationalist resistance. Although it is difficult to determine how many Filipinos died resisting occupying U.S. troops, estimates of the combined death toll from fighting, disease, and starvation ranged from several hundred thousands to one million (see Espiritu 1995:2).
34. San Buenaventura 1998:2.
35. San Buenaventura 1998:6; Lipsitz 1998:189–90.
36. See, for example, Mohanty 1991; Stoler 1991; Yegenoglu 1998.
37. This paragraph and the next are drawn from Hoganson 1998.
38. To demonstrate Filipino men's "effeminacy," imperialists portrayed them as unwilling to assume the role of the "breadwinner," preferring instead to tend

to domestic work such as child care. Some accounts used Filipino women to discredit Filipino men, depicting them as the more economically productive, assimilative, and intelligent members of society. At the same time, Filipinas were sexualized and racialized as alluring and willing belles, eager to secure the attention and service the needs of American men (Hoganson 1998:137).

39. The following report typifies the American reaction to the Filipino people at that time: "They are not *men*. Honesty, truth, justice, pity—are either extinct among these people, or else still undeveloped" (cited in Hoganson 1998:134).

40. Another level of gender is involved in imperialism, in addition to the binary construction of otherness and the gender anxieties of white men. In *Orientalism,* Edward Said (1979) shows how Asia itself became feminized in the Euro-American imagination because it seemed a source of "luxury" goods. In Europe, where production was considered manly and virtuous and consumption was suspect as female and decadent, the riches of Asia could be and were coded as "female." I thank George Lipsitz for reminding me of this point.

41. Stoler 1995:97.

42. George Chauncey (1994) likewise argues that the growing antipathy of middle-class men toward gay men at the turn of the twentieth century was closely tied to their growing concern that the gender arrangements of their culture were in crisis.

43. Ickstadt 1990:14

44. Ickstadt 1990:10.

45. Hoganson 1998:155. Dean Worcester, ethnologist from the university of Michigan and personal representative of President McKinley in the Philippines, explicitly drew a sexual distinction between Spaniards and Anglo-Americans as conquerors. He argued that when the Spaniards arrived in the Philippines in 1565, they had made commendable progress "in subduing" the tribes, but then had slowed down and "seemed to have lost much of their virility." On the other hand, the Americans "had grown more virile in subduing all the tribes across a vast continent over the same centuries and were more than potent to consummate what the Spanish colonizers had only begun" (cited in Drinnon 1980:285).

46. Hoganson 1998:134.

47. Hoganson 1998:10–11, 139.

48. Gotanda 1999:132.

49. Yegenoglu 1988:1.

50. Rafael 2000.

51. Rafael 2000:14.

52. San Buenaventura 1998:21

53. Mills 1997.

54. Mills 1997:48.

55. Goldberg 1993:185.

56. Mills 1997:48, emphasis in original.

57. The information for this paragraph is based on Blumentritt 1998 and Drinnon 1980:344–45.

58. See Lowe 1996; Bredbenner 1998; Mohanty 1991.

59. Lee 1999:109–10.

60. Palumbo-Liu 1999:37.

61. Cabranes 1979:37.

62. Cited in Cabranes 1979:29–30.

63. The relatively positive treatment accorded to Puerto Ricans may be partially explained be questionable census reports showing that whites outnumbered by nearly two to one the combined total of Negroes and mulattos (Cabranes 1979:31).

64. Cited in Cabranes 1979:33–34.

65. Cited in Cabranes 1979:83.

66. Cabranes 1979:6.

67. Cabranes 1979:96. Puerto Rico subsequently became a model for the smaller territories of the American empire. The Virgin Islands in 1927, Guam in 1950, and the Northern Mariana Islands in 1976 successfully claimed for their people the U.S. citizenship extended in 1917 to the people of Puerto Rico.

68. San Buenaventura 1998:10.

69. Sharma 1984:604–9.

70. Espiritu 1995; Jung 1999.

71. Jung 1999a:119.

72. Jung 1999a:120.

73. Jung 1999a:120.

74. Lowe 1996:80; Lipsitz 1998:70.

75. Palumbo-Liu 1999:33.

76. Bulosan 1946:121.

77. Espiritu 1997.

78. Lai 1992:165.

79. Cited in Takaki, 1989:321. See also Glenn 1986:194–95 and Chan 1991:104.

80. Scharlin and Villanueva 1992:5.

81. Cited in Sharma 1984:583, emphasis added.

82. Wallovitts 1972:21; Kitano and Daniels 1988:79–80.

83. See Agbayani-Siewert and Revilla 1995.

84. *Manong* literally means "uncle," a term of respect used to refer to old-timers. For the complete life history of Connie Tirona, please see chapter 3 in Espiritu 1995.

85. Cited in Espana-Maram 1996:186. See also Parrenas 1998.

86. Espana-Maram 1996:187–89.

87. Parrenas 1998.

88. Cited in Espana-Maram 1996:206–7.

89. Bogardus 1976.

90. See Frankenberg 1993:74–75.

91. Osumi 1982.

92. See Hondagneu-Sotelo 1995:183–84.

93. Omi and Winant (1994:123) note that since the 1960s, racial, ethnic, and other social identities have been reproduced and deployed through the use of "code words," those "phrases and symbols that refer indirectly to racial themes but do not directly challenge popular democratic or egalitarian ideals (for example, justice, equal opportunity)."

94. Lowe 1996:5.
95. Lowe 1996:27.

CHAPTER 4. MOBILE HOMES

1. Gupta and Ferguson 1992:10.
2. De Manuel 1997:42.
3. See Davis 1997:124.
4. This argument is influenced by Nina Glick Schiller and George Furon's (2001) argument that we need to redefine the "second generation" to include the entire generation in both homeland and new land that grow up within transnational social fields linked by familial, economic, religious, social, and political networks.
5. I base my discussion in this chapter on my respondents' recollections of life in the Philippines and not on actual interviews with Filipinos in the Philippines.
6. San Juan 1991:118.
7. Constantino 1975:3.
8. Sibayan 1991:73.
9. Constantino 1975:4.
10. Constantino 1975:4.
11. Pido 1986:49.
12. Ong and Azores 1994:171.
13. Chan 1991:149.
14. See, for example, Kim 1977; "The Loneliest Brides" 1952; Kim 1991.
15. Williams 1991.
16. See Lipsitz 1998:190; Peery 1994: 277–78.
17. Constantino 1975:1.
18. Cited in Rafael 1997:271.
19. Rafael 1997:271.
20. The term *balikbayan* joins the Tagalog words *balik,* "to return," with *bayan,* meaning both "town" and, at least from the late-nineteenth century on, "nation."
21. See Okamura 1998:122–23; Basch, Glick Schiller, and Szanton Blanc 1994:257. The definition of the *balikbayan* has varied over the years. As of December 1989, the Philippine Consulate defines a *balikbayan* as "a. a Filipino citizen who has been continuously out of the Philippines for a period of at least a year from date of last departure; b. a Filipino overseas worker; c. a former Filipino citizen and his family as this term is defined hereunder (spouse and children) who had been naturalized in a foreign country and comes or returns to the Philippines" (cited in Basch, Glick Schiller, and Szanton Blanc 1994:265).
22. Okamura 1998:26.
23. Basch, Glick Schiller, and Szanton Blanc 1994:256–58; Rafael 1997:270; Guarzino and Smith 1998:8.
24. Basch, Glick Schiller, and Szanton Blanc 1994; Lessinger 1992; Mahler 1996; Smith 1994; Laguerre 1998.
25. Basch, Glick Schiller, and Szanton Blanc 1994:257; Okamura 1998:122; Rafael 1997:270.

26. This is not to suggest that the anti-Marcos movement was homogeneous. The first U.S.-based opposition group was the National Committee for the Restoration of Civil Liberties in the Philippines (NCRCLP). NCRCLP was replaced in 1974 by the Anti-Martial Law Coalition, which later became the Coalition Against the Marcos Dictatorship/Philippine Solidarity Network (CAMD/PSN). Another important organization was the Movement for a Free Philippines (MFP), organized by exiled former Philippine senator Raul Manglapus. (When martial law was declared in the Philippines, Senator Manglapus had just left Manila and was on his way to a speaking engagement in California. Instead of returning to the Philippines, he remained in the United States in self-imposed exile and led the movement against the Marcos government from outside the Philippines.) For an informed account of the different camps within the movement, see Bello and Reyes 1986–87.

27. The information in this paragraph is based on Basch, Glick Schiller, and Szanton Blanc 1994, and Bello and Reyes 1986–87.

28. Gamboa's profile was featured in chapter 2. For a more comprehensive account of Gamboa's life, please see chapter 8 in Espiritu 1995.

29. Basch, Glick Schiller, and Szanton Blanc 1994:234.

30. Basch, Glick Schiller, and Szanton Blanc 1994:281; Laguerre 1998:157–58.

31. Bello and Reyes 1986–87:77.

32. Basch, Glick Schiller, and Szanton Blanc 1994:275; Bello and Reyes 1986–87.

33. Bello and Reyes 1986–87:75.

34. Okamura 1998:123.

35. See Goldring 1998:185.

36. Rafael 1997:270.

37. Francia 1999:213.

38. Goldring 1998:173.

39. See Small 1997:192.

40. Guarzino and Smith 1999.

41. Small 1997.

42. Small 1997:173.

43. Okamura 1998:126.

44. Basch, Glick Schiller, and Szanton Blanc 1994:257–58.

45. Okamura 1998:44.

46. Small 1997:196.

47. Basch, Glick Schiller, and Szanton Blanc 1994:81.

48. Small 1997:196.

49. Carino, Fawcett, Gardner, and Arnold 1990:78–79.

50. I am fully aware that there is a large gap between migrants' subjective description of their intentions to return "home" and the actual course of action they pursue. Past immigration studies have found little correlation between what migrants say and what they actually do: some migrants report that they intend to return home but end up staying, while others see their stay as permanent and yet one day pack up and "go home." So I ask this question not to determine how many individuals will or will not return home to live, but rather to learn more

about *why* they do or do not desire to return home. That is, my interest is qualitative rather than quantitative. Through looking at the migrants' stated preferences, I hope to gain some insight into their differential feelings and perceptions about life in the Philippines and in the United States.

51. Hondagneu-Sotelo 1994; Goldring 1998; Pessar 1986.

52. San Juan 1998a:190.

53. Diaz 2001.

CHAPTER 5. MAKING HOME

1. Massey 1999:41.

2. Even in the current era of post–Cold War military downsizing, San Diego retains its status as a Navy town. Between the payrolls for active-duty personnel and the local defense industry, the military establishment contributes in excess of 9.6 billion dollars per year to the local economy, accounting for one-fifth of the gross regional income (Shragge 1998:578). However, the Federal Base Realignment and Closing Program (BRAC), which began in 1989, has not left the city unscathed: the Naval Training Center graduated its last recruit in 1994 and closed its doors in 1998 and a number of commands have also either relocated or disappeared altogether (Shragge 1998:578).

3. The information in this paragraph is derived from Shragge 1998 and Killory 1993.

4. Shragge 1998:431.

5. Indeed, the city prides itself as having the largest collection of U.S. Navy (and Marine) installations in the world.

6. Lipsitz 1998.

7. Harris 1974.

8. These figures were derived from the annual reports of the Secretary of the Navy to the U.S. Congress, various years.

9. Killory 1993:42. The mass removal of San Diego's Japanese population during World War II exemplifies the virulent racism of the time. On New Year's Day, 1942, the *San Diego Union* reported the first of what would become a series of hate crimes directed at the Japanese community. The story also noted that local Filipinos, apparently wary of mistaken identity, "were passing out free identification buttons to members of their community" (cited in Estes 1993:4). While the federal, state, and local governments were still working out how best to intern Japanese Americans, the San Diego's Chamber of Commerce acted on its own. At a crucial Chamber board meeting, the county agricultural commissioner proclaimed that his department was intent on "protect[ing] the people of San Diego from the possibility of poisoning of fruits and vegetables by Japanese farmers" (cited in Shragge 1998: 526). The County Agricultural Department then instituted a program to test all shipments from local Japanese farmers; it also sent inspectors out to all the Japanese farms "in order to keep a close watch on the crops in the fields." At this same board meeting, the city's district attorney informed the Chamber's directors that the San Diego County Defense Council had decided that "all Japanese, both alien and American-born, [should] be evacuated from the State of California and sent to the interior of the United

States." Accordingly, his office was tracking down the Japanese wherever they might be in the county (cited in Shragge 1998:526). April 1942 saw the wholesale removal of San Diego's Japanese population from the county. As happened elsewhere, the mass evacuation of San Diego's Japanese population devastated the community—economically, physically, and emotionally. Although many of the evacuees returned to the county at war's end in 1945, their prewar livelihood, lifestyles, and sense of community had been shattered. As Shragge (1998) reports, after the war, the Japanese community in San Diego existed only in the abstract and not in the physical sense.

10. Hewes 1946:13; Harris 1974:128.

11. Quinsaat 1976:104.

12. As in other parts of the U.S. mainland, the first Filipinos in San Diego were students. According to Adelaida Castillo (1976), school records indicate that in 1903 a group of Filipinos between the ages of sixteen and twenty-five enrolled at the State Normal School (now San Diego State University). Lawrence Lawcock (1975) reported that nineteen Filipinos organized a Filipino Students' Club in San Diego that same year. Presumably arriving on government scholarship, these *pensionados* stayed only for one year, during which they studied algebra, drawing, botany, English, and music. Nonsponsored students—students who came on their own without government sponsorship—also came to San Diego.

13. See Espiritu 1995.

14. 1964—Naval Training Center, San Diego: Rhett Asis, Victor Campos, Jose Cruz, A. B. Funtanilla, D. M. Garces, Librado Gascon, E. P. Gratil, G. G. Hermosa, Manuel Sarte, R. N. Valdez, A. V. Villacorte.

1975—Naval Training Center, San Diego: Eleazar Baltazar, Eladio Bareng, Renato Batalla, Jeffrey Becasen, Carlos Bituin, Florante Cabanatan, Onofre Dauz, Aquilino Elane, Angelito Garcia, Jose A. Navea Jr., Manuel Nunez, Jose Morales.

1979—Naval Training Center, San Diego: F. A. Atienza, Henry Abanes, Winston Almacen, Irwin Bacuita, Laredo Gois, Danio Ibarra, Feliz Lozada, Christopher Olis, Melvin Odonez, Cesar Paradeza, Miguelito Sakay, Fredo Tolentino, Angelito Torres.

15. Szalay and Bryson 1977:11.

16. *The Anchors* are not paginated; therefore, I am unable to include page numbers for the quotes taken from these three publications; emphasis added.

17. Lowe 1996.

18. A 1977 U.S. Navy-sponsored study found that the large majority of Filipinos were stewards, cooks, or clerks in the field of food service or processing. In contrast, the Americans enjoyed a broad diversity of assignments in the fields of communication, weaponry, aviation, maintenance, and administration. (Szalay and Bryson 1977:18).

19. Unlike earlier years, when there was relatively little competition to join the U.S. Navy, by the time that Leo Sicat and his friends submitted their application in 1965, they were among some one hundred thousand Filipinos who applied to the U.S. Navy that year. For a published life history of Leo Sicat, see chapter 6 in Espiritu 1995.

20. Mills 1997.
21. These ideas were developed in a conversation with Rick Bonus.
22. Pido 1986:106; Posadas and Guyotte 1990:41–42.
23. Bulosan 1973:98.
24. Castillo-Tsuchida 1979:97.
25. Szalay and Bryson 1977:52.
26. On September 11, 1969, the importance of Cavite City was confirmed when the Council of the City of San Diego adopted Resolution No. 19769 establishing a sister-city relationship between the City of San Diego and Cavite City.
27. Duff and Ransom 1973:203.
28. Ingram 1970.
29. Quinsaat 1976:108.
30. Szalay and Bryson 1977:30.
31. Duff and Ransom 1973.
32. In their review of contemporary immigration to the United States, Portes and Rumbaut (1996:29) report that geographical propinquity plays a significant role in the settlement decisions of contemporary immigrants.
33. Rumbaut 1991:220.
34. Portes and Rumbaut 1996:32–34.
35. Carino, Fawcett, Gardner, and Arnold 1990:63.
36. At the time of my interview in the early 1990s, only three women of the original thirteen were left.
37. The *sampaguita* is the national flower of the Philippines.
38. In a 1937 study of the composition of the Filipino married population in Los Angeles, Severino Corpus found that the majority of the Filipino immigrant men married non-Filipinas such as Mexicans, Germans, Jews, Poles, Spaniards, Japanese, and "whites."
39. Although clearly not every Filipino/a in the labor force was in a white-collar or upper-blue-collar occupation, almost 75 percent of the CILS sample (see note 39) came from families that owned their own home—a strong indicator of middle-class status, one that many working-class Filipinos strived to achieve and maintain by taking on multiple jobs and working multiple shifts.
40. The Children of Immigrants Longitudinal Study (CILS) is the largest survey of its kind to date in the United States. The study has followed the progress of a large sample of teenage youths representing seventy-seven nationalities in two main areas of immigrant settlement in the United States: Southern California (San Diego) and South Florida (Miami and Fort Lauderdale). The initial survey, conducted in Spring 1992 ("T1"), interviewed 5,262 students enrolled in the eighth and ninth grades in schools of the San Diego Unified

School District (N = 2,420), and of the Dade and Broward County Unified School Districts (N = 2,296 and 339, respectively, with another 207 enrolled in private bilingual schools in the Miami area). The sample was drawn in the junior high grades. For purposes of the study, students were eligible to enter the sample if they were U.S. born but had at least one immigrant (foreign-born) parent, or if they themselves were foreign born and had come to the U.S. at an early age (most before age ten). More than three years later, in 1995–96 ("T2"), a second survey of the same group of children of immigrants was conducted—this time supplemented by in-depth interviews with a stratified sample of their parents (the interviews with the parents were conducted separately in their homes and in their native languages).

The principal nationalities represented in the San Diego CILS sample are Mexican, Filipino, Vietnamese, Laotian, Cambodian, and smaller groups of other children of immigrants from Asia (mostly Chinese, Japanese, Korean, and Indian) and Latin America. The number of Filipino youth surveyed was 808 at T1 (1992) and 716 at T2 (1995–96). Reflecting long-established migration histories, the vast majority of the CILS Filipino sample—75 percent—were either born in the United States or arrived before the age of five, meaning that much if not all of their socialization occurred while in the United States and all of their schooling took place in the United States. Of the 808 Filipino youth first surveyed, over half were born in the US; 20 percent came to the States between infancy and age five; and another quarter came to the States after the age of five.

For further information on the CILS survey results, see Portes and Rumbaut 2001 and Rumbaut and Portes 2001.

41. *Samahan* means working together in Tagalog.

42. Liu, Ong, and Rosenstein 1991:501. Other local professional organizations include the Filipino Nurses Association, Filipino Accountants of Southern California, and the Filipino American Educators Association. The relative class homogeneity of these associations suggests that these professionals limit their contact largely to Filipinos of the same socioeconomic background.

43. Bonus 2000.

44. My estimate of the number of Filipino American organizations is derived from the official membership list of the Council of Pilipino American Organizations (COPAO) and from the announcements of community organizations in the local Filipino American newspapers.

45. In a study of Filipino hometown associations in Hawaii, Jonathan Okamura (1983) likewise argues that organizational divisiveness within the Filipino community is not manifest between associations as much as it may be within the same association. Most organizations extend membership to non–town mates and, through their officers, are supportive of the activities of other associations.

46. Okamura 1983.

47. Bonus 2000:102.

48. Quoted in Bonus 2000:111.

49. Bonus 2000.

CHAPTER 6. HOME, SWEET HOME

1. Tyner 1999.

2. Espiritu 1997.

3. See Espiritu and Wolf 2001. Other health-care occupations include dietician, health record technician, physician, practical nurse, health technician, nursing attendant, orderly, and dental-medical technician.

4. But this is not unique to the Filipino community. In a review of the family life of African slaves, Chinese migrants, and colonized Mexicans, Bonnie Thornton Dill (1994) concludes that race has been fundamental to the construction and destruction of families in the United States.

5. Glenn 1986:218.
6. George 1996.
7. Collins 1991.
8. Espiritu 1997:90–91.
9. Kim 1990:70.
10. Romero 1992.
11. See Espiritu 1997:35–36.
12. Espiritu 1997:22.
13. After World War II, the largely male Filipino community in the United States was revitalized by the arrival of sixteen thousand women—almost all wives of U.S. servicemen, a sizeable number of whom were Filipinos serving in the U.S. Navy (Agbayani-Siewert and Revilla 1995).
14. This interview of Reynaldo Cablay was conducted by his daughter to fulfill a class assignment for an Ethnic Studies course entitled Filipino American Lives, in the fall of 1996, University of California, San Diego.
15. Francia 1999:205.
16. The experiences of Navy families echo those of other "split-household" families. The spotty information on the lives of the wives who stayed behind in Asia (before World War II) suggests that the split-household arrangement was both liberating and oppressive: it gave some women more independence but also increased their burden (Espiritu 1997:25–27). Pierette Hondagneu-Sotelo (1994) recorded similar findings: the absence of their husbands expanded women's work routines and responsibilities but also enabled them to act more decisively and autonomously.
17. The interview was conducted by this daughter as a part of an Ethnic Studies class assignment.
18. Kaplan 1997.
19. Between 1975 and 1980, women (twenty years and older) constituted more than 50 percent of the immigrants from China, Burma, Indonesia, Taiwan, Hong Kong, Malaysia, Korea, Japan, Thailand, and the Philippines (Donato 1992).
20. Tyner 1999:678.
21. Donato 1992:164.
22. See U.S. Bureau of the Census 1993:figure 6.
23. Ong and Azores 1994:154. Owing to the dominance of nurses, Filipinas are more likely than other women and than Filipino men to be in professional jobs. According to the 1990 Census, 20 percent of Filipino women but only 12 percent of Filipino men had professional occupations. The same pattern exists for San Diego Filipinos. Of the approximately eight hundred students sampled for CILS, 30 percent of their fathers but almost 50 percent of their mothers had at least a college degree or more. The proportion of parents in white-collar occupations matches closely their educational attainment with almost 60 percent of the mothers but only about 40 percent of the fathers in white-collar positions (Espiritu and Wolf 2001).
24. See, for example, Caspari and Giles 1986; Davis and Heyl 1986. Sheba George's (2000) dissertation—a study of female nurses from India—is among the few to investigate the phenomenon of female-led migration, and possibly the first to explore in details the gender implications of the female-led migration of professionally trained women to the United States.

25. By the late 1960s, 80 percent of EVP participants in the United States were from the Philippines. Between 1956 and 1969, Filipino health personnel dominated Filipino participation in the program, with nurses comprising more than 50 percent (11,136) of the total number (20,420) of exchange visitors from the Philippines (Choy 2003).

26. Exchange visitors are allowed to stay in the United States for a maximum of only two years, after which they are supposed to leave the country and return to their countries of origin.

27. Hondagneu-Sotelo 1994.

28. Choy 2003.

29. In this chapter, I argue that my interviewees report distinctively gendered motivations for migration. I understand that these are clearly post-facto responses. On the other hand, I believe that they deserve to be taken seriously, because they add nuance to the prevailing economistic explanations of migration.

30. See Choy 2003.

31. In her study of Filipina exchange nurses, Catherine Choy (2003) reports that her interviews reveal that some Filipino families utilized the exchange program to increase family surveillance and discipline. For example, one family sent a daughter to the United States to monitor the activities of a younger daughter already abroad; another wanted their daughter to leave to temporarily separate her from her boyfriend in the Philippines. While important, these cases are examples of family-initiated migrations; in this section, I am interested in migration movements that have been initiated by the women themselves.

32. Choy 2003.

33. Choy 2003.

34. Dill 1988; Glenn 1986; Hondagneu-Sotelo and Avila 1997. See Parreñas (2001) for an eloquent discussion of the pain of family separation experienced by Filipina domestic workers in Rome and Los Angeles.

35. Min 1998:52.

36. Hondagneu-Sotelo 1994; Espiritu 1997; Menjivar 1999.

37. Chen 1992; Min 1998; Pesquera 1993.

38. Ong and Azores 1994:183–84.

39. Pressner 1998.

40. Hondagneu-Sotelo and Avila 1997:562.

41. Chen 1992; Min 1998; Pesquera 1993.

42. Pesquera 1993:185.

43. Romero 1992:15.

CHAPTER 7. “WE DON’T SLEEP AROUND”

1. Eastmond 1993:40.
2. San Juan 1991:117.
3. George 1996:2.
4. George 1996:189.
5. Lipsitz 1998:1.
6. Lowe 1996.
7. Tuan 1998.

8. Lowe 1996:8.
9. Lee 1996:24.
10. Tuan 1998.
11. Alexander 1991:133.
12. Lamont 1997.
13. Collins 1991; Marchetti 1993; Hamamoto 1994.
14. A few studies have documented the ways racialized communities have represented white Americans. For example, in his anthropological work on Chicano joking, José Limón (1982) reports that young Mexican Americans elevate themselves over whites through telling "stupid American" jokes in which an Anglo-American is consistently duped by a Mexican character. In her interviews with African American working-class men, Michele Lamont (1997) finds that these men tend to perceive white Americans as immoral, sneaky, and untrustworthy. Although these studies provide an interesting and compelling window into racialized communities' views of white Americans, they do not analyze how the rhetoric of moral superiority often depends on gender categories.
15. Orsi 1985.
16. Indeed, people around the world often believe that Americans have no real family ties. For example, during a visit to my family in Vietnam, my cousin asked me earnestly if it was true that American children put their elderly parents in nursing homes instead of caring for them at home. She was horrified at this practice and proclaimed that, because they care for their elders, Vietnamese families are morally superior to American families.
17. See di Leonardo 1984; Kibria 1993; Hickey 1996; and Lamont 1997.
18. There was evidence that some respondents gave self-legitimating answers. In one such example, a Filipino man spoke glowingly about his "close-knit" family and his three well-adjusted and successful daughters. It was only when I interviewed one of the daughters that I learned that this man had a previous marriage that had ended in divorce and that this daughter was in the process of divorcing her own husband. In his conversations with me, the father did not mention either of these divorces. In another example, when I asked a Filipina mother if she experienced conflict with her daughter, she replied without hesitation, "No, we always had a good relationship." However, her son, who was in the room at the time, questioned this statement: "Are you sure about that, Mom? I remember a lot of conflict between you two." When his mother continued to insist that they had a conflict-free relationship, the son whispered to me, "I think you should interview my sister." I interviewed the sister (Amanda Flores) and found out that she considered her relationship with her mother to have been very "difficult." These examples underscore the importance of interviewing multiple members of the same family, if at all possible.
19. Di Leonardo 1984:229.
20. Di Leonardo 1984:222.
21. Alexander 1991:133.
22. Gilman 1985; Stoler 1991.
23. Writing on the objectification of black women, Collins (1991) argues that popular representations of black females—the mammy, the welfare queen, and the Jezebel—all pivot around their sexuality, either desexualizing or hypersexu-

alizing them. Along the same lines, Native American women have been portrayed as sexually excessive (Green 1975); Chicano women as "exotic and erotic" (Mirande 1980); and Puerto Rican and Cuban women as "tropical bombshells . . . sexy, sexed and interested" (Tafolla 1985:39).

24. Alexander 1991:133.
25. Gilman 1985:89.
26. Stoler 1991.
27. Mazumdar 1989:3–4; Espiritu 1997:93.
28. Halualani 1995; Egan 1996.
29. Coronel and Rosca 1993; Warren 1993.
30. Villanueva 1991.
31. Wong 1993:53.
32. According to Filipino cultural historian Nicanor G. Tiongson (2001), during the early decades of U.S. colonial regime, Philippine community theater denounced U.S. colonialism through depicting Filipinas who pursued American men as "Americanized" and as sexually immoral.
33. Halualani 1995:49; also Ordonez 1997:122.
34. Dasgupta and DasGupta 1996:229–31.
35. The relationship between immigrant parents and their sons deserves a study of its own. According to Gabaccia (1994:70), "immigrant parents fought with sons, too, but over different issues: parents' complaints about rebellious sons focused more on criminal activity than on male sexuality or independent courtship." Moreover, because of their mobility, young men have more means to escape—at least temporarily—the pressures of the family than young women. In his study of Italian American families, Orsi (1985) reports that young men rebelled by sleeping in cars or joining the army; but young women did not have such opportunities.
36. Billson 1995.
37. Gabaccia 1994:xi.
38. Orsi 1985:135
39. Gabaccia 1994:113.
40. Yung 1995; Orsi 1985; Ruiz 1992; Waters 1996; Dasgupta and DasGupta 1996.
41. Rumbaut and Ima 1988; Woldemikael 1989; Matute-Bianchi 1991; Gibson 1995.
42. Waters 1996:75–76; Haddad and Smith 1996:22–24.
43. See, for example, Wolf 1997.
44. Wolf 1997.
45. Dasgupta and DasGupta 1996:230.
46. Wolf 1997:467.
47. The names of the two high schools cited in this excerpt are fictitious.
48. See Kibria 1993.
49. See Maglin and Perry 1996.
50. Tolman and Higgins 1996:206.
51. Tolman and Higgins 1996.
52. Dasgupta and DasGupta 1996:236.
53. According to a 1992 health-assessment report of Filipinos in San Fran-

cisco, Filipino teens have the highest pregnancy rates among all Asian groups and, in 1991, the highest rate of increase in the number of births compared to all other racial or ethnic groups (Tiongson 1997:257).

54. See Wolf 1997. In the CILS data, the ideology of the family as an important primary group was expressed as well, but was not necessarily matched by the actual practice of feelings of family cohesion and consensus. It is important to note that female respondents appeared to experience more familial conflicts than male respondents. In 1995, while almost two-thirds of the sample felt strongly that family togetherness was always or often important, only about half lived in families in which family members felt close, and not quite 40 percent lived in families that enjoyed spending time together. In other words, while the great majority of the respondents indicated that the ideology of family togetherness and cohesion was extremely important to them, few actually experienced this cohesion in their family life (Espiritu and Wolf 2001).

55. Espiritu 1994.

56. I thank Rosemary George for reminding me of this point.

57. The few available studies on Filipino American intermarriage indicate that Filipinos intermarry at a high rate relative to other Asian groups. In 1980, Filipino men in California recorded the highest rate of intermarriage rate among all Asian groups, and Filipino women had the second highest rate after Japanese women (Agbayani-Siewert and Revilla 1995:156).

58. See Lau 1995.

59. See Frankenberg 1993; Lipsitz 1998.

60. See Gabaccia 1994:113.

CHAPTER 8. "WHAT OF THE CHILDREN?"

1. See Espiritu 1994 for an elaboration of this argument.
2. Rosaldo 1994:244.
3. Espiritu and Wolf 2001.
4. Espiritu and Wolf 2001.
5. Harris 1974; Hewes 1946.
6. Espiritu and Wolf 2001
7. Aguilar-San Juan 1998.
8. Espiritu, Fujita Rony, Kibria, and Lipsitz 2000:136.
9. Davis 1997:318.
10. Lipsitz 2000:64.
11. Espiritu and Wolf 2001.
12. Carlston 1983:18; Takaki 1989: 432; Portes and Rumbaut 1996.
13. Espiritu 1994:256.
14. Mura 1988:137.
15. San Juan 1991:123.
16. Espiritu and Wolf 2001.
17. Francia 1999:212.
18. Lowe 1996:64.
19. Gonzalves 1997:176.
20. Williams 1989:428.

21. Lowe 1996:64, emphasis in original.
22. Lipsitz 2000:264

CHAPTER 9. HOMES, BORDERS, AND POSSIBILITIES

1. Dunn 1996; Palafox 1996. In 1996, as an example of the escalation of military involvement in domestic law enforcement, in the San Diego sector alone, some 350 members of marine and army units helped "monitor electric sensors, staff night-vision scopes, assist with communications and transportation, and conduct aerial surveillance" (Palafox 1996:14).
2. Gross 1999.
3. Cacho 2000:402; also Hondagneu-Sotelo 1995; Lipsitz 1998:47–54.
4. Cited in Rose 1985:205.
5. Starr and Roberts 1981.
6. Roberts 1988:81.
7. U.S. Commission on Civil Rights 1992:22–48.
8. Lowe 1996; Lipsitz 1998; Ong, Bonacich, and Cheng 1994; Fernández-Kelly 1983.
9. Feagin 1997:28.
10. Smith 1992.
11. Chavez 1997:66.
12. Rodriquez 1997:225.
13. Grewal and Kaplan 1994.
14. Mahmud 1997:633.
15. For example, in 1996 the Committee on International Migration of the Social Science Research Council organized a conference entitled "Becoming Americans/America Becoming." According to the organizers, the conference was organized to provide an interdisciplinary overview and assessment of the socio-cultural and political aspects of immigrant incorporation and responses by native-born Americans. A selection of revised conference papers was published in a special issue of the *International Migration Review* 31 (winter 1997). The organizing theme of the issue was "Immigrant Adaptation and Native-Born Responses in the Making of Americans."
16. Schlesinger 1991; Brimelow 1995.
17. Feagin 1997; Portes and Rumbaut 1996.
18. Feagin 1997:32, 37.
19. Portes 1994:634. Portes (1994:632) contends that it is the second generation, not the first, that is the key to establishing the long-term consequences of immigration. The issues to be permanently decided by the second generation include "the continuing dominance of English, the growth of a welfare-dependent population, the resilience of culturally distinct urban enclaves, and the decline or growth of ethnic intermarriages."
20. By "ethnic studies" scholars, I do not mean scholars in Ethnic Studies departments, but rather scholars who take an ethnic studies approach to their work. For a discussion on the ethnic studies approach, please see Espiritu 1999.
21. Muller 1997:109.

22. Kumar 2000:xi, emphasis in original.
23. Mahmud 1997:633.
24. Lowe 1996.
25. Roberts 1997:211.
26. Chavez 1997:62.
27. Lowe 1996:5.
28. Chavez 1997:67.
29. Kaplan 1993.
30. Lipsitz 1998:70–72.
31. Kaplan 1993.
32. Mills 1997:53.
33. Chang 1997.
34. Cacho 2000:390.
35. Chang 1997:249–51.
36. Patricia Pessar (1999) has made the same point regarding immigration studies. She argues that classical theories of migration emphasize movements of capital and labor and envision migrants as adult men acting primarily from economic motives. In so doing, these theories conceptualize women and children as appendages to male migration or as occasional exceptions to the adult male model.
37. Nonini and Ong 1997:23.
38. Rosaldo 1994:239.
39. Francia 1999:205.
40. Bourdieu 1990:22.
41. Small 1997.
42. Mahler (1999) and Hondagneu-Sotelo (1994) also report that most Salvadoran and Mexican immigrants, respectively, were here to stay.
43. Hobsbawm and Ranger 1983.
44. Francia 1999:212.
45. Fanon 1963:170.
46. Ong 1996.
47. Lloyd 1994:229.
48. Hall 1990.
49. Hall 1990:225.
50. Ong 1987; Williams 1989; Collins 1991; Grewal and Kaplan 1994.
51. Foucault 1991.
52. Friday 1994; Scharlin and Villanueva 1992; Fujita Rony 2000.
53. Nonini and Ong 1997:26.
54. Mohanty 1991:13, emphasis in original.
55. Ong 1997:194–95.
56. In 1994, the California electorate voted in favor of Proposition 187, a measure designed to deny medical treatment and education to undocumented workers and their families. In 1995, the University of California Regents voted to eliminate affirmative action for minorities and women in admissions. A year later, state voters passed Proposition 209 to end statewide affirmative action practices.
57. These three women prefer to identify themselves as *Pinays*, a term used

to connote politically conscious Filipina Americans. As Melany explained, "To me, *Pinay* is like the term *Chicana;* it is a term used when you have a certain sense of consciousness of your history, your people, that you are respectful. It's a political term, too."

58. But they have not always been this confident about their identities. Growing up in the suburbs, Jennifer felt culturally empty: "When we moved to the suburbs, the language, the food, the culture began to disappear, and I was left empty. There's a void there full of questions of what is Filipino? You feel embarrassed 'cuz you're Filipino, but you don't know what Filipino is. A country, a land, a culture, a way of life, a language, a food?" In the same way, Melany related an "identity crisis" that she experienced during her sophomore and junior years in high school:

> I felt the pressure to *act* white because this is what would get me into college. All of my life, my best friends and people I grew up with were either Filipino or Mexican. As I started thinking about college, I realized I needed to start studying and *acting* more like the white students in my classes because they were the ones who were also pursuing a higher education. The white students were the most motivated, most prepared, and I wanted to surround myself and create relationships with those people and as a result, ended up spending less time with my friends of color.

Unlike Jennifer and Melany, Strela attended a high school with a sizeable Filipino student population. There she helped to found Halo-Halo, the first Filipino American student club on campus. But the club did not meet her expectations: it became primarily a social space rather than an educational space where she and other Filipino students could learn about their history, language, and culture—the tangible facts and tidbits that they felt they had not been taught at home or at school.

59. These were the names used to describe participants in the Integration/Exposure Program.

60. The Exposure Program to the Philippines is about thirty years old. During the late 1960s and early 1970s, there was a strong and growing movement in the Philippines calling for an end to feudalism and fascism and U.S. imperialism in the Philippines. Movement supporters were among those Filipinos who migrated to the United States during the 1970s. These migrants took frequent trips back to the Philippines to renew and revitalize their support for the fight for the liberation of the Philippines and its people. U.S.-born and/or -raised Filipinos have also gone through these U.S.-based support groups. Their purpose was to go back to their roots, to view firsthand the conditions of the people, and to meet peasants, students, workers and others who are struggling for national democracy. Some Filipino students have gone on medical missions with pro-people health organizations. The past few years have seen an increase in the number of Filipino youth taking exposure trips. Many of them get involved in local Filipino groups that organize locally and support the National Democratic Movement in the Philippines. The exposure trip program depends highly on the wants and needs of the exposurists. If they want to be exposed to progressive artists, they will be programmed with an artist group as their host. If they are interested in issues affecting women and children, then their program will have that emphasis. Other programs focus on students and youth, national minorities, church,

peasants, workers, teachers, medical workers. No matter what the focus is, the exposurist will be encouraged to have a minimum exposure to the peasants, workers, and urban poor. The length of the exposure depends on the exposurist. Some last for a couple of days while others have lasted for more than a year. Educational workshops, ideally before and during the trip, are an integral component of the exposure experience. These workshops give the exposurists an opportunity to learn comprehensively about the history and current economical, political, and social situation of the Philippines. As testified by Melany, Strela, and Jennifer, the exposure programs have often been life-changing as exposurists experience firsthand the harsh poverty and survival-level of life in the Philippines *and* the incredibly strong and vital movement that is transforming society. Finally, part of the Exposure Program is to understand Filipino culture and to bridge gaps between Filipinos and Filipino Americans. This means trying to ascertain where Filipino Americans fit into Filipino culture and how we they can be a part of the Filipino struggle as a whole.

61. In Hacienda Looc, peasant farmers were fighting to keep their land from being converted into a golf resort—an investment venture financed by such foreign investors as Jack Nicholas and Michael Jackson.

62. Mills 1997.

63. Smith 1994.

64. Boggs 1998:255.

Bibliography

Abelmann, Nancy, and John Lie. 1995. *Blue Dreams: Korean Americans and the Los Angeles Riots*. Cambridge, Mass.: Harvard University Press.

Agbayani-Siewert, Pauline, and Linda Revilla. 1995. "Filipino Americans." In *Asian Americans: Contemporary Trends and Issues,* edited by Pyong Gap Min. Thousand Oaks, Calif.: Sage.

Aguilar-San Juan, Karin. 1998. "Going Home: Enacting Justice in Queer Asian America." In *Q & A: Queer in Asian America,* edited by David L. Eng and Alice Y. Hom. Philadelphia: Temple University Press.

Alexander, Jacqui M. 1991. "Redrafting Morality: The Postcolonial State and the Sexual Offences Bill of Trinidad and Tobango." In *Third World Women and the Politics of Feminism,* edited by Chandra Talpade Mohanty, Ann Russo, and Lourdes Torres. Bloomington: Indiana University Press.

The Anchor. 1964. San Diego, Calif.: U.S. Naval Training Center.

Anderson, Benedict. 1983. *Imagined Communities: Reflections on the Origin and Spread of Nationalism*. London and New York: Verso.

Anderson, Warwick. 1995. " 'Where Every Prospect Pleases and Only Man Is Vile': Laboratory Medicine as Colonial Discourse." In *Discrepant Histories: Translocal Essays on Filipino Cultures,* edited by Vicente Rafael. Philadelphia: Temple University Press.

Anzaldúa, Gloria. 1987. *Borderlands = La Frontera: The New Mestiza.* San Francisco: Spinsters/Aunt Lute.

Appadurai, Arjun. 1991. "Disjunction and Difference in the Global Cultural Economy." *Public Culture* 2 (2): 1–24.

———. 1996. "Sovereignty Without Territoriality: Notes for a Postnational Geography, in the Geography of Identity." In *The Geography of Identity,* edited by Patricia Yaeger. Ann Arbor: University of Michigan Press.

Archdeacon, Thomas. 1983. *Becoming American: An Ethnic History.* New York: Free Press.

Basch, Linda, Nina Glick Schiller, and Cristina Szanton Blanc. 1994. *Nations Unbound: Transnational Projects, Postcolonial Predicaments, and Deterritorialized Nation-States.* Langhorn, Pa.: Gordon and Breach.

Bello, Madge, and Vince Reyes. 1986–87. "Filipino Americans and the Marcos Overthrow: The Transformation of Political Consciousness." *Amerasia Journal* 13: 73–83.

Berry, William E., Jr. 1989. *U.S. Bases in the Philippines: The Evolution of a Special Relationship.* Boulder, Colo.: Westview Press.

Billson, Janet Mancini. 1995. *Keepers of the Culture: The Power of Tradition in Women's Lives.* New York: Lexington Books.

Blumentritt, Mia. 1998. "Bontoc Eulogy, History, and the Craft of Memory: An Extended Conversation with Marlon E. Fuentes." *Amerasia Journal* 24 (3): 75–90.

Bogardus, Emory S. 1930. "Filipino Immigrant Attitudes." *Sociology and Social Research* 14: 469–79.

———. 1976. "Anti-Filipino Race Riots." In *Letters in Exile: An Introductory Reader on the History of Pilipinos in America.* Los Angeles: U.C.L.A. Asian American Studies Center.

Boggs, Grace Lee. 1998. *Living for Change: An Autobiography.* Minneapolis: University of Minnesota Press.

Bonacich, Edna, and Lucie Cheng. 1984. "Introduction: A Theoretical Orientation to International Labor Migration." In *Labor Immigration Under Capitalism: Asian Workers in the United States Before World War II,* edited by Lucie Cheng and Edna Bonacich. Berkeley and Los Angeles: University of California Press.

Bonus, Rick. 2000. *Locating Filipino Americans: Ethnicity and the Cultural Politics of Space.* Philadelphia: Temple University Press.

Borjas, George. 1990. *Friends or Strangers: The Impact of Immigrants on the U.S. Economy.* New York: Basic Books.

Bourdieu, Pierre. 1990. *In Other Worlds: Essays Toward a Reflexive Sociology.* Palo Alto, Calif.: Stanford University Press.

Bouvier, Leon, and Robert Gardner. 1986. "Immigration to the U.S.: the Unfinished Story." *Population Bulletin* 4: 1–50.

Bredbenner, Candice Lewis. 1998. *A Nationality of Her Own: Women, Marriage, and the Law of Citizenship.* Berkeley and Los Angeles: University of California Press.

Brimelow, Peter. 1995. *Alien Nation: Common Sense About America's Immigration Disaster.* New York: Random House.

Bulosan, Carlos. 1946. *America Is in the Heart.* Reprint, Seattle: University of Washington Press, 1973.

Burawoy, Michael. 1976. "The Functions and Reproduction of Migrant Labor: Comparative Material from Southern Africa and the United States." *American Journal of Sociology* 81: 1050–87.

Cabezas, Amado, Larry H. Shinagawa, and Gary Kawaguchi. 1986–87. "New

Inquiries into the Socioeconomic Status of Pilipino Americans in California." *Amerasia Journal* 13 (1): 1–21.

Cabranes, Jose. 1979. *Citizenship and the American Empire*. New Haven and London: Yale University Press.

Cacho, Lisa Marie. 2000. " 'The People of California Are Suffering': The Ideology of White Injury and Discourses of Immigration." *Cultural Values* 4 (4): 389–418.

Campomanes, Oscar. 1993. "The Institutional Invisibility of American Imperialism, the Philippines, and Filipino Americans." Paper presented at the Annual Meeting of the Association for Asian Studies, Los Angeles, March 25.

———. 1995. "The New Empire's Forgetful and Forgotten Citizens: Unrepresentability and Unassimilability in Filipino American Postcolonialities." *Critical Mass* 2 (2): 145–200.

———. 1997. "New Formations of Asian American Studies and the Question of U.S. Imperialism." *Positions* 5 (2): 523–50.

Carino, Benjamin, James T. Fawcett, Robert W. Gardner, and Fred Arnold. 1990. *The New Filipino Immigrants to the United States: Increasing Diversity and Change*. Honolulu: East-West Center.

Carlson, Alvar W. 1983. "The Settling of Recent Filipino Immigrants in Midwestern Metropolitan Areas." *Crossroads* 1 (1): 13–19.

Caspari, Andrea, and Wenona Giles. 1986. "Immigration Policy and the Employment of Portuguese Migrant Women in the UK and France: A Comparative Analysis." In *International Migration: The Female Experience*, edited by Rita James Simon and Caroline Brettell. Totowa, N.J.: Rowman & Allanheld.

Castillo, Adelaida. 1976. "Filipino Migrants in San Diego, 1900–1946." *Journal of San Diego History* 12: 27–35.

Castillo-Tsuchida, Adelaida. 1979. *Filipino Migrants in San Diego, 1900–1946*. San Diego: San Diego Society, Title Insurance and Trust Collection.

Chan, Sucheng. 1991. *Asian Americans: An Interpretive History*. Boston: Twayne.

Chang, Robert S. 1997. "A Meditation on Borders." In *Immigrants Out! The New Nativism and the Anti-Immigrant Impulse in the United States*, edited by Juan F. Perea. New York: New York University Press.

Chauncey, George. 1994. *Gay New York: Gender, Urban Culture, and the Making of the Gay Male World, 1890–1940*. New York: Basic Books.

Chavez, Leo R. 1997. "Immigration Reform and Nativism: The Nationalist Response to the Transnational Challenge." In *Immigrants Out! The New Nativism and the Anti-Immigrant Impulse in the United States*, edited by Juan F. Perea. New York: New York University Press.

———. 2001. *Covering Immigration: Popular Images and the Politics of the Nation*. Berkeley and Los Angeles: University of California Press.

Chen, H. S. 1992. *Chinatown No More: Taiwan Immigrants in Contemporary New York*. Ithaca, N.Y.: Cornell University Press.

Choy, Catherine Ceniza. 2003. *Empire of Care: Nursing and Migration in Filipino American History*. Durham, N.C., and London: Duke University Press.

Ciria-Cruz, Rene. 2000. "Why Image Counts." *Filipinas Magazine,* September, 7.

Clifford, James. 1994. "Diasporas." *Cultural Anthropology* 9 (3): 302–38.

Collins, Patricia Hill. 1991. *Black Feminist Thought: Knowledge, Consciousness, and the Politics of Empowerment.* New York: Routledge.

Constantino, Renato. 1975. "Our Captive Minds." In *Iriri Ti Pagsayaatan Ti Sapasap: A Reader on the History of Pilipinos in America,* edited by Pilipinos in America History Workgroup. San Francisco: Pilipinos in America History Workgroup.

———. 1994. "Identity and Consciousness: The Philippine Experience." Paper presented in Symposium 3 of the VIII World Sociology Congress, Toronto, Canada.

Cordova, Fred. 1983. *Filipinos: Forgotten Asian Americans, A Pictorial Essay, 1763–1963.* Dubuque, Iowa: Kendall/Hunt Publishing.

Coronel, Sheila, and Ninotchka Rosca. 1993. "For the Boys: Filipinas Expose Years of Sexual Slavery by the U.S. and Japan." *Ms.,* November/December, 11.

Corpus, Severino. 1937. "Second Generation Filipinos in Los Angeles." *Sociology and Social Research* 22: 446–51.

Cottrell, Alvin, and Robert Hanks. 1980. *The Military Utility of the U.S. Facilities in the Philippines.* Washington, D.C.: Center for Strategic and International Studies.

Crouchett, Loraine Jacobs. 1982. *Filipinos in California: From the Days of the Galleons to the Present.* El Cerrito, Calif.: Downey Place Publishing House.

Das Gupta, Monisha. 1997. " 'What Is Indian About You?' A Gendered, Transnational Approach to Ethnicity." *Gender and Society* 11 (5): 572–96.

Dasgupta, Shamita Das, and Sayantani DasGupta. 1996. "Public Face, Private Face: Asian Indian Women and Sexuality." In *"Bad Girls"/"Good Girls": Women, Sex, and Power in the Nineties,* edited by Nan Bauer Maglin and Donna Perry. New Brunswick, N.J.: Rutgers University Press.

Davis, Angela. 1997. "Interview with Lisa Lowe: Reflections on Race, Class, and Gender in the U.S.A." In *The Politics of Culture in the Shadow of Capital,* edited by Lisa Lowe and David Lloyd. Durham, N.C.: Duke University Press.

Davis, F. James, and Barbara Sherman Heyl. 1986. "Turkish Women and Guestworker Migration to West Germany." In *International Migration: The Female Experience,* edited by Rita James Simon and Caroline B. Brettell. Towata, N.J.: Rowman & Allanheld.

Davis, Rocio G. 1997. "Ninotchka Rosca's State of War and Jessica Hagedorn's Dogeaters: Revisioning the Philippines." In *Ideas of Home: Literature of Asian Migration,* edited by Geoffrey Kain. East Lansing: Michigan State University Press.

dela Cruz, Enrique. 1998. "Introduction: Essays into American Empire in the Philippines." *Amerasia Journal* 24 (2): vii–xv.

De Manuel, Dolores. 1997. "Imagined Homecomings: Strategies for Reconnection in the Writing of Asian Exiles." In *Ideas of Home: Literature of Asian Migration,* edited by Geoffrey Kain. East Lansing: Michigan State University Press.

De Quiros, Conrado. 1990. "Bracing for Balikbayans." In *Flowers from the Rubble*. Pasig City, Metro Manila, Philippines: Anvil Publishing.

De Witt, Howard A. 1976. *Anti-Filipino Movements in California: A History, Bibliography, and Study Guide*. San Francisco: R & E Research Associates.

Diaz, Vince. 2001. "Pacific Islander Roundtable: Theorizing Oceanic Identity." Paper presented at the East of California conference, Oberlin College, Oberlin, Ohio, October 12–13.

"A Different Kind of Foreign Policy." 1998. *Economist*, 24 October, 38.

Di Leonardo, Micaela. 1984. *The Varieties of Ethnic Experience: Kinship, Class, and Gender Among California Italian-Americans*. Ithaca and London: Cornell University Press.

Dill, Bonnie Thornton. 1988. "Our Mother's Grief: Racial-Ethnic Women and the Maintenance of Families." *Journal of Family History* 13: 415–31.

Dirlik, Arif. 1996. "Asians on the Rim: Transnational Capital and Local Community in the Making of Contemporary Asian America." *Amerasia Journal* 22 (3): 1–24.

Donato, K. M. 1992. "Understanding U.S. Immigration: Why Some Countries Send Women and Others Send Men." In *Seeking Common Ground: Multidisciplinary Studies of Immigrant Women in the United States*, edited by Donna Gabbacia. Westport, Conn.: Greenwood.

Dorita, Mary. 1975. *Filipino Immigration to Hawaii*. San Francisco: R & E Research Associates.

Drinnon, Richard. 1980. *Facing West: The Metaphysics of Indian-Hating and Empire-Building*. Minneapolis: University of Minnesota Press.

Drogin, Bob. 1992. "Hopeful Filipinos Foresee a Boom as U.S. Exits Subic Bay." *Los Angeles Times*, 18 August.

Duff, Donald, and Arthur Ransom. 1973. "Between Two Worlds: Filipinos in the U.S. Navy." In *Asian Americans*, edited by Stanley Sue and Nathan Wagner. Palo Alto, Calif.: Science and Behavior Books.

Dunn, Timothy. 1996. *The Militarization of the U.S.-Mexico Border, 1978–1992: Low-Intensity Conflict Doctrine Comes Home*. Austin, Tex.: Center for Mexican American Studies, University of Texas at Austin.

Eastmond, Marita. 1993. "Reconstructing Life: Chilean Refugee Women and the Dilemmas of Exile." In *Migrant Women: Crossing Boundaries and Changing Identities*, edited by Gina Buijs. Oxford: Berg.

Egan, Timothy. 1996. "Mail-Order Marriage, Immigrant Dreams, and Death." *New York Times*, 26 May, 12.

Espana-Maram, Linda Nueva. 1996. "Negotiating Identity: Youth, Gender, and Popular Culture in Los Angeles's Little Manila, 1920s–1940s." Ph.D. diss., University of California, Los Angeles.

Espina, Maria. 1988. *Filipinos in Louisiana*. New Orleans: A F. Laborde & Sons.

Espiritu, Yen Le. 1994. "The Intersection of Race, Ethnicity, and Class: The Multiple Identities of Second Generation Filipinos." *Identities* 1 (2–3): 249–73.

———. 1995. *Filipino American Lives*. Philadelphia: Temple University Press.

———. 1996. "Colonial Oppression, Labour Importation, and Group Formation: Filipinos in the United States." *Ethnic and Racial Studies* 19 (1): 29–47.

———. 1997. *Asian American Women and Men: Labor, Laws, and Love*. Thousand Oaks, Calif.: Sage.

———. 1999. "Disciplines Unbound: Notes on Sociology and Ethnic Studies." *Contemporary Sociology: A Journal of Reviews* 28 (5): 510–14.

Espiritu, Yen Le, Dorothy Fujita Rony, Nazli Kibria, and George Lipsitz. 2000. "The Role of Race and Its Articulations for Asian Pacific Americans." *Journal of Asian American Studies* 3 (2): 127–37.

Espiritu, Yen Le, and Diane L. Wolf. 2001. "The Paradox of Assimilation: Children of Filipino Immigrants in San Diego." In *Ethnicities: Children of Immigrants in America*, edited by Ruben Rumbaut and Alejandro Portes. Berkeley and New York: University of California Press and Russell Sage Foundation.

Estes, Donald H., and Matthew T. Estes. 1993. "Further and Further Away: The Relocation of San Diego's Nikkei Community, 1942." *Journal of San Diego History* 39 (1–2): 1–31.

Fanon, Frantz. 1963. "On National Culture." *The Wretched of the Earth*. New York: Grove Press.

Feagin, Joe R. 1997. "Old Poison in Old Bottles: The Deep Roots of Modern Nativism." In *Immigrants Out! The New Nativism and the Anti-Immigrant Impulse in the United States*, edited by Juan F. Perea. New York: New York University Press.

Fernández-Kelly, Maria Patricia. 1983. *For We Are Sold, I and My People: Women and Industry in Mexico's Frontier*. Albany: State University of New York Press.

Foley, Neil. 1997. *The White Scourge: Mexicans, Blacks, and Poor Whites in Texas Cotton Culture*. Berkeley and Los Angeles: University of California Press.

Foucault, Michel. 1991. "Governmentality." In *The Foucault Effect: Studies in Governmentality*, edited by Graham Burchell, Colin Gordon, and Peter Miller. Chicago: University of Chicago Press.

Francia, Luis. 1999. "Inventing the Earth: The Notion of 'Home' in Asian American Literature." In *Across the Pacific: Asian Americans and Globalization*, edited by Evelyn Hu-DeHart. New York: Asia Society; Philadelphia: Temple University Press.

Frankenberg, Ruth. 1993. *White Women, Race Matters: The Social Construction of Whiteness*. Minneapolis: University of Minnesota Press.

Friday, Chris. 1994. *Organizing Asian American Labor: The Pacific Coast Canned-Salmon Industry, 1870–1942*. Philadelphia: Temple University Press.

Fujita Rony, Dorothy. 2000. "Coalitions, Race, and Labor: Rereading Philip Vera Cruz." *Journal of Asian American Studies* 3 (2): 139–62.

Gabaccia, Donna. 1994. *From the Other Side: Women, Gender, and Immigrant Life in the U.S., 1820–1990*. Bloomington and Indianapolis: Indiana University Press.

Garcia, Voltaire E., II. 1967. "U.S. Military Bases and Philippine-American Relations." *Journal of East Asiatic Studies* 11: 1–116.

George, Rosemary Marangoly. 1996. *The Politics of Home: Postcolonial Relocations and Twentieth-Century Fiction*. Cambridge: Cambridge University Press.

George, Sheba. 2000. "When the Women Come First." Ph.D. diss., University of California, Berkeley.

Gibson, Margaret A. 1995. "Additive Acculturation as a Strategy for School Improvement." In *California's Immigrant Children: Theory, Research, and Implications for Educational Policy,* edited by Ruben Rumbaut and Wayne Cornelius. La Jolla: Center for U.S.-Mexican Studies, University of California, San Diego.

Gilman, Sander L. 1985. *Difference and Pathology: Stereotypes of Sexuality, Race, and Madness.* Ithaca: Cornell University Press.

Glenn, Evelyn Nakano. 1986. *Issei, Nisei, War Bride: Three Generations of Japanese American Women at Domestic Services.* Philadelphia: Temple University Press.

Glick Schiller, Nina. 1997. "The Situation of Transnational Studies." *Identities* 4 (2): 155–66.

Glick Schiller, Nina, Linda Basch, and Cristina Szanton Blanc. 1992. "Transnationalism: A New Analytic Framework for Understanding Migration." In *Towards a Transnational Perspective on Migration: Race, Class, Ethnicity, and Nationalism Reconsidered,* edited by Nina Glick Schiller, Linda Basch, and Cristina Szanton Blanc. Annals of the New York Academy of Sciences, vol. 645. New York: New York Academy of Sciences.

Glick Schiller, Nina, and Georges Fouron. 2001. "The Generation of Identity: Redefining the Second Generation within a Transnational Field." In *Migration, Transnationalism, and Race in a Changing New York,* edited by Hector Cordero-Guzman, Robert Smith, and Ramon Grosfogel. Philadelphia: Temple University Press.

Gmelch, George. 1992. *Double Passage: The Lives of Caribbean Migrants Abroad and Back Home.* Ann Arbor: University of Michigan Press.

Gold, Steve, and Nazli Kibria. 1993. "Vietnamese Refugees and Blocked Mobility." *Asian and Pacific Migration Review* 2: 27–56.

Goldberg, Barry. 1992. "Historical Reflections on Transnationalism, Race, and the American Immigrant Saga." *Annals of the New York Academy of Sciences* 645: 201–15.

Goldberg, Theo David. 1993. *Racist Culture: Philosophy and the Politics of Meaning.* Cambridge: Blackwell.

Goldring, Luin. 1998. "The Power of Status in Transnational Social Fields." In *Transnationalism from Below,* edited by Michael Peter Smith and Luis Eduardo Guarnizo. New Brunswick: Transactions.

Gonzalves, Theodore S. 1997. "The Day the Dancers Stayed: On Pilipino Cultural Nights." In *Filipino Americans: Transformation and Identity,* edited by Maria P. P. Root. Thousand Oaks, Calif.: Sage.

Gordon, Avery F. 1997. *Ghostly Matters: Haunting and the Sociological Imagination.* Minneapolis: University of Minnesota Press.

Gotanda, Neil. 1999. "Exclusion and Inclusion: Immigration and American Orientalism." In *Across the Pacific: Asian Americans and Globalization,* edited by Evelyn Hu-DeHart. Philadelphia: Temple University Press.

Green, Rayna. 1975. "The Pocahontas Perplex: The Image of Indian Women in American Culture." *Massachusetts Review* 16 (4): 698–714.

Grewal, Inderpal, and Caren Kaplan. 1994. "Introduction: Transnational Feminist Practices and Questions of Postmodernity." In *Scattered Hegemonies: Postmodernity and Transnational Feminist Practices,* edited by Inderpal Grewal and Caren Kaplan. Minneapolis: University of Minnesota Press.

Gross, Gregory Alan. 1999. "5-Year-Old Gatekeeper Is Praised, Denounced: Critics Say It Makes Border More Dangerous." *San Diego Union Tribune,* 7 June.

Guarzino, Luis Eduardo, and Michael Peter Smith. 1998. "The Location of Transnationalism." In *Transnationalism from Below,* edited by Michael Peter Smith and Luis Eduardo Guarnizo. New Brunswick, N.J., and London: Transaction Publishers.

Gupta, Akhil, and James Ferguson. 1992. " 'Beyond 'Culture': Space, Identity, and the Politics of Difference." *Cultural Anthropology* 7 (1): 6–23.

Gutierrez, David. 1995. *Walls and Mirrors: Mexican Americans, Mexican Immigrants, and the Politics of Ethnicity.* Berkeley and Los Angeles: University of California Press.

Haddad, Yvonne Y., and Jane I. Smith. 1996. "Islamic Values Among American Muslims." In *Family and Gender Among American Muslims: Issues Facing Middle Eastern Immigrants and Their Descendants,* edited by Barbara C. Aswad and Barbara Bilge. Philadelphia: Temple University Press.

Hagedorn, Jessica. 1990. *Dogeaters.* New York: Penguin.

Hall, Stewart. 1990. "Cultural Identity and Diaspora." In *Identity, Community, Culture, Difference,* edited by Jonathan Rutherford. London: Lawrence and Wishart.

Halualani, Rona Tamiko. 1995. "The Intersecting Hegemonic Discourses of an Asian Mail-Order Bride Catalog: Pilipina 'Oriental Butterfly' Dolls for Sale." *Women's Studies in Communication* 18 (1): 45–64.

Hamamoto, Darrell Y. 1994. *Monitored Peril: Asian Americans and the Politics of Representation.* Minneapolis: University of Minnesota Press.

Handlin, Oscar. 1973. *The Uprooted.* 2nd ed. Boston: Little Brown.

Harkavy, Robert E. 1982. *Great Power Competition for Overseas Bases: The Geopolitics of Access Diplomacy.* New York: Pergamon Press.

Harris, Leroy. 1974. "The Other Side of the Freeway: A Study of Settlement Patterns of Negroes and Mexican Americans in San Diego, California." Ph.D. diss., Carnegie-Mellon University.

Hayles, Robert, and Ronald W. Perry. 1981. "Racial Equality in the American Naval Justice System: An Analysis of Incarceration Differentials." *Ethnic and Racial Studies* 4 (1): 44–55.

Hewes, Laurence. 1946. "Intergroup Relations in San Diego: Some Aspects of Community Life in San Diego Which Particularly Affect Minority Groups, with Recommendations for a Program of Community Action/Prepared at the Joint Request of the Mayor, the City Council, the Superintendent of Schools, and the Board of Education of San Diego." San Francisco: American Council on Race Relations.

Hickey, M. Gail. 1996. " 'Go to College, Get a Job, and Don't Leave the House Without Your Brother': Oral Histories with Immigrant Women and Their Daughters." *Oral History Review* 23 (2): 63–92.

Hobsbawm, E. J. 1987. *The Age of Empire, 1875–1914*. London: Weidenfeld and Nicolson.

Hobsbawm, E. J., and Terence Ranger. 1983. *The Invention of Tradition*. New York: Cambridge University Press.

Hochschild, Arlie, with Anne Machung. 1989. *The Second Shift: Working Parents and the Revolution at Home*. New York: Viking.

Hoganson, Kristin L. 1998. *Fighting for American Manhood: How Gender Politics Provoked the Spanish-American and Philippine-American Wars*. New Haven and London: Yale University Press.

Hondagneu-Sotelo, Pierette. 1994. *Gendered Transitions: Mexican Experiences of Immigration*. Berkeley and Los Angeles: University of California Press.

———. 1995. "Women and Children First: New Directions in Anti-Immigrant Politics." *Socialist Review* 25 (1): 169–90.

Hondagneu-Sotelo, Pierette, and Ernestine Avila. 1997. " 'I'm Here, But I'm There': The Meanings of Latina Transnational Motherhood." *Gender and Society* 11 (5): 548–71.

Horlacher, Friedrich W. 1990. "The Language of Late Nineteenth-Century American Expansionism." In *An American Empire: Expansionist Cultures and Policies, 1881–1917*, edited by Serge Ricard. Aix-en-Provence, France: Université de Provence Service des Publications.

Horsman, Reginald. 1981. *Race and Manifest Destiny: The Origins of American Anglo-Saxonism*. Cambridge: Harvard University Press.

Hurtado, Aida. 1998. "Relating to Privilege: Seduction and Rejection in the Subordination of White Women and Women of Color." *Signs: Journal of Women in Culture and Society* 14: 833–55.

Ickstadt, Heinz. 1990. "The Rhetoric of Expansionism in Painting and Fiction (1880–1910)." In *An American Empire: Expansionist Cultures and Policies, 1881–1917*, edited by Serge Ricard. Aix-en-Provence: Université de Provence Service des Publications.

Ingram, Timothy. 1970. "The Floating Plantation." *Washington Monthly*, October, 17–20.

Jones, R. C. 1995. *Ambivalent Journey*. Tucson: University of Arizona Press.

Jung, Moon-Kie. 1999a. "The Making of Hawaii's Interracial Working Class." Ph.D. diss., University of Michigan.

———. 1999b. "No Whites, No Asians: Race, Marxism and Hawaii's Preemergent Working Class." *Social Science History* 23 (3): 357–93.

Kaplan, Amy. 1993. " 'Left Alone with America': The Absence of Empire in the Study of American Culture." In *Cultures of United States Imperialism*, edited by Amy Kaplan and Donald E. Pease. Durham, N.C., and London: Duke University Press.

Kaplan, Elaine Bell. 1997. *Not Our Kind of Girl: Unraveling the Myths of Black Teenage Motherhood*. Berkeley and Los Angeles: University of California Press.

Katrak, Ketu. 1996. "South Asian American Writers: Geography and Memory." *Amerasia Journal* 22 (3): 121–38.

Kearney, Michael. 1995. "The Effects of Transnational Culture, Economy, and Migration on Mixtec Identity on Oxacalifornia." In *The Bubbling Cauldron:*

Race, Ethnicity, and the Urban Crisis, edited by Michael Peter Smith and Joe Feagin. Minneapolis: University of Minnesota Press.

Khan, Aisha. 1995. "Motherland: Authenticity, Legitimacy, and Ideologies of Place Among Muslims in Trinidad." In *Nation and Migration,* edited by Peter van der Veer. Philadelphia: University of Philadelphia Press.

Kibria, Nazli. 1993. *Family Tightrope: The Changing Lives of Vietnamese Immigrant Community.* Princeton, N.J.: Princeton University Press.

Killory, Christine. 1993. "Temporary Suburbs: The Lost Opportunity of San Diego's National Defense Housing Projects." *Journal of San Diego History* 39 (1–2): 33–49.

Kim, Bok-Lim. 1997. "Asian Wives of American Servicemen: Women in Shadows." *Amerasia Journal* 4 (1): 91–116.

Kim, Claire Jean. 2000. *Bitter Fruit: The Politics of Black-Korean Conflict in New York City.* New Haven, Conn.: Yale University Press.

Kim, Elaine. 1990. " 'Such Opposite Creatures': Men and Women in Asian American Literature." *Michigan Quarterly Review* 29: 68–93.

———. 1993. Preface to *Charlie Chan Is Dead: An Anthology of Contemporary Asian American Fiction,* edited by Jessica Hagedorn. New York: Penguin.

Kim, Haeyun Juliana. 1991. "Voices from the Shadows: The Lives of Korean War Brides." *Amerasia Journal* 17 (1): 15–30.

Kitano, Harry, and Roger Daniels. 1988. *Asian Americans: Emerging Minorities.* Englewood Cliffs, N.J.: Prentice-Hall.

Kolko, Gabriel. 1976. *Main Currents in Modern American History.* New York: Pantheon.

Kondo, Dorinne. 1996. *The Narrative Production of "Home," Community, and Political Identity in Asian American Theater.* Durham, N.C., and London: Duke University Press.

Kumar, Amitava. 2000. *Passport Photos.* Berkeley and Los Angeles: University of California Press.

Lafeber, Walter. 1998. *The New Empire: An Interpretation of American Expansion, 1860–1898.* Ithaca, N.Y.: Cornell University Press.

Laguerre, Michel S. 1998. *Diasporic Citizenship: Haitian Americans in Transnational America.* New York: St. Martin's Press.

Lai, T. 1992. "Asian American Women: Not for Sale." In *Race, Class, and Gender: An Anthology,* edited by Margaret Andersen and Patricia Hill Collins. Belmont, Calif.: Wadsworth.

Lamont, Michèle. 1997. "Colliding Moralities Between Black and White Workers." In *From Sociology to Cultural Studies: New Perspectives,* edited by Elisabeth Long. New York: Blackwell.

Lasker, Bruno. 1969. *Filipino Immigration to the United States and to Hawaii.* New York: Arno.

Lau, Angela. 1995. "Filipino Girls Think Suicide at Number One Rate." *San Diego Union-Tribune,* 11 February.

Lawcock, Larry Arden. 1975. "Filipino Students in the United States and the Philippine Independence Movement: 1900–1935." Ph.D. diss., University of California, Berkeley.

Lee, Robert. 1999. *Orientals: Asian Americans in Popular Culture*. Philadelphia: Temple University Press.

Lee, Stacey J. 1996. *Unraveling the "Model Minority" Stereotype: Listening to Asian American Youth*. New York and London: Teachers' College Press.

Lessinger, Johanna. 1992. "Investing or Going Home? A Transnational Strategy Among Indian Immigrants in the United States." In *Toward a Transnational Perspective on Migration: Race, Class, Ethnicity, and Nationalism Reconsidered*, edited by Nina Glick Schiller, Linda Basch, and Cristina Szanton Blanc. Annals of the New York Academy of Sciences, vol. 645. New York: New York Academy of Sciences.

Levitt, Peggy. 2001. *The Transnational Villagers*. Berkeley and Los Angeles: University of California Press.

Limón, José E. 1982. "History, Chicano Joking, and the Varieties of Higher Education: Tradition and Performance as Critical Symbolic Action." *Journal of the Folklore Institute* (2–3): 141–66.

Lipsitz, George. 1998. *The Possessive Investment in Whiteness: How White People Profit from Identity Politics*. Philadelphia: Temple University Press.

———. 1999. "No Shining City on a Hill: American Studies and the Problem of Place." *American Studies* 40 (2): 53–69.

———. 2000. Review of Vijay Prashad's *Karma of Brown Folks*. *Journal of Asian American Studies* 3 (2): 263–65.

Liu, John, and Lucie Cheng. 1994. "Pacific Rim Development and the Duality of Post-1965 Asian Immigration to the United States." In *The New Asian Immigration in Los Angeles and Global Restructuring*, edited by Paul Ong, Edna Bonacich, and Lucie Cheng. Philadelphia: Temple University Press.

Liu, John, Paul Ong, and Carolyn Rosenstein. 1991. "Dual Chain Migration: Post-1965 Filipino Immigration to the United States." *International Migration Review* 25 (3): 487–513.

Lloyd, David. 1994. "Ethnic Cultures, Minority Discourse and the State." In *Colonial Discourse/Postcolonial Theory*, edited by Francis Barker, Peter Hulme, and Margaret Iversen. Manchester, England, and New York: St. Martin's Press.

"The Loneliest Brides in America." 1952. *Ebony*, April, 50.

Lowe, Lisa. 1996. *Immigrant Acts: On Asian American Cultural Politics*. Durham, N.C.: Duke University Press.

———. 1998. "Comparative Asian Racial Formations." Paper presented at the Annual Meeting of the Association of Asian American Studies, Honolulu, Hawaii, June.

Maglin, Nan Bauer, and Donna Perry. 1996. Introduction to *"Bad Girls"/"Good Girls": Women, Sex, and Power in the Nineties*, edited by Nan Bauer Maglin and Donna Perry. New Brunswick, N.J.: Rutgers University Press.

Mahler, Sarah. 1996. *American Dreaming: Immigrant Life on the Margins*. Princeton, N.J.: Princeton University Press.

———. 1999. "Engendering Transnational Migration: A Case Study of Salvadorans." *American Behavioral Scientist* 42 (4): 690–719.

Mahmud, Tayyab. 1997. "Migration, Identity, and the Colonial Encounter." *Oregon Law Review* 76 (Fall): 633–90.

Malkki, Liisa. 1995. *Purity and Exile: Violence, Memory, and National Cosmology Among Hutu Refugees in Tanzania.* Chicago and London: University of Chicago Press.

Marchetti, Gina. 1993. *Romance and the "Yellow Peril": Race, Sex, and Discursive Strategies in Hollywood Fiction.* Berkeley and Los Angeles: University of California Press.

Martin, Biddy, and Chandra Talpade Mohanty. 1986. "Feminist Politics: What's Home Got to Do with It?" In *Feminist Studies/Critical Studies,* edited by Teresa de Lauretis. Bloomington: Indiana University Press.

Massey, Doreen. 1999. "Imagining Globalization: Power-Geometries of Time-Space." In *Global Futures: Migration, Environment and Globalization,* edited by Avtar Brah, Mary J. Hickman, and Mairtin Mac an Ghaill. New York: St. Martin's Press.

Matute-Bianchi, M. E. 1991. "Situational Ethnicity and Patterns of School Performance Among Immigrant and Nonimmigrant Mexican-Descent Students." In *Minority Status and Schooling: A Comparative Study of Immigrant and Involuntary Minorities,* edited by M. Gibson and J. U. Ogbu. New York: Garland.

Mazumdar, Suchetta. 1989. "General Introduction: A Woman-Centered Perspective on Asian American History." In *Making Waves: An Anthology by and About Asian American Women,* edited by Asian Women United of California. Boston: Beacon.

McCormick, Thomas. 1967. *China Market: America's Quest for Informal Empire, 1893–1901.* Chicago: Quadrangle Books.

Melendy, H. Brett. 1977. *Asians in America: Filipinos, Koreans, and East Indians.* Boston: Twayne.

Menjivar, Cecilia. 1999. "The Intersection of Work and Gender: Central American Women and Employment in California." *American Behavioral Scientist* 42 (2): 601–27.

Millet, Kate. 1970. *Sexual Politics.* Garden City, N.Y.: Doubleday.

Mills, Charles. 1997. *The Racial Contract.* Ithaca, N.Y.: Cornell University Press.

Min, Pyong Gap. 1996. *Caught in the Middle: Korean Merchants in America's Multiethnic Cities.* Berkeley and Los Angeles: University of California Press.

———. 1998. *Changes and Conflicts: Korean Immigrant Families in New York.* Needham Heights, Mass.: Allyn and Bacon.

Mirande, Alfredo. 1980. "The Chicano Family: A Reanalysis of Conflicting Views." In *Rethinking Marriage, Child Rearing, and Family Organization,* edited by Arlene S. Skolnick and Jerome H. Skolnick. Berkeley and Los Angeles: University of California Press.

Mitchell, Timothy. 1988. *Colonizing Egypt.* Cambridge: Cambridge University Press.

Mohanty, Chandra. 1991. "Cartographies of Struggle: Third World Women and the Politics of Feminism." In *Third World Women and the Politics of Feminism,* edited by Chandra Mohanty, Ann Russo, and Lourdes Torres. Bloomington: University of Indiana Press.

Moore, Henrietta. 1994. *A Passion for Difference.* Bloomington: Indiana University Press.

Moore, Stephen. 1997. *Immigration and the Rise and Decline of American Cities*. Stanford, Calif.: Hoover Institution on War, Revolution and Peace, Stanford University.

Moraga, Cherríe. 1983. Preface to *This Bridge Called My Back: Writings by Radical Women of Color,* edited by Cherríe Moraga and Gloria Anzaldúa. New York: Kitchen Table, Women of Color Press.

Morley, David. 1999. "Bounded Realms: Household, Family, Community, and Nation." In *Home, Exile, Homeland: Film, Media, and the Politics of Place,* edited by Hamid Naficy. New York and London: Routledge.

Muller, Thomas. 1997. "Nativism in the Mid-1990s: Why Now?" In *Immigrants Out! The New Nativism and the Anti-Immigrant Impulse in the United States,* edited by Juan F. Perea. New York: New York University Press.

Mura, David. 1988. "Strangers in the Village." In *Multi-Cultural Literacy,* edited by Rick Simonson and Scott Walker. Graywolf Annual, vol. 5. St. Paul, Minn.: Graywolf Press.

Naficy, Hamid. 1999. "Framing Exile: From Homeland to Homepage." In *Home, Exile, Homeland: Film, Media, and the Politics of Place,* edited by Hamid Naficy. London and New York: Routledge.

The Nation. 1974. 14 December, 614.

Nguyen, Viet Thanh. 1997. "Representing Reconciliation: Le Ly Hayslip and the Victimized Body." *Positions* 5 (2): 605–42.

Nonini, Donald M., and Aihwa Ong. 1997. "Introduction: Chinese Transnationalism as an Alternative Modernity." In *Ungrounded Empires: The Cultural Politics of Modern Chinese Transnationalism,* edited by Aihwa Ong and Donald M. Nonini. New York: Routledge.

Okamura, Jonathan Y. 1983. "Filipino Hometown Associations in Hawaii." *Ethnology* 22: 341–53.

———. 1998. *Imagining the Filipino American Diaspora: Transnational Relations, Identities, and Communities*. New York and London: Garland Publishing.

Okamura, Jonathan Y., and Amefil Agbayani. 1997. "Pamantasan: Filipino American Higher Education." In *Filipino Americans: Transformation and Identity,* edited by Maria P. P. Root. Thousand Oaks, Calif.: Sage.

Okihiro, Gary. 1994. *Margins and Mainstreams: Asians in American History and Culture*. Seattle: University of Washington Press.

Oliver, Melvin, and James H. Johnson Jr. 1984. "Inter-Ethnic Conflict in an Urban Ghetto: The Case of Blacks and Latinos in Los Angeles." *Research in Social Movements, Conflicts, and Change* 6: 57–94.

Omi, Michael, and Howard Winant. 1994. *Racial Formation in the United States: From the 1960s to the 1990s*. New York and London: Routledge.

Ong, Aihwa. 1987. *Spirits of Resistance and Capitalist Discipline: Factory Women in Malaysia*. Albany: State University of New York Press.

———. 1996. "Cultural Citizenship as Subject-Making." *Current Anthropology* 37 (5): 737–62.

———. 1997. "Chinese Modernities: Narratives of Nation and of Capitalism." In *Ungrounded Empires: The Culture and Politics of Modern Chinese Transnationalism,* edited by Aihwa Ong and Donald Nonini. New York: Routledge.

Ong, Paul. 1993. *Beyond Asian American Poverty: Community Economic Development Policies and Strategies.* Los Angeles: Leadership Education for Asian Pacifics.

Ong, Paul, and Tania Azores. 1994. "The Migration and Incorporation of Filipino Nurses." In *The New Asian Immigration in Los Angeles and Global Restructuring,* edited by Paul Ong, Edna Bonacich, and Lucie Cheng. Philadelphia: Temple University Press.

Ong, Paul, Edna Bonacich, and Lucie Cheng. 1994. "The Political Economy of Capitalist Restructuring and the New Asian Immigration." In *The New Asian Immigration in Los Angeles and Global Restructuring,* edited by Paul Ong, Edna Bonacich, and Lucie Cheng. Philadelphia: Temple University Press.

Ong, Paul, and Karen Umemoto. 1994. "Life and Work in the Inner City." In *The State of Asian Pacific America: Economic Diversity, Issues, and Policies,* edited by Paul Ong. Los Angeles: LEAP Asian Pacific American Public Policy Institute and the University of California at Los Angeles Asian American Studies Center.

Ordonez, Raquel Z. 1997. "Mail-Order Brides: An Emerging Community." In *Filipino Americans: Transformation and Identity,* edited by Maria P. P. Root. Thousand Oaks, Calif.: Sage.

Orsi, Robert Anthony. 1985. *The Madonna of 115th Street: Faith and Community in Italian Harlem, 1880–1950.* New Haven and London: Yale University Press.

Osumi, Megumi Dick. 1982. "Asians and California's Anti-Miscegenation Laws." In *Asian and Pacific American Experiences: Women's Perspectives,* edited by Nobuya Tsuchida. Minneapolis: University of Minnesota, Asian/Pacific Learning Resources Center.

Paisano, Edna L. 1993. *We the American Asians.* Washington, D.C.: Government Printing Office.

Palafox, Jose. 1996. "Militarizing the Border." *CAQ* 56 (Spring), 14–19.

Palumbo-Liu, David. 1999. *Asian/American: Historical Crossings of a Racial Frontier.* Stanford, Calif.: Stanford University Press.

Parrenas, Rhacel Salazar. 1998. " 'White Trash' Meets the 'Little Brown Monkeys': The Taxi Dance Hall as a Site of Interracial and Gender Alliances Between White Working Class Women and Filipino Immigrant Men in the 1920s and 1930s." *Amerasia Journal* 24 (2): 115–34.

Peery, Nelson. 1994. *Black Fire: The Making of an American Revolutionary.* New York: New Press.

Penaranda, Oscar, Serafin Syquia, and San Tagatac. 1974. "An Introduction to Filipino American Literature." In *Aiiieeeee! An Anthology of Asian American Writers,* edited by Frank Chin et al. Washington, D.C.: Howard University Press.

Perminow, A. A. 1993. *The Long Way Home: Dilemmas of Everyday Life in a Tongan Village.* Oslo: Scandinavian University Press.

Perrier, Hubert. 1990. "The U.S. Left on War and Empire, 1880–1920." In *American Empire: Expansionist Cultures and Policies, 1881–1917,* edited by Serge Ricard. Aix-en-Provence: Université de Provence Service des Publications.

Personal Narratives Group. 1989. "Origins." In *Interpreting Women's Lives: Feminist Theory and Personal Narratives,* edited by the Personal Narratives Group. Bloomington: Indiana University Press.

Pesquera, Beatriz M. 1993. " 'In the Beginning He Wouldn't Lift a Spoon': The

Division of Household Labor." In *Building with Our Hands: New Directions in Chicana Studies,* edited by Adela de la Torre and Beatriz M. Pesquera. Berkeley and Los Angeles: University of California Press.

Pessar, Patricia. 1986. "The Role of Gender in Dominican Settlement in the United States." In *Women and Change in Latin America,* edited by June Nash and Helen Safa. South Hadley, Mass.: Bergin and Garvey.

———. 1999. "Engendering Migration Studies: The Case of New Immigrants in the United States." *American Behavioral Scientist* 42: 577–600.

Petras, James. 1978. *Critical Perspectives on Imperialism and Social Class in the Third World.* New York: Monthly Review Press.

Pido, Antonio. 1986. *The Pilipinos in America.* New York: Center for Migration Studies.

Portes, Alejandro. 1978. "Migration and Underdevelopment." *Politics and Society* 8: 1–48.

———. 1987. "The Social Origins of the Cuban Enclave Economy of Miami." *Sociological Perspectives* 30 (October): 340–72.

———. 1994. "Introduction: Immigration and Its Aftermath." *International Migration Review* 28 (4): 632–39.

Portes, Alejandro, and Ruben Rumbaut. 1996. *Immigrant America: A Portrait.* 2nd ed. Berkeley and Los Angeles: University of California Press.

Portes, Alejandro, Luis E. Guarzino, and Patricia Landolt. 1999. "The Study of Transnationalism: Pitfalls and Promises of an Emergent Research Field." *Ethnic and Racial Studies* 22 (2): 217–37.

Posadas, Barbara M., and Roland L. Guyotte. 1990. "Unintentional Immigrants: Chicago's Filipino Foreign Students Become Settlers, 1900–1941." *Journal of American Ethnic History* 9 (Spring), 26–48.

Pressner, Harriet. 1988. "Shift Work and Child Care Among Young Dual-Earner American Parents." *Journal of Marriage and the Family* 50: 133–48.

Quinsaat, Jesse. 1976. "An Exercise on How to Join the Navy and Still Not See the World." In *Letters in Exile,* edited by Jesse Quinsaat. Los Angeles: University of California, Los Angeles, Asian American Studies Center.

Rafael, Vicente L. 1997. " 'Your Grief Is Our Gossip': Overseas Filipinos and Other Spectral Presences." *Public Culture* 9 (2): 267–91.

———. 2000. *White Love and Other Events in Filipino History.* Durham, N.C., and London: Duke University Press.

Reza, H. G. 1992. "Navy to Stop Recruiting Filipino Nationals." *Los Angeles Times,* 27 February.

Roberts, Alden. 1988. "Racism Sent and Received: Americans and Vietnamese View One Another." *Research in Race and Ethnic Relations* 5: 75–97.

Roberts, Dorothy E. 1997. "Who May Give Birth to Citizens? Reproduction, Eugenics, and Immigration." In *Immigrants Out! The New Nativism and the Anti-Immigrant Impulse in the United States,* edited by Juan F. Perea. New York: New York University Press.

Rodriquez, Nestor P. 1997. "The Social Construction of the U.S.-Mexico Border." In *Immigrants Out! The New Nativism and the Anti-Immigrant Impulse in the United States,* edited by Juan F. Perea. New York: New York University Press.

Romero, Mary. 1992. *Maid in the U.S.A.* New York: Routledge.
Rosaldo, Renato. 1994. "Social Justice and the Crisis of National Communities." In *Colonial Discourse/Postcolonial Theory,* edited by Francis Barker, Peter Hulme, and Margaret Iversen. New York: St. Martin's Press.
Rose, Peter. 1985. "Asian Americans: From Pariahs to Paragons." In *Clamor at the Gates: The New Immigration,* edited by Nathan Glazer. San Francisco: Institute of Contemporary Studies.
Rouse, Roger. 1991. "Mexican Migration and the Social Space of Postmodernism." *Diaspora* 1: 8–23.
———. 1995. "Questions of Identity: Personhood and Collectivity in Transnational Migration to the United States." *Critique of Anthropology* 15 (1): 351–80.
Ruiz, Vicki L. 1992. "The Flapper and the Chaperone: Historical Memory Among Mexican-American Women." In *Seeking Common Ground: Multidisciplinary Studies,* edited by Donna Gabbacia. Westport, Conn.: Greenwood Press.
Rumbaut, Ruben. 1991. "Passages to America: Perspectives on the New Immigration." In *America at Century's End,* edited by Alan Wolfe. Berkeley and Los Angeles: University of California Press.
———. 1994. "The Crucible Within: Ethnic Identity, Self-Esteem, and Segmented Assimilation Among Children of Immigrants." *International Migration Review* 28 (4): 748–94.
Rumbaut, Ruben, and Kenji Ima. 1988. *The Adaptation of Southeast Asian Refugee Youth: A Comparative Study.* Washington, D.C.: U.S. Office of Refugee Resettlement.
Ruth, Heather Low. 1970. "Philippines." In *The International Migration of High-Level Manpower: Its Impact on the Development Process,* edited by the Committee on the International Migration of Talent. New York: Praeger.
Said, Edward. 1979. *Orientalism.* New York: Random.
———. 1993. *Culture and Imperialism.* New York: Alfred A. Knopf.
Saito, Leland. 2000. *Race and Politics: Asian Americans, Latinos, and Whites in a Los Angeles Suburb.* Urbana: University of Illinois Press.
San Buenaventura, Steffi. 1998. "The Colors of Manifest Destiny: Filipinos and the American Other(s)." *Amerasia Journal* 24 (3): 117–31.
San Juan, E., Jr. 1991. "Mapping the Boundaries: The Filipino Writer in the U.S." *Journal of Ethnic Studies* 19 (1): 117–31.
———. 1998a. *Beyond Postcolonial Theory.* New York: St. Martin's Press.
———. 1998b. "One Hundred Years of Producing and Reproducing the 'Filipino.' " *Amerasia Journal* 24 (2): 1–33.
Sanchez, George. 1993. *Becoming Mexican American: Ethnicity, Culture, and Identity in Chicano Los Angeles, 1900–1945.* New York and Oxford: Oxford University Press.
———. 1997. "Face the Nation." *International Migration Review* 31 (4): 1009–29.
Santos, Bienvenido. 1982. "Words from a Writer in Exile." In *Asian Writers on Literature and Justice,* edited by Leopoldo Yabes. Manila: Philippine Center of International PEN.

Sawada, Mitziko. 1996. *Tokyo Life, New York Dreams: Urban Japanese Visions of America, 1890–1924*. Berkeley and Los Angeles: University of California Press.

Saxton, Alexander. 1977. "Nathan Glazer, Daniel Moynihan, and the Cult of Ethnicity." *Amerasia Journal* 4 (2): 141–50.

Scharlin, Craig, and Lilia V. Villanueva. 1992. *Philip Vera Cruz: A Personal History of Filipino Immigrants and the Farmworkers Movement*. Los Angeles: UCLA Labor Center, Institute of Labor Relations, and U.C.L.A. Asian American Studies Center.

Schlesinger, Arthur. 1991. *The Disuniting of America: Reflections on a Multicultural Society*. New York: Norton.

Shammas, Anton. 1996. "Autocartography: The Case of Palestine, Michigan." In *The Geography of Identity*, edited by Patricia Yaeger. Ann Arbor: University of Michigan Press

Sharma, Miriam. 1984. "Labor Migration and Class Formation Among the Filipinos in Hawaii, 1906–1946." In *Labor Immigration Under Capitalism: Asian Workers in the United States Before World War II*, edited by Lucie Cheng and Edna Bonacich. Berkeley and Los Angeles: University of California Press.

Sheffer, G. 1986. "A New Field of Study: Modern Diasporas in International Politics." In *Modern Diasporas in International Politics*, edited by G. Sheffer. Beckenham, London: Croom Helm.

Shragge, Abraham. 1998. "Boosters and Bluejackets: The Civic Culture of Militarism in San Diego, California, 1900–1945." Ph.D. diss., University of California, San Diego.

Shukla, Sandhya. 1996. "Ethnic Nationalism Beyond the State: The Non-Resident Indian (NRI) as a Category for Transnational Identities." Paper presented at the American Studies Association Conference, Kansas City, Missouri, October 31–November 3.

Sibayan, Bonifacio P. 1991. "The Intellectualization of Filipino." *International Journal of Social Language* 88: 69–82.

Simbulan, Roland G. 1989. *A Guide to Nuclear Philippines*. Manila: IBON Databank Philippines.

Small, Cathy. 1997. *Voyages: From Tongan Villages to American Suburbs*. Ithaca, N.Y.: Cornell University Press.

Smith, James P., and Barry Edmonston, eds. 1997. *The New Americans: Economic, Demographic, and Fiscal Effects of Immigration*. Washington, D.C.: National Academy Press.

Smith, Michael Peter. 1992. "Postmodernism, Urban Ethnography, and the New Social Space of Ethnic Identity." *Theory and Society* 21: 493–531.

———. 1994. "Can You Imagine? Transnational Migration and the Globalization of Grassroots Politics." *Social Text* 39: 15–33.

———. 2001. *Transnational Urbanism: Locating Globalization*. Malden, Mass.: Blackwell.

Sorensen, Ninna Nyberg. 1999. "Narrating Identity Across Dominican Worlds." In *Transnationalism from Below*, edited by Michael Peter Smith and Luis Eduardo Guarnizo. New Brunswick, N.J.: Transaction Publishers.

Starr, Paul D., and Alden Roberts. 1981. "Attitudes Toward Indochinese Refugees: An Empirical Study." *Journal of Refugee Resettlement* 1 (4): 51–61.

Steinberg, David Joel. 1990. *The Philippines: A Singular and a Plural Place.* Boulder, Colo.: Westview Press.

Steinberg, Stephen. 1989. *The Ethnic Myth: Race, Ethnicity, and Class in America.* Boston: Beacon Press.

Stoler, Ann Laura. 1991. "Carnal Knowledge and Imperial Power: Gender, Race, and Morality in Colonial Asia." In *Gender at the Crossroads of Knowledge: Feminist Anthropology in the Postmodern Era,* edited by Micaela di Leonardo. Berkeley and Los Angeles: University of California Press.

———. 1995. *Race and the Education of Desire: Foucault's History of Sexuality and the Colonial Order of Things.* Durham, N.C.: Duke University Press.

Suarez-Orozco, C., and M. Suarez-Orozco. 1995. *Transformations: Immigration, Family Life, and Achievement Motivation Among Latino Adolescents.* Stanford, Calif.: Stanford University Press.

Szalay, Lorand B., and Jean A. Bryson. 1997. *Filipinos in the Navy: Service, Interpersonal Relations, and Cultural Adaptation.* Washington, D.C.: American Institutes for Research.

Tafolla, Carmen. 1985. *To Split a Human: Mitos, Machos, y la Mujer Chicana.* San Antonio, Tex.: Mexican American Cultural Center.

Takaki, Ronald. 1989. *Strangers from a Different Shore: A History of Asian Americans.* Boston: Little, Brown.

Tapia, Ruby. 1997. "Studying Other 'Others.' " Paper presented at the Association of Pacific Americans in Higher Education, San Diego, California, April 4.

Thomas, Brinley. 1973. *Migration and Economic Growth: A Study of Great Britain and the Atlantic Economy.* Cambridge: Cambridge University Press.

Tiongson, Antonio T., Jr. 1997. "Throwing the Baby Out with the Bath Water." In *Filipino Americans: Transformation and Identity,* edited by Maria P. P. Root. Thousand Oaks, Calif.: Sage.

Tiongson, Nicanor. 2001. "Laughter as Subversion: The Pusong (Trickster) in Tagalog Theater." Paper presented at the University of California, San Diego, Literature Department Colloquium Series, La Jolla, Calif., October 17.

Tolman, Deborah L., and Tracy E. Higgins. 1996. "How Being a Good Girl Can Be Bad for Girls." In *"Bad Girls"/"Good Girls": Women. Sex, and Power in the Nineties,* edited by Nan Bauer Maglin and Donna Perry. New Brunswick, N.J.: Rutgers University Press.

Tuan, Mia. 1998. *Forever Foreigners or Honorary Whites? The Asian Ethnic Experience Today.* New Brunswick, N.J.: Rutgers University Press.

Tyner, James A. 1999. "The Global Context of Gendered Labor: Migration from the Philippines to the United States." *American Behavioral Scientist* 42 (4): 671–89.

U.S. Bureau of the Census. 2001. "Profiles of General Demographic Characteristics: 2000, Table DP-1, Geographic Area: San Diego County, California." Washington, D.C.: Government Printing Office.

U.S. Commission on Civil Rights. 1992. *Civil Rights Issues Facing Asian Americans in the 1990s.* Washington, D.C.: Government Printing Office.

U.S. House. 1973. Committee on the Judiciary House of Representatives. Special Study Subcommittee of the Committee on the Judiciary to Review Certain Immigration, Refugee, and Nationality Problems. *Report of Special Study Subcommittee of the Committee on the Judiciary to Review Immigration, Refugee, and Nationality Problems.* 93rd Cong., 1st sess. (December).

Vassanji, M. G. 1996. "Life at the Margins: In the Thick of Multiplicity." In *Between the Lines: South Asians and Postcoloniality,* edited by Deepika Bahri and Mary Vasudeva. Philadelphia: Temple University Press.

Vaughan, Christopher A. 1995. "The 'Discovery' of the Philippines by the U.S. Press, 1898–1902." *The Historian* 57 (2): 303–14.

Villanueva, M. 1991. *Ginseng and Other Tales from Manila.* Corvallis, Oreg.: Calyx.

Wallovitts, Sonia Emily. 1972. *The Filipinos in California.* San Francisco: R & E Associates.

Warren, Jenifer. 1993. "Suit Asks Navy to Aid Children Left in Philippines." *Los Angeles Times,* 5 March.

Waters, Mary C. 1996. "The Intersection of Gender, Race, and Ethnicity in Identity Development of Caribbean American Teens." In *Urban Girls: Resisting Stereotypes, Creating Identities,* edited by Bonnie J. Ross Leadbeater and Niobe Way. New York: New York University Press.

Williams, Brackette. 1989. "A Class Act: Anthropology and the Race to Nation Across Ethnic Terrain." *Annual Review of Anthropology* 18: 401–44.

Williams, Teresa. K. 1991. "Marriage Between Japanese Women and U.S. Servicemen Since World War II." *Amerasia Journal* 17 (1): 135–54.

Woldemikael, T. M. 1989. *Becoming Black American: Haitians and American Institutions in Evanston, Illinois.* New York: AMS Press.

Wolf, Diane L. 1997. "Family Secrets: Transnational Struggles Among Children of Filipino Immigrants." *Sociological Perspectives* 40 (3): 457–82.

Wong, Sau-ling. 1993. *Reading Asian American Literature: From Necessity to Extravagance.* Princeton, N.J.: Princeton University Press.

———. 1995. "Denationalization Reconsidered: Asian American Cultural Criticism at a Theoretical Crossroads." *Amerasia Journal* 21 (1–2): 1–28.

Yegenoglu, Meyda. 1998. *Colonial Fantasies: Towards a Feminist Reading of Orientalism.* Cambridge: Cambridge University Press.

Yung, Judy. 1995. *Unbound Feet: A Social History of Chinese Women in San Francisco.* Berkeley and Los Angeles: Berkeley University Press.

Zolberg, Aristide. 1986. "International Factors in the Formation of Refugee Movements." *International Migration Review* 20 (Summer): 151–69.

Index

Compositor: Binghamton Valley Composition, LLC
Text: 10/13 Sabon
Display: Sabon
Printer and binder: Maple-Vail Manufacturing Group